MULES AND MEN

Courtesy of Jane Belo estate and Margaret Mead

Zora Neale Hurston collecting folklore in the late 1930s.

MULES
AND MEN

ZORA NEALE HURSTON

PREFACE BY FRANZ BOAS
WITH A NEW FOREWORD BY ARNOLD RAMPERSAD
ILLUSTRATIONS BY MIGUEL COVARRUBIAS
SERIES EDITOR: HENRY LOUIS GATES, JR.

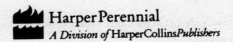

HarperPerennial
A Division of HarperCollinsPublishers

A hardcover edition of this book was originally published by J. B. Lippincott, Inc.

First PERENNIAL LIBRARY edition published 1990.

Designed by Cassandra J. Pappas

LIBRARY OF CONGRESS CATALOG CARD NUMBER 89-45672

ISBN 0-06-091648-6

02 03 04 05 RRD(H)   33 34 35 36 37 38 39 40

To
my dear friend
Mrs. Annie Nathan Meyer
who hauled the mud to make me
but loves me just the same

CONTENTS

Part II
HOODOO

PREFACE

ver since the time of Uncle Remus, Negro folklore has exerted a strong attraction upon the imagination of the American public. Negro tales, songs and sayings without end, as well as descriptions of Negro magic and voodoo, have appeared; but in all of them the intimate setting in the social life of the Negro has been given very inadequately.

It is the great merit of Miss Hurston's work that she entered into the homely life of the southern Negro as one of them and was fully accepted as such by the companions of her childhood. Thus she has been able to penetrate through that affected demeanor by which the Negro excludes the White observer effectively from participating in his true inner life. Miss Hurston has been equally successful in gaining the confidence of the voodoo doctors and she gives us much that throws a new light upon the much discussed voodoo beliefs and practices. Added to all this is the charm of a loveable personality and of a revealing style which makes Miss Hurston's work an unusual contribution to our knowledge of the true inner life of the Negro.

To the student of cultural history the material presented is valuable not only by giving the Negro's reaction to everyday events, to his emotional life, his humor and passions, but it throws into relief also the peculiar amalgamation of African and European tradition which is so important for understanding historically the character of American Negro life, with its strong African background in the West Indies, the importance of which diminishes with increasing distance from the south.

FRANZ BOAS

FOREWORD

On December 14, 1927, according to her biographer Robert Hemenway, Zora Neale Hurston boarded a midafternoon train at Pennsylvania Station in New York City, bound for Mobile, Alabama. From Mobile she would travel on to Florida and then to Louisiana, in a major effort to gather material on African-American folklore and other folk practices, including voodoo.

Hurston did not begin her project with the utmost confidence. After all, her first significant venture as a collector of folklore in the South had ended earlier that year with a frank admission on her part of failure. That professional setback was particularly galling for two reasons. First, Hurston was no stranger to the South, having been born and reared in Eatonville, Florida; as she later boasted in her autobiography *Dust Tracks on a Road* (1942), she had "the map of Dixie on my tongue." Secondly, she had carried out this first project collecting folklore in the South with the solid backing and encouragement of Franz Boas, unquestionably the dominant figure in American anthropology and Hurston's most influential professor at Barnard College, which she had entered as a student in 1925.

Still, Hurston had been unable to make the most of these advantages and had returned to New York with raw material in her notebooks rather than with a mature, complex grasp of the implications of that material that would have enabled her to move from being simply a transcriber to becoming a profound interpreter of Southern folklore's place in the culture of black America. She had returned to Boas with little to show for her efforts. However, her second expedition into the South as a gatherer of folklore would end differently, even though several years passed before its success was crowned with the publication in 1935 of *Mules and Men*. Filtered through a matured consciousness, and organized according to effective journalistic and literary strategies, the material she gathered mainly between 1927 and 1928 (with additional work up to 1931 and 1932) resulted in one of the outstanding books of its kind ever published in the United States. In 1960, the year Hurston died, the celebrated American collector Alan Lomax appraised *Mules and Men* as "the most engaging, genuine, and skillfully written book in the field of folklore."

Although Hurston is far better known for the publication of her feminist novel *Their Eyes Were Watching God* (1937), no understanding of her mind and her art, or of her contribution to African-American culture or to the study of folklore, can ignore the achievement of *Mules and Men*. Almost certainly, there would have been no *Their Eyes Were Watching God* without the process of growth and maturation that resulted first from *Mules and Men*. In this book, Hurston first effected a genuine reconciliation between herself and her past, which is to say between herself as a growing individual with literary ambitions on the one hand and the evolving African-American culture and history on the other. Here, in an extended literary act—her most ambitious to date—she found at last the proper form for depicting herself in relationship to the broad range of forces within the African-American culture that had produced her, as well as for portraying the people of which she was but one member. Here she came to terms at last with the full range of black folk traditions, practices, expressions, and types of behavior, and began to trust her understanding of their multiple meanings as an index to the African-American world. "From the earliest rocking of my cradle," she wrote in *Mules and Men,* "I had known about the capers Brer Rabbit is apt to cut and what the Squinch Owl says from the house top. But it was fitting me like a tight chemise. I couldn't see it for wearing it. It was only when I was off in college, away from my native surroundings, that I could see myself like somebody else and stand off and look at my garment. Then I had to have the spy-glass of Anthropology to look through at that."

In the case of Zora Neale Hurston, one speaks of this "coming to terms" with black folk culture carefully or not at all. Struggling to find a lofty place for herself in the world, she nevertheless arrived in New York in 1925 displaying from the start little ambivalence about traditional black culture. She was one of W.E.B. Du Bois's talented tenth—the gifted and educated leadership of the race on whom Du Bois based his hopes for African-American ascendance—without seeing herself, as members of the tenth often saw themselves, as victim caught tragically between two worlds, black and white. Instead, she draped black folk culture about herself like a fabulous robe, creating an inimitable and unforgettable personality, according to virtually everyone who recalled her, based on her mastery of jokes and stories, insights and attitudes, that derived almost directly from the black folk experience. As a fledgling writer, too, her earliest stories depended proudly—and shrewdly—on the black voices she had heard as a child growing up in Florida, the people who had taught her how to speak. She moved ambitiously among whites, often with guile and not infrequently in a servile manner; but consistently she offered herself as a child of the black South who had little desire ever to forget, much less repudiate, her folk and country roots.

This degree of identification set her apart from virtually all other writers, black and white. In his landmark study *The Souls of Black Folk* (1903), Du Bois had delved into folk culture to illustrate his thesis of black dignity and historicity. However, he had concentrated almost exclusively, in the area of psychology and philosophy, on approaches by blacks to Christianity;

in the area of art, he clung almost entirely to the noble and transcendent music of the spirituals. Other black writers, such as William Wells Brown and Charles Chesnutt, had drawn on black folkways, including both in music and in religion, in certain areas of their work, but none approached Hurston's knowledge of and commitment to folk culture. By far the best-known explorer of the black folk tradition among writers was Joel Chandler Harris, whose Uncle Remus stories, in tying animal tales to the plantation tradition, severely limited their applicability to black culture as a whole. Within what passed in those days for folklore science (as Hemenway points out, not one American university then boasted a department of folklore), efforts by white collectors to gather black material were often stymied by preconceptions about black character and by the reticence of blacks to lower their guard before such strangers. Notable among such work available in Hurston's days as a student were Guy Johnson and Howard Odum's *The Negro and His Sons* (1925) and *Negro Workaday Songs* (1926), as well as the white Mississippi folklorist Newbell Niles Puckett's *Folk Beliefs of the Southern Negro* (1927), in which Puckett had masqueraded as a voodoo priest himself in order to gain information.

As her letters to her academic mentor Franz Boas attest, Hurston had little regard for the work of these writers, especially Odum and Johnson, whom she saw as presumptuous in their confidence that they understood fully the black folk material. "Folklore is not as easy to collect as it sounds," she warned. "The best source is where there are the least outside influences and these people, being usually under-privileged, are the shyest." She was fortunate in that Boas, although a white man himself, was perhaps the outstanding champion of the notion of cultural relativism. He urged that cultures be seen on their own terms and not according to a scale that held European civilization to be the supreme standard. For all her advantages, however, Hurston still found it difficult to effect a breakthrough. In part, this was owing to the complexity of the task of understanding the material; in part, it derived from

Hurston's personal life experience, and especially from the fact that she was living at least one major lie as a student at Barnard. The two elements—the scholarly or intellectual, on the one hand, and the "purely" personal, on the other—were perhaps finally inseparable.

Hurston was born in the black town of Eatonville, Florida, on January 7, 1891—but so willfully misrepresented herself later that even her diligent biographer believed that her year of birth was 1901. This lost decade is perhaps only the major mystery of her life. What happened to Hurston between 1891 and 1917, when she started high school at Morgan Academy (later Morgan State University) in Baltimore, Maryland, is barely illuminated either by independent research or by her autobiography *Dust Tracks on a Road* (1942). Both, however, tell of a loving mother who urged her to "jump at de sun" and a dominating father, an Eatonville preacher and carpenter, whose remarriage following his wife's death began a long season of sorrow for Hurston. Apparently unable to find common ground with her new stepmother, Zora was passed around among relatives before she struck out on her own. She worked variously as a maid and a waitress, and may even have been married for a while, before she entered Morgan Academy in 1917. After being graduated from Morgan, she briefly attended Howard University in Washington, D.C., before going to New York in 1925 to study at Barnard College. *Mules and Men* is dedicated to Annie Nathan Meyer ("who hauled the mud to make me but loves me just the same"), the founder and a trustee of the college and the person directly responsible for Hurston's presence there.

As Hurston wrote, "the spy-glass of Anthropology" offered at Barnard and Columbia, especially in the persons of Boas and his associates Melville Herskovits and Ruth Benedict, enabled her to begin to see her Southern black culture accurately and comprehensively. And yet her deliberate obscuring of a decade of her life suggests that she could have approached her past, which is to say the wellspring of her folkloric knowledge, only with a certain amount of caution, perhaps even distaste. In dropping a decade from her life, she was almost certainly denying the existence of experiences and involvements that, however unpalatable to her later on as she strove for success, had been a major part of her knowledge of her world. However, one other person was at least as important as these academics in pushing Hurston not only back into the arms of her past, as exemplified by her literal reentry into Eatonville to gather the material for the first part of *Mules and Men,* but also toward the radical belief in parapsychology and occultism, in voodoo and other forms of African religion, that generated the second, even more extraordinary part of the volume. That person was her patron Mrs. R. Osgood Mason, as Hurston reveals in *Mules and Men,* who "backed my falling in a hearty way, in a spiritual way, and in addition, financed the whole expedition in the manner of the Great Soul that she is. The world's most gallant woman."

This tribute appears at the end of Hurston's introduction, which places her in a motorcar (paid for by Mrs. Mason) precisely on the border of Eatonville—home. The wealthy septuagenarian widow of a doctor who had been himself an expert in parapsychology, Mrs. Mason was already "Godmother" to various Harlem Renaissance figures, including Alain Locke and Langston Hughes, when she took up Zora Neale Hurston and bankrolled her second folklore expedition into the South. As with Langston Hughes, whose novel *Not Without Laughter* (1930) Mrs. Mason virtually commissioned and edited, she did much more than provide Hurston with money. Volatile in personality, contemptuous of European rationalism and radically devoted to the idea of extrasensory communication, and a champion of the notion of the artistic and spiritual superiority of the darker races, Mrs. Mason, more than any of Hurston's academic advisers, paved the way for Hurston's plunging not simply into the Eatonville community of her childhood but, far more radically, into voodoo and black magic in Louisiana.

Although the voodoo section (a slightly edited version of her 1931 article "Hoodoo in America" in the *Journal of Ameri-*

can Folklore) was added at the last minute to the book in 1934 to please its publisher, Lippincott, the two sections are intimately related. The world of Eatonville and Florida in general—the world of tales spun by black men and women—is linked directly in this book to the world of New Orleans and Louisiana, where "two-headed doctors" preside over a community that believes devoutly in spells and conjures, hexes and divinations. Linking Eatonville and New Orleans is the communality and adaptability, the indomitable resilience of the imagination of Africans terrorized in the New World by objective reality in the form of slavery, segregation, and poverty. And both elements, I believe, were linked integrally to Hurston's interior world, to the fantastic personality and the altered personal history she had created for herself. "I thought about the tales I had heard as a child," Hurston recalled fancifully but pointedly during her approach by car to Eatonville. "How even the Bible was made over to suit our vivid imagination. How the devil always outsmarted God and how that over-noble hero Jack or John—not *John Henry,* who occupies the same place in Negro folklore that Casey Jones does in white lore and if anything is more recent—outsmarted the devil."

She who had been living to some extent by her wits, by her imagination, by the "lies" she created for her empowerment and salvation, as well as by her more structured, conventionally disciplined intelligence as a college student, now had begun to see her personal predicament and her imaginative response to it in a broader historical and cultural sense. To her black sources, their marvelous tales were—"lies." (" 'Zora,' George Thomas informed me, 'you come to de right place if lies is what you want. Ah'm gointer lie up a nation.' ") In one sense, it is possible to say that Hurston had become more of an African-American cultural nationalist, seeing more of the world and herself in terms of race and her own blackness. This would be true only to a limited degree, as Hurston's later involvement with reactionary political forces and personalities suggests. The power she gained from seeing her life in coherence with the storytelling imagination of country blacks and with the world of conjure and black magic represented by voodoo was placed largely in a different service—self-empoweringly, to facilitate her emergence as a writer of fiction. Even before *Mules and Men* appeared in 1935, she published her first novel, *Jonah's Gourd Vine* (1934), which drew on her parents' history for inspiration. Two years after *Mules and Men* came *Their Eyes Were Watching God,* in which she effected her most harmonious blending of the themes of folklore and individualism, in a story now recognized as one of the main foundations of African-American literature.

In both main sections of *Mules and Men*—the seventy stories that make up "Folk Tales" and her encounters with five doctors in "Hoodoo"—the most fertile single device is the portrait of the narrator, Hurston herself. In both cases, she is both familiar with the culture into which she is moving and also an initiate. She is known in Eatonville, but everywhere else she must ingratiate herself into the confidence of the people, her great source. ("I stood there awkwardly, knowing that the too-ready laughter and aimless talk was a window-dressing for my benefit. The brother in black puts a laugh in every vacant place in his mind. His laugh has a hundred meanings.") So, too, with the world of hoodoo, which she approaches not as a scientific scholar, taking notes, or fraudulently, as Newbell Niles Puckett had done for his own book in representing himself as a conjure man. "None may wear the crown of power," she writes of her initiation, "without preparation. *It must be earned.*" Instead, she would be a true believer. "Belief in magic is older than writing," she declared tellingly. In the end, her teacher Luke Turner (called elsewhere Samuel Thompson by Hurston), who offered himself as the grandnephew of Marie Leveau, the most fabled figure in New Orleans hoodoo lore, invites Hurston to devote her life to the field. "He wanted me to stay with him to the end," she soberly reveals. "It has been a great sorrow to me that I could not say yes."

Much has been made about Hurston's scholarly shortcomings in compiling *Mules and Men.* It seems certain that not all the stories and anecdotes in the book originated in the course of her research. Some of them, picked up elsewhere, may have been substantially ornamented by Hurston, and perhaps she invented a few. Rival versions of certain passages, published elsewhere by her, raise questions about her scholarly integrity. For the sake of symmetry, she appears to have telescoped certain periods of time into more convenient arrangements. "I had spent a year in gathering and culling over folk-tales," she wrote, when in fact she had spent a much longer period. Above all, some readers find Hurston insufficiently analytical and too much a part of her text, without that text revealing her definitively. Her shifts from the third person to the first are sometimes disconcerting. Scientific purists may find her language at times too colloquial and even racy, her sense of humor often reckless, her poetic license too frequently invoked. Her approach, some would say, was journalistic rather than scientific, self-indulgent rather than profound.

I would respond that the key to *Mules and Men* is precisely Hurston's finding of herself in the black folk world she described, and finding that black folk world, approached first by her as a student of anthropology, finally to be an unmistakable, ineradicable part of herself, her intimate psychology and history, and her desires, especially her desire to be an artist.

ARNOLD RAMPERSAD

MULES AND MEN

INTRODUCTION

I was glad when somebody told me, "You may go and collect
Negro folklore."

In a way it would not be a new experience for me. When
I pitched headforemost into the world I landed in the crib of
negroism. From the earliest rocking of my cradle, I had known
about the capers Brer Rabbit is apt to cut and what the Squinch
Owl says from the house top. But it was fitting me like a tight
chemise. I couldn't see it for wearing it. It was only when I
was off in college, away from my native surroundings, that I
could see myself like somebody else and stand off and look at
my garment. Then I had to have the spy-glass of Anthropology
to look through at that.

Dr. Boas asked me where I wanted to work and I said,
"Florida," and gave, as my big reason, that "Florida is a place
that draws people—white people from all over the world, and
Negroes from every Southern state surely and some from the
North and West." So I knew that it was possible for me to get
a cross section of the Negro South in the one state. And then
I realized that I was new myself, so it looked sensible for me
to choose familiar ground.

First place I aimed to stop to collect material was Eatonville,
Florida.

And now, I'm going to tell you why I decided to go to my

native village first. I didn't go back there so that the home folks could make admiration over me because I had been up North to college and come back with a diploma and a Chevrolet. I knew they were not going to pay either one of these items too much mind. I was just Lucy Hurston's daughter, Zora, and even if I had—to use one of our down-home expressions—had a Kaiser baby,[1] and that's something that hasn't been done in this Country yet, I'd still be just Zora to the neighbors. If I had exalted myself to impress the town, somebody would have sent me word in a match-box that I had been up North there and had rubbed the hair off of my head against some college wall, and then come back there with a lot of form and fashion and outside show to the world. But they'd stand flat-footed and tell me that they didn't have me, neither my sham-polish, to study 'bout. And that would have been that.

I hurried back to Eatonville because I knew that the town was full of material and that I could get it without hurt, harm or danger. As early as I could remember it was the habit of the men folks particularly to gather on the store porch of evenings and swap stories. Even the women folks would stop and break a breath with them at times. As a child when I was sent down to Joe Clarke's store, I'd drag out my leaving as long as possible in order to hear more.

Folklore is not as easy to collect as it sounds. The best source is where there are the least outside influences and these people, being usually under-privileged, are the shyest. They are most reluctant at times to reveal that which the soul lives by. And the Negro, in spite of his open-faced laughter, his seeming acquiescence, is particularly evasive. You see we are a polite people and we do not say to our questioner, "Get out of here!" We smile and tell him or her something that satisfies the white person because, knowing so little about us, he doesn't know what he is missing. The Indian resists curiosity by a stony silence. The Negro offers a feather-bed resistance. That is, we let the probe enter, but it never comes out. It gets

[1]Have a child by the Kaiser.

2

smothered under a lot of laughter and pleasantries.

The theory behind our tactics: "The white man is always trying to know into somebody else's business. All right, I'll set something outside the door of my mind for him to play with and handle. He can read my writing but he sho' can't read my mind. I'll put this play toy in his hand, and he will seize it and go away. Then I'll say my say and sing my song."

I knew that even *I* was going to have some hindrance among strangers. But here in Eatonville I knew everybody was going to help me. So below Palatka I began to feel eager to be there and I kicked the little Chevrolet right along.

I thought about the tales I had heard as a child. How even the Bible was made over to suit our vivid imagination. How the devil always outsmarted God and how that over-noble hero Jack or John—not *John Henry,* who occupies the same place in Negro folk-lore that Casey Jones does in white lore and if anything is more recent—outsmarted the devil. Brer Fox, Brer Deer, Brer 'Gator, Brer Dawg, Brer Rabbit, Ole Massa and his wife were walking the earth like natural men way back in the days when God himself was on the ground and men could talk with him. Way back there before God weighed up the dirt to make the mountains. When I was rounding Lily Lake I was remembering how God had made the world and the elements and people. He made souls for people, but he didn't give them out because he said:

"Folks ain't ready for souls yet. De clay ain't dry. It's de strongest thing Ah ever made. Don't aim to waste none thru loose cracks. And then men got to grow strong enough to stand it. De way things is now, if Ah give it out it would tear them shackly bodies to pieces. Bimeby, Ah give it out."

So folks went round thousands of years without no souls. All de time de soul-piece, it was setting 'round covered up wid God's loose raiment. Every now and then de wind would blow and hist up de cover and then de elements would be full of lightning and de winds would talk. So

3

people told one 'nother that God was talking in de mountains.

De white man passed by it way off and he looked but he wouldn't go close enough to touch. De Indian and de Negro, they tipped by cautious too, and all of 'em seen de light of diamonds when de winds shook de cover, and de wind dat passed over it sung songs. De Jew come past and heard de song from de soul-piece then he kept on passin' and all of a sudden he grabbed up de soul-piece and hid it under his clothes, and run off down de road. It burnt him and tore him and throwed him down and lifted him up and toted him across de mountain and he tried to break loose but he couldn't do it. He kept on hollerin' for help but de rest of 'em run hid 'way from him. Way after while they come out of holes and corners and picked up little chips and pieces that fell back on de ground. So God mixed it up wid feelings and give it out to 'em. 'Way after while when He ketch dat Jew, He's goin' to 'vide things up more ekal'.

So I rounded Park Lake and came speeding down the straight stretch into Eatonville, the city of five lakes, three croquet courts, three hundred brown skins, three hundred good swimmers, plenty guavas, two schools, and no jail-house.

Before I enter the township, I wish to make acknowledgments to Mrs. R. Osgood Mason of New York City. She backed my falling in a hearty way, in a spiritual way, and in addition, financed the whole expedition in the manner of the Great Soul that she is. The world's most gallant woman.

PART I

❖

FOLK TALES

ONE

As I crossed the Maitland-Eatonville township line I could see a group on the store porch. I was delighted. The town had not changed. Same love of talk and song. So I drove on down there before I stopped. Yes, there was George Thomas, Calvin Daniels, Jack and Charlie Jones, Gene Brazzle, B. Moseley and "Seaboard." Deep in a game of Florida-flip. All of those who were not actually playing were giving advice—"bet straightening" they call it.

"Hello, boys," I hailed them as I went into neutral.

They looked up from the game and for a moment it looked as if they had forgotten me. Then B. Moseley said, "Well, if it ain't Zora Hurston!" Then everybody crowded around the car to help greet me.

"You gointer stay awhile, Zora?"

"Yep. Several months."

"Where you gointer stay, Zora?"

"With Mett and Ellis, I reckon."

"Mett" was Mrs. Armetta Jones, an intimate friend of mine since childhood and Ellis was her husband. Their house stands under the huge camphor tree on the front street.

"Hello, heart-string," Mayor Hiram Lester yelled as he hurried up the street. "We heard all about you up North. You back home for good, I hope."

7

"Nope, Ah come to collect some old stories and tales and Ah know y'all know a plenty of 'em and that's why Ah headed straight for home."

"What you mean, Zora, them big old lies we tell when we're jus' sittin' around here on the store porch doin' nothin'?" asked B. Moseley.

"Yeah, those same ones about Ole Massa, and colored folks in heaven, and—oh, y'all know the kind I mean."

"Aw shucks," exclaimed George Thomas doubtfully. "Zora, don't you come here and tell de biggest lie first thing. Who you reckon want to read all them old-time tales about Brer Rabbit and Brer Bear?"

"Plenty of people, George. They are a lot more valuable than you might think. We want to set them down before it's too late."

"Too late for what?"

"Before everybody forgets all of 'em."

"No danger of that. That's all some people is good for—set 'round and lie and murder groceries."

"Ah know one right now," Calvin Daniels announced cheerfully. "It's a tale 'bout John and de frog."

"Wait till she get out her car, Calvin. Let her get settled at 'Met's' and cook a pan of ginger bread then we'll all go down and tell lies and eat ginger bread. Dat's de way to do. She's tired now from all dat drivin'."

"All right, boys," I agreed. "But Ah'll be rested by night. Be lookin' for everybody."

So I unloaded the car and crowded it into Ellis' garage and got settled. Armetta made me lie down and rest while she cooked a big pan of ginger bread for the company we expected.

Calvin Daniels and James Moseley were the first to show up.

"Calvin, Ah sure am glad that you got here. Ah'm crazy to hear about John and dat frog," I said.

"That's why Ah come so early so Ah could tell it to you and go. Ah got to go over to Wood Bridge a little later on."

"Ah'm glad you remembered me first, Calvin."

8

"Ah always like to be good as my word, and Ah just heard about a toe-party over to Wood Bridge tonight and Ah decided to make it."

"A toe-party! What on earth is that?"

"Come go with me and James and you'll see!"

"But, everybody will be here lookin' for me. They'll think Ah'm crazy—tellin' them to come and then gettin' out and goin' to Wood Bridge myself. But Ah certainly would like to go to that toe-party."

"Aw, come on. They kin come back another night. You gointer like this party."

"Well, you tell me the story first, and by that time, Ah'll know what to do."

"Ah, come on, Zora," James urged. "Git de car out. Calvin kin tell you dat one while we're on de way. Come on, let's go to de toe-party."

"No, let 'im tell me this one first, then, if Ah go he can tell me some more on de way over."

James motioned to his friend. "Hurry up and tell it, Calvin, so we kin go before somebody else come."

"Aw, most of 'em ain't comin' nohow. They all 'bout goin' to Wood Bridge, too. Lemme tell you 'bout John and dis frog:

It was night and Ole Massa sent John,[1] his favorite slave, down to the spring to get him a cool drink of water. He called John to him.

"John!"

"What you want, Massa?"

"John, I'm thirsty. Ah wants a cool drink of water, and Ah wants you to go down to de spring and dip me up a nice cool pitcher of water."

John didn't like to be sent nowhere at night, but he always tried to do everything Ole Massa told him to do, so he said, "Yessuh, Massa, Ah'll go git you some!"

Ole Massa said: "Hurry up, John. Ah'm mighty thirsty."

John took de pitcher and went on down to de spring.

[1]Negro story-hero name. See glossary.

9

There was a great big ole bull frog settin' right on de edge of de spring, and when John dipped up de water de noise skeered de frog and he hollered and jumped over in de spring.

John dropped de water pitcher and tore out for de big house, hollerin' "Massa! Massa! A big ole booger[2] done got after me!"

Ole Massa told him, "Why, John, there's no such thing as a booger."

"Oh, yes it is, Massa. He down at dat Spring."

"Don't tell me, John. Youse just excited. Furthermore, you go git me dat water Ah sent you after."

"No, indeed, Massa, you and nobody else can't send me back there so dat booger kin git me."

Ole Massa begin to figger dat John musta seen somethin' sho nuff because John never had disobeyed him before, so he ast: "John, you say you seen a booger. What did it look like?"

John tole him, "Massa, he had two great big eyes lak balls of fire, and when he was standin' up he was sittin' down and when he moved, he moved by jerks, and he had most no tail."

Long before Calvin had ended his story James had lost his air of impatience.

"Now, Ah'll tell one," he said. "That is, if you so desire."

"Sure, Ah want to hear you tell 'em till daybreak if you will," I said eagerly.

"But where's the ginger bread?" James stopped to ask.

"It's out in the kitchen," I said. "Ah'm waiting for de others to come."

"Aw, naw, give us ours now. Them others may not get here before forty o'clock and Ah'll be done et mine and be in Wood Bridge. Anyhow Ah want a corner piece and some of them others will beat me to it."

So I served them with ginger bread and buttermilk.

[2]A bogey man.

"You sure going to Wood Bridge with us after Ah git thru tellin' this one?" James asked.

"Yeah, if the others don't show up by then," I conceded. So James told the story about the man who went to Heaven from Johnstown.

You know, when it lightnings, de angels is peepin' in de lookin' glass; when it thunders, they's rollin' out de rain-barrels; and when it rains, somebody done dropped a barrel or two and bust it.

One time, you know, there was going to be big doin's in Glory and all de angels had brand new clothes to wear and so they was all peepin' in the lookin' glasses, and therefore it got to lightning all over de sky. God tole some of de angels to roll in all de full rain barrels and they was in such a hurry that it was thunderin' from the east to the west and the zig-zag lightning went to join the mutterin' thunder and, next thing you know, some of them angels got careless and dropped a whole heap of them rain barrels, and didn't it rain!

In one place they call Johnstown they had a great flood. And so many folks got drownded that it looked jus' like Judgment day.

So some of de folks that got drownded in that flood went one place and some went another. You know, everything that happen, they got to be a nigger in it—and so one of de brothers in black went up to Heben from de flood.

When he got to the gate, Ole Peter let 'im in and made 'im welcome. De colored man was named John, so John ast Peter, says, "Is it dry in dere?"

Ole Peter tole 'im, "Why, yes it's dry in here. How come you ast that?"

"Well, you know Ah jus' come out of one flood, and Ah don't want to run into no mo'. Ooh, man! You ain't *seen* no water. You just oughter seen dat flood we had at Johnstown."

Peter says, "Yeah, we know all about it. Jus' go wid Gabriel and let him give you some new clothes."

So John went on off wid Gabriel and come back all dressed up in brand new clothes and all de time he was changin' his clothes he was tellin' Ole Gabriel all about dat flood, jus' like he didn't know already.

So when he come back from changin' his clothes, they give him a brand new gold harp and handed him to a gold bench and made him welcome. They was so tired of hearing about dat flood they was glad to see him wid his harp 'cause they figgered he'd get to playin' and forget all about it. So Peter tole him, "Now you jus' make yo'self at home and play all de music you please."

John went and took a seat on de bench and commenced to tune up his harp. By dat time, two angels come walkin' by where John was settin' so he throwed down his harp and tackled 'em.

"Say," he hollered, "Y'all want to hear 'bout de big flood Ah was in down on earth? Lawd, Lawd! It sho rained, and talkin' 'bout water!"

Dem two angels hurried on off from 'im jus' as quick as they could. He started to tellin' another one and he took to flyin'. Gab'ull went over to 'im and tried to get 'im to take it easy, but John kept right on stoppin' every angel dat he could find to tell 'im about dat flood of water.

Way after while he went over to Ole Peter and said: "Thought you said everybody would be nice and polite?"

Peter said, "Yeah, Ah said it. Ain't everybody treatin' you right?"

John said, "Naw. Ah jus' walked up to a man as nice and friendly as Ah could be and started to tell 'im 'bout all dat water Ah left back there in Johnstown and instead of him turnin' me a friendly answer he said, 'Shucks! You ain't seen no water!' and walked off and left me standin' by myself."

"Was he a *ole* man wid a crooked walkin' stick?" Peter ast John.

"Yeah."

"Did he have whiskers down to here?" Peter measured down to his waist.

"He sho did," John tol' 'im.

"Aw shucks," Peter tol' 'im. "Dat was Ole Nora.[3] You can't tell *him* nothin' 'bout no flood."

There was a lot of horn-honking outside and I went to the door. The crowd drew up under the mothering camphor tree in four old cars. Everybody in boisterous spirits.

"Come on, Zora! Le's go to Wood Bridge. Great toe-party goin' on. All kinds of 'freshments. We kin tell you some lies most any ole time. We never run outer lies and lovin'. Tell 'em tomorrow night. Come on if you comin'—le's go if you gwine."

So I loaded up my car with neighbors and we all went to Wood Bridge. It is a Negro community joining Maitland on the north as Eatonville does on the west, but no enterprising souls have ever organized it. They have no schoolhouse, no post office, no mayor. It is lacking in Eatonville's feeling of unity. In fact, a white woman lives there.

While we rolled along Florida No. 3, I asked Armetta where was the shindig going to be in Wood Bridge. "At Edna Pitts' house," she told me. "But she ain't givin' it by herself; it's for the lodge."

"Think it's gointer be lively?"

"Oh, yeah. Ah heard that a lot of folks from Altamonte and Longwood is comin'. Maybe from Winter Park too."

We were the tail end of the line and as we turned off the highway we could hear the boys in the first car doing what Ellis Jones called bookooing[4] before they even hit the ground. Charlie Jones was woofing[5] louder than anybody else. "Don't y'all sell off all dem pretty li'l pink toes befo' Ah git dere."

Peter Stagg: "Save me de best one!"

Soddy Sewell: "Hey, you mullet heads! Get out de way

---

[3]Noah.

[4]Loud talking, bullying, woofing. From French *beaucoup*.

[5]Aimless talking. See glossary.

there and let a real man smoke them toes over."

Gene Brazzle: "Come to my pick, gimme a vaseline brown!"

Big Willie Sewell: "Gimme any kind so long as you gimme more'n one."

Babe Brown, riding a running-board, guitar in hand, said, "Ah want a toe, but if it ain't got a good looking face on to it, don't bring de mess up."

When we got there the party was young. The house was swept and garnished, the refreshments on display, several people sitting around; but the spot needed some social juices to mix the ingredients. In other words, they had the carcass of a party lying around up until the minute Eatonville burst in on it. Then it woke up.

"Y'all done sold off any toes yet?" George Brown wanted to know.

Willie Mae Clarke gave him a certain look and asked him, "What's dat got to do with you, George Brown?" And he shut up. Everybody knows that Willie Mae's got the business with George Brown.

"Nope. We ain't had enough crowd, but I reckon we kin start now," Edna said. Edna and a sort of committee went inside and hung up a sheet across one end of the room. Then she came outside and called all of the young women inside. She had to coax and drag some of the girls.

"Oh, Ah'm shame-face-ted!" some of them said.

"Nobody don't want to buy *mah* ole rusty toe." Others fished around for denials from the male side.

I went on in with the rest and was herded behind the curtain.

"Say, what *is* this toe-party business?" I asked one of the girls.

"Good gracious, Zora! Ain't you never been to a toe-party before?"

"Nope. They don't have 'em up North where Ah been and Ah just got back today."

"Well, they hides all de girls behind a curtain and you stick out yo' toe. Some places you take off yo' shoes and some places you keep 'em on, but most all de time you keep 'em on. When all de toes is in a line, sticking out from behind de sheet they let de men folks in and they looks over all de toes and buys de ones they want for a dime. Then they got to treat de lady dat owns dat toe to everything she want. Sometime they play it so's you keep de same partner for de whole thing and sometime they fix it so they put de girls back every hour or so and sell de toes agin."

Well, my toe went on the line with the rest and it was sold five times during the party. Everytime a toe was sold there was a great flurry before the curtain. Each man eager to see what he had got, and whether the other men would envy him or ridicule him. One or two fellows ungallantly ran out of the door rather than treat the girls whose toe they had bought sight unseen.

Babe Brown got off on his guitar and the dancing was hilarious. There was plenty of chicken perleau and baked chicken and fried chicken and rabbit. Pig feet and chitterlings[6] and hot peanuts and drinkables. Everybody was treating wildly.

"Come on, Zora, and have a treat on me!" Charlie Jones insisted. "You done et chicken-ham and chicken-bosom wid every shag-leg in Orange County *but* me. Come on and spend some of *my* money."

"Thanks, Charlie, but Ah got five helpin's of chicken inside already. Ah either got to get another stomach or quit eatin'."

"Quit eatin' then and go to thinking. Quit thinkin' and start to drinkin'. What you want?"

"Coca-Cola right off de ice, Charlie, and put some salt in it. Ah got a slight headache."

"Aw naw, my money don't buy no sweet slop. Choose some coon dick."

"What is coon dick?"

"Aw, Zora, jus' somethin' to make de drunk come. Made

<hr>

[6]Hog intestines.

out uh grape fruit juice, corn meal mash, beef bones and a few mo' things. Come on le's git some together. It might make our love come down."

As soon as we started over into the next yard where coon dick was to be had, Charlie yelled to the barkeep, "Hey, Seymore! fix up another quart of dat low wine—here come de boom!"

It was handed to us in a quart fruit jar and we went outside to try it.

The raw likker known locally as coon dick was too much. The minute it touched my lips, the top of my head flew off. I spat it out and "choosed" some peanuts. Big Willie Sewell said, "Come on, heart-string, and have some gospel-bird[7] on me. My money spends too." His Honor, Hiram Lester, the Mayor, heard him and said, "There's no mo' chicken left, Willie. Why don't you offer her something she can get?"

"Well there *was* some chicken there when Ah passed the table a little while ago."

"Oh, so you offerin' her some chicken *was*. She can't eat that. What she want is some chicken *is*."

"Aw shut up, Hiram. Come on, Zora, le's go inside and make out we dancin'." We went on inside but it wasn't a party any more. Just some people herded together. The high spirits were simmering down and nobody had a dime left to cry so the toe-business suffered a slump. The heaped-up tables of refreshments had become shambles of chicken bones and empty platters anyway so that there was no longer any point in getting your toe sold, so when Columbus Montgomery said, "Le's go to Eatonville," Soddy Sewell jumped up and grabbed his hat and said, "I heard you, buddy."

Eatonville began to move back home right then. Nearly everybody was packed in one of the five cars when the delegation from Altamonte arrived. Johnny Barton and Georgia Burke. Everybody piled out again.

"Got yo' guitar wid you, Johnnie?"

[7]Chicken. Preachers are supposed to be fond of them.

"Man, you know Ah don't go nowhere unless Ah take my box wid me," said Johnnie in his starched blue shirt, collar pin with heart bangles hanging on each end and his cream pants with the black stripe. "And what make it so cool, Ah don't go nowhere unless I play it."

"And when you git to strowin' yo' mess and Georgy gits to singin' her alto, man it's hot as seven hells. Man, play dat 'Palm Beach.'"

Babe Brown took the guitar and Johnnie Barton grabbed the piano stool. He sung. Georgia Burke and George Thomas singing about Polk County where the water taste like wine.

My heart struck sorrow, tears come running down.

At about the thirty-seventh verse, something about:

Ah'd ruther be in Tampa with the Whip-poor-will,
Ruther be in Tampa with the Whip-poor-will
Than to be 'round here—
Honey with a hundred dollar bill,

I staggered sleepily forth to the little Chevrolet for Eatonville. The car was overflowing with passengers but I was so dull from lack of sleep that I didn't know who they were. All I knew is they belonged in Eatonville.

Somebody was woofing in my car about love and I asked him about his buddy—I don't know why now. He said, "Ah ain't got no buddy. They kilt my buddy so they could raise me. Jus' so Ah be yo' man Ah don't want no damn buddy. Ah hope they kill every man dat ever cried, 'titty-mamma' but me. Lemme be yo' kid."

Some voice from somewhere else in the car commented, "You sho' Lawd is gointer have a lot of hindrance."

Then somehow I got home and to bed and Armetta had Georgia syrup and waffles for breakfast.

TWO

The very next afternoon, as usual, the gregarious part of
the town's population gathered on the store porch. All
the Florida-flip players, all the eleven-card layers.[1] But
they yelled over to me they'd be over that night in full. And
they were.

"Zora," George Thomas informed me, "you come to de
right place if lies is what you want. Ah'm gointer lie up a
nation."

Charlie Jones said, "Yeah, man. Me and my sworn buddy
Gene Brazzle is here. Big Moose done come down from de
mountain."[2]

"Now, you gointer hear lies above suspicion," Gene added.

It was a hilarious night with a pinch of everything social
mixed with the story-telling. Everybody ate ginger bread;
some drank the buttermilk provided and some provided coon
dick for themselves. Nobody guzzled it—just took it in social
sips.

But they told stories enough for a volume by itself. Some
of the stories were the familiar drummer-type of tale about
two Irishmen, Pat and Mike, or two Jews as the case might be.

[1]Coon-can players. A two-handed card game popular among Southern Negroes.
[2]Important things are about to happen.

19

Some were the European folk-tales undiluted, like Jack and the Beanstalk. Others had slight local variations, but Negro imagination is so facile that there was little need for outside help. A'nt Hagar's son, like Joseph, put on his many-colored coat an paraded before his brethren and every man there was a Joseph.

Steve Nixon was holding class meeting across the way at St. Lawrence Church and we could hear the testimony and the songs.[3] So we began to talk about church and preachers.

"Aw, Ah don't pay all dese ole preachers no rabbit-foot,"[4] said Ellis Jones. "Some of 'em is all right but everybody dats up in de pulpit whoopin' and hollerin' ain't called to preach."

"They ain't no different from nobody else," added B. Moseley. "They mouth is cut cross ways, ain't it? Well, long as you don't see no man wid they mouth cut up and down, you know they'll all lie jus' like de rest of us."

"Yeah; and hard work in de hot sun done called a many a man to preach," said a woman called Gold, for no evident reason. "Ah heard about one man out clearin' off some new ground. De sun was so hot till a grindstone melted and run off in de shade to cool off. De man was so tired till he went and sit down on a log. 'Work, work, work! Everywhere Ah go de boss say hurry, de cap' say run. Ah got a durn good notion not to do nary one. Wisht Ah was one of dese preachers wid a whole lot of folks makin' my support for me.' He looked back over his shoulder and seen a narrer li'l strip of shade along side of de log, so he got over dere and laid down right close up to de log in de shade and said, 'Now, Lawd, if you don't pick me up and chunk me on de other side of dis log, Ah know you done called me to preach.'

"You know God never picked 'im up, so he went off and tol' everybody dat he was called to preach."

"There's many a one been called just lak dat," Ellis corroborated. "Ah knowed a man dat was called by a mule."

[3]See glossary.

[4]I ignore these preachers.

20

"A mule, Ellis? All dem b'lieve dat, stand on they head," said Little Ida.

"Yeah, a mule did call a man to preach. Ah'll show you how it was done, if you'll stand a straightenin'."

"Now, Ellis, don't mislay de truth. Sense us into dis mule-callin' business."

Ellis: These was two brothers and one of 'em was a big preacher and had good collections every Sunday. He didn't pastor nothin' but big charges. De other brother decided he wanted to preach so he went way down in de swamp behind a big plantation to de place they call de prayin' ground, and got down on his knees.

"O Lawd, Ah wants to preach. Ah feel lak Ah got a message. If you done called me to preach, gimme a sign."

Just 'bout dat time he heard a voice, "Wanh, uh wanh! Go preach, go preach, go preach!"

He went and tol' everybody, but look lak he never could git no big charge. All he ever got called was on some saw-mill, half-pint church or some turpentine still. He knocked around lak dat for ten years and then he seen his brother. De big preacher says, "Brother, you don't look like you gittin' holt of much."

"You tellin' dat right, brother. Groceries is scarce. Ah ain't dirtied a plate today."

"Whut's de matter? Don't you git no support from your church?"

"Yeah, Ah gits it such as it is, but Ah ain't never pastored no big church. Ah don't git called to nothin' but saw-mill camps and turpentine stills."

De big preacher reared back and thought a while, then he ast de other one, "Is you sure you was called to preach? Maybe you ain't cut out for no preacher."

"Oh, yeah," he told him. "Ah *know* Ah been called to de ministry. A voice spoke and tol' me so."

"Well, seem lak if God called you He is mighty slow in puttin' yo' foot on de ladder. If Ah was you Ah'd go back and ast 'im agin."

21

So de po' man went on back to de prayin' ground agin and got down on his knees. But there wasn't no big woods like it used to be. It has been all cleared off. He prayed and said, "Oh, Lawd, right here on dis spot ten years ago Ah ast you if Ah was called to preach and a voice tole me to go preach. Since dat time Ah been strugglin' in Yo' moral vineyard, but Ah ain't gathered no grapes. Now, if you really called me to preach Christ and Him crucified, please gimme another sign."

Sho nuff, jus' as soon as he said dat, de voice said "Wanh-uh! Go preach! Go preach! Go preach!"

De man jumped up and says, "Ah knowed Ah been called. Dat's de same voice. Dis time Ah'm goin ter ast Him where *must* Ah go preach."

By dat time de voice come agin and he looked 'way off and seen a mule in de plantation lot wid his head all stuck out to bray agin, and he said, "Unh hunh, youse de very son of a gun dat called me to preach befo'."

So he went on off and got a job plowin'. Dat's whut he was called to do in de first place.

Armetta said, "A many one been called to de plough and they run off and got up in de pulpit. Ah wish dese mules knowed how to take a pair of plow-lines and go to de church and ketch some of 'em like they go to de lot with a bridle and ketch mules."

Ellis: Ah knowed one preacher dat was called to preach at one of dese split-off churches. De members had done split off from a big church because they was all mean and couldn't git along wid nobody.

Dis preacher was a good man, but de congregation was so tough he couldn't make a convert in a whole year. So he sent and invited another preacher to come and conduct a revival meeting for him. De man he ast to come was a powerful hard preacher wid a good strainin' voice. He was known to get converts.

Well, he come and preached at dis split-off for two whole weeks. De people would all turn out to church and jus' set dere and look at de man up dere strainin' his lungs out and nobody would give de man no encouragement by sayin' "Amen," and not a soul bowed down.

It was a narrer church wid one winder and dat was in de pulpit and de door was in de front end. Dey had a mean ole sexton wid a wooden leg. So de last night of de protracted meetin' de preacher come to church wid his gripsack in his hand and went on up in de pulpit. When he got up to preach he says, "Brother Sexton, dis bein' de last night of de meetin' Ah wants you to lock de do' and bring me de key. Ah want everybody to stay and hear whut Ah got to say."

De sexton brought him de key and he took his tex and went to preachin'. He preached and he reared and pitched, but nobody said "Amen" and nobody bowed down. So 'way after while he stooped down and opened his suitsatchel and out wid his .44 Special. "Now," he said, "you rounders and brick-bats—yeah, you women, Ah'm talkin' to you. If you ain't a whole brick, den you must be a bat— and gamblers and 'leven-card layers. Ah done preached to you for two whole weeks and not one of you has said 'Amen,' and nobody has bowed down."

He thowed de gun on 'em. "And now Ah say bow down!" And they beginned to bow all over dat church.

De sexton looked at his wooden leg and figgered he couldn't bow because his leg was cut off above de knee. So he ast, "Me too, Elder?"

"Yeah, you too, you peg-leg son of a gun. You bow down too."

Therefo' dat sexton bent dat wooden leg and bowed down. De preacher fired a couple of shots over they heads and stepped out de window and went on 'bout his business. But he skeered dem people so bad till they all rushed to one side of de church tryin' to git out and carried dat church buildin' twenty-eight miles befo' they thought to turn it loose.

"Now Ellis," chided Gold when she was thru her laughter, "You know dat's a lie. Folks over there in St. Lawrence hol-

23

din' class meetin' and you over here lyin' like de crossties from Jacksonville to Key West."

"Naw, dat ain't no lie!" Ellis contended, still laughing himself.

"Aw, yes it 'tis," Gold said. "Dat's all you men is good for—settin' 'round and lyin'. Some of you done quit lyin' and gone to flyin'."

Gene Brazzle said, "Get off of us mens now. We *is* some good. Plenty good too if you git de right one. De trouble is you women ain't good for nothin' exceptin' readin' Sears and Roebuck's bible and hollerin' 'bout, 'gimme dis and gimme dat' as soon as we draw our pay."

Shug[5] said, "Well, we don't git it by astin' you mens for it. If we work for it we kin git it. You mens don't draw no pay. You don't do nothin' but stand around and draw lightnin'."

"Ah don't say Ah'm detrimental," Gene said dryly, "but if Gold and Shug don't stop crackin' us, Ah'm gointer get 'em to go."

Gold: "Man, if you want me any, some or none, do whut you gointer do and stop cryin'."

Gene: "You ain't seen me cryin'. See me cryin', it's sign of a funeral. If Ah even look cross somebody gointer bleed."

Gold: "Aw, shut up, Gene, you ain't no big hen's biddy if you do lay gobbler eggs. You tryin' to talk like big wood when you ain't nothin' but brush."

Armetta sensed a hard anger creepin' into the teasing so she laughed to make Gene and Gold laugh and asked, "Did y'all have any words before you fell out?"

"We ain't mad wid one 'nother," Gene defended. "We jus' jokin'."

"Well, stop blowin' it and let de lyin' go on," said Charlie Jones. "Zora's gittin' restless. She think she ain't gointer hear no more."

"Oh, no Ah ain't," I lied. After a short spell of quiet, good

[5]Short for sugar.

humor was restored to the porch. In the pause we could hear Pa Henry over in the church house sending up a prayer:

. . . You have been with me from the earliest rocking of my
   cradle up until this present moment.
You know our hearts, our Father,
And all de range of our deceitful minds,
And if you find anything like sin lurking
In and around our hearts,
Ah ast you, My Father, and my Wonder-workin' God
To pluck it out
And cast it into de sea of Fuhgitfulness
Where it will never rise to harm us in dis world
Nor condemn us in de judgment.
You heard me when Ah laid at hell's dark door
With no weapon in my hand
And no God in my heart,
And cried for three long days and nights.
You heard me, Lawd,
And stooped so low
And snatched me from the hell
Of eternal death and damnation.
You cut loose my stammerin' tongue;

You established my feet on de rock of Salvation
And yo' voice was heard in rumblin' judgment.
I thank Thee that my last night's sleepin' couch
Was not my coolin' board
And my cover
Was not my windin' sheet.
Speak to de sinner-man and bless 'im.
Touch all those
Who have been down to de doors of degradation.
Ketch de man dat's layin' in danger of consumin' fire;
And Lawd,
When Ah kin pray no mo';
When Ah done drunk down de last cup of sorrow
Look on me, yo' weak servant who feels de least of all;
'Point my soul a restin' place
Where Ah kin set down and praise yo' name forever
Is my prayer for Jesus sake
Amen and thank God.

As the prayer ended the bell of Macedonia, the Baptist
church, began to ring.

"Prayer meetin' night at Macedony," George Thomas said.

"It's too bad that it must be two churches in Eatonville," I
commented. "De town's too little. Everybody ought to go to
one."

"Dey wouldn't do dat, Zora, and you know better. Fack is,
de Christian churches nowhere don't stick together," this
from Charlie.

Everybody agreed that this was true. So Charlie went on.
"Look at all de kind of denominations we got. But de people
can't help dat 'cause de church wasn't built on no solid foundation to start wid."

"Oh yes, it 'twas!" Johnnie Mae disputed him. "It was built
on solid rock. Didn't Jesus say 'On dis rock Ah build my
church?'"

"Yeah," chimed in Antie Hoyt. "And de songs says, 'On
Christ de solid rock I stand' and 'Rock of Ages.'"

Charlie was calm and patient. "Yeah, he built it on a rock,

but it wasn't solid. It was a pieced-up rock and that's how come de church split up now. Here's de very way it was:

Christ was walkin' long one day wid all his disciples and he said, "We're goin' for a walk today. Everybody pick up a rock and come along." So everybody got their selves a nice big rock 'ceptin' Peter. He was lazy so he picked up a li'l bit of a pebble and dropped it in his side pocket and come along.

Well, they walked all day long and de other 'leven disciples changed them rocks from one arm to de other but they kept on totin' 'em. Long towards sundown they come 'long by de Sea of Galilee and Jesus tole 'em, "Well, le's fish awhile. Cast in yo' nets right here." They done like he tole 'em and caught a great big mess of fish. Then they cooked 'em and Christ said, "Now, all y'all bring up yo' rocks." So they all brought they rocks and Christ turned 'em into bread and they all had a plenty to eat wid they fish exceptin' Peter. He couldn't hardly make a moufful offa de li'l bread he had and he didn't like dat a bit.

Two or three days after dat Christ went out doors and looked up at de sky and says, "Well, we're goin' for another walk today. Everybody git yo'self a rock and come along."

They all picked up a rock apiece and was ready to go. All but Peter. He went and tore down half a mountain. It was so big he couldn't move it wid his hands. He had to take a pinch-bar to move it. All day long Christ walked and talked to his disciples and Peter sweated and strained wid dat rock of his'n.

Way long in de evenin' Christ went up under a great big ole tree and set down and called all of his disciples around 'im and said, "Now everybody bring up yo' rocks."

So everybody brought theirs but Peter. Peter was about a mile down de road punchin' dat half a mountain he was bringin'. So Christ waited till he got dere. He looked at de rocks dat de other 'leven disciples had, den he seen dis great big mountain dat Peter had and so he got up and walked over to it and put one foot up on it and said, "Why

27

Peter, dis is a fine rock you got here! It's a noble rock! And Peter, on dis rock Ah'm gointer build my church."

Peter says, "Naw you ain't neither. You won't build no church house on *dis* rock. You gointer turn dis rock into bread."

Christ knowed dat Peter meant dat thing so he turnt de hillside into bread and dat mountain is de bread he fed de 5,000 wid. Den he took dem 'leven other rocks and glued 'em together and built his church on it.

And that's how come de Christian churches is split up into so many different kinds—cause it's built on pieced-up rock.

There was a storm of laughter following Charlie's tale. "Zora, you come talkin' bout puttin' de two churches together and not havin' but one in dis town," Armetta said chidingly. "You know better'n dat. Baptis' and Methdis' always got a pick out at one 'nother. One time two preachers—one Methdis' an de other one Baptis' wuz on uh train and de engine blowed up and bein' in de colored coach right back of de engine they got blowed up too. When they saw theyself startin' up in de air de Baptis' preacher hollered, 'Ah bet Ah go higher than you!' "

Then Gold spoke up and said, "Now, lemme tell one. Ah know one about a man as black as Gene."

"Whut you always crackin' me for?" Gene wanted to know. "Ah ain't a bit blacker than you."

"Oh, yes you is, Gene. Youse a whole heap blacker than Ah is."

"Aw, go head on, Gold. Youse blacker than me. You jus' look my color cause youse fat. If you wasn't no fatter than me you'd be so black till lightnin' bugs would follow you at twelve o'clock in de day, thinkin' it's midnight."

"Dat's a lie, youse blacker than Ah ever dared to be. Youse lam' black. Youse so black till they have to throw a sheet over yo' head so de sun kin rise every mornin'. Ah know yo' ma cried when she seen *you*."

28

"Well, anyhow, Gold, youse blacker than me. If Ah was as fat as you Ah'd be a yaller man."

"Youse a liar. Youse as yaller as you ever gointer git. When a person is poor he look bright and de fatter you git de darker you look."

"Is dat yo' excuse for being so black, Gold?"

Armetta soothed Gold's feelings and stopped the war. When the air cleared Gold asked, "Do y'all know how come we are black?"

"Yeah," said Ellis. "It's because two black niggers got together."

"Aw, naw," Gold disputed petulantly. "Well, since you so smart, tell me where dem two black niggers come from in de first beginnin'."

"They musta come from Zar, and dat's on de other side of far."

"Uh, hunh!" Gold gloated. "Ah knowed you didn't know whut you was talkin' about. Now Ah'm goin' ter tell you how come we so black:

Long before they got thru makin' de Atlantic Ocean and haulin' de rocks for de mountains, God was makin' up de people.[6] But He didn't finish 'em all at one time. Ah'm compelled to say dat some folks is walkin' 'round dis town right now ain't finished yet and never will be.

Well, He give out eyes one day. All de nations come up and got they eyes. Then He give out teeth and so on. Then He set a day to give out color. So seven o'clock dat mornin' everybody was due to git they color except de niggers. So God give everybody they color and they went on off. Then He set there for three hours and one-half and no niggers. It was gettin' hot and God wanted to git His work done and go set in de cool. So He sent de angels. Rayfield and Gab'ull[7] to go git 'em so He could 'tend some mo' business.

[6]See glossary.

[7]The angels Raphael and Gabriel.

29

They hunted all over Heben till dey found de colored folks. All stretched out sleep on de grass under de tree of life. So Rayfield woke 'em up and tole 'em God wanted 'em.

They all jumped up and run on up to de th'one and they was so skeered they might miss sumpin' they begin to push and shove one 'nother, bumpin' against all de angels and turnin' over foot-stools. They even had de th'one all pushed one-sided.

So God hollered "Git back! Git back!" And they misunderstood Him and thought He said, "Git black," and they been black ever since.

Gene rolled his eyeballs into one corner of his head.

"Now Gold call herself gettin' even wid me—tellin' dat lie. 'Tain't no such a story nowhere. She jus' made dat one up herself."

"Naw, she didn't," Armetta defended. "Ah *been* knowin' dat ole tale."

"Me too," said Shoo-pie.

"Don't you know you can't git de best of no woman in de talkin' game? Her tongue is all de weapon a woman got," George Thomas chided Gene. "She could have had mo' sense, but she told God no, she'd ruther take it out in hips. So God give her her ruthers. She got plenty hips, plenty mouf and no brains."

"Oh, yes, womens is got sense too," Mathilda Moseley jumped in. "But they got too much sense to go 'round braggin' about it like y'all do. De lady people always got de advantage of mens because God fixed it dat way."

"Whut ole black advantage is y'all got?" B. Moseley asked indignantly. "We got all de strength and all de law and all de money and you can't git a thing but whut we jes' take pity on you and give you."

"And dat's jus' de point," said Mathilda triumphantly. "You *do* give it to us, but how come you do it?" And without waiting for an answer Mathilda began to tell why women always take advantage of men.

You see in de very first days, God made a man and a woman and put "em in a house together to live. 'Way back in them days de woman was just as strong as de man and both of 'em did de same things. They useter get to fussin' 'bout who gointer do this and that and sometime they'd fight, but they was even balanced and neither one could whip de other one.

One day de man said to hisself, "B'lieve Ah'm gointer go see God and ast Him for a li'l mo' strength so Ah kin whip dis 'oman and make her mind. Ah'm tired of de way things is." So he went on up to God.

"Good mawnin', Ole Father."

"Howdy man. Whut you doin' 'round my throne so soon dis mawnin'?"

"Ah'm troubled in mind, and nobody can't ease mah spirit 'ceptin' you."

God said: "Put yo' plea in de right form and Ah'll hear and answer."

"Ole Maker, wid de mawnin' stars glitterin' in yo' shinin' crown, wid de dust from yo' footsteps makin' worlds upon worlds, wid de blazin' bird we call de sun flyin' out of yo' right hand in de mawnin' and consumin' all day de flesh and blood of stump-black darkness, and comes flyin' home every evenin' to rest on yo' left hand, and never once in all yo' eternal years, mistood de left hand for de right, Ah ast you *please* to give me mo' strength than dat woman you give me, so Ah kin make her mind. Ah know you don't want to be always comin' down way past de moon and stars to be straightenin' her out and its got to be done. So give me a li'l mo' strength, Ole Maker and Ah'll do it."

"All right, Man, you got mo' strength than woman."

So de man run all de way down de stairs from Heben till he got home. He was so anxious to try his strength on de woman dat he couldn't take his time. Soon's he got in de house he hollered "Woman! Here's yo' boss. God done

31

tole me to handle you in which ever way Ah please. Ah'm yo' boss.''

De woman flew to fightin' 'im right off. She fought 'im frightenin' but he beat her. She got her wind and tried 'im agin but he whipped her agin. She got herself together and made de third try on him vigorous but he beat her every time. He was so proud he could whip 'er at last, dat he just crowed over her and made her do a lot of things she didn't like. He told her, "Long as you obey me, Ah'll be good to yuh, but every time yuh rear up Ah'm gointer put plenty wood on yo' back and plenty water in yo' eyes.''

De woman was so mad she went straight up to Heben and stood befo' de Lawd. She didn't waste no words. She said, "Lawd, Ah come befo' you mighty mad t'day. Ah want back my strength and power Ah useter have.''

"Woman, you got de same power you had since de beginnin'.''

"Why is it then, dat de man kin beat me now and he useter couldn't do it?''

"He got mo' strength than he useter have. He come and ast me for it and Ah give it to 'im. Ah gives to them that ast, and you ain't never ast me for no mo' power.''

"Please suh, God, Ah'm astin' you for it now. Jus' gimme de same as you give him.''

God shook his head. "It's too late now, woman. Whut Ah give, Ah never take back. Ah give him mo' strength than you and no matter how much Ah give you, he'll have mo'.''

De woman was so mad she wheeled around and went on off. She went straight to de devil and told him what had happened.

He said, "Don't be dis-incouraged, woman. You listen to me and you'll come out mo' than conqueror. Take dem frowns out yo' face and turn round and go right on back to Heben and ast God to give you dat bunch of keys hangin' by de mantel-piece. Then you bring 'em to me and Ah'll show you what to do wid 'em.''

So de woman climbed back up to Heben agin. She was mighty tired but she was more out-done that she was tired so she climbed all night long and got back up to Heben agin. When she got befo' de throne, butter wouldn't melt in her mouf.

"O Lawd and Master of de rainbow, Ah know yo' power. You never make two mountains without you put a valley in between. Ah know you kin hit a straight lick wid a crooked stick."

"Ast for whut you want, woman."

"God, gimme dat bunch of keys hangin' by yo' mantelpiece."

"Take 'em."

So de woman took de keys and hurried on back to de devil wid 'em. There was three keys on de bunch. Devil say, "See dese three keys? They got mo' power in 'em than all de strength de man kin ever git if you handle 'em right. Now dis first big key is to de do' of de kitchen, and you know a man always favors his stomach. Dis second one is de key to de bedroom and he don't like to be shut out from dat neither and dis last key is de key to de cradle and he don't want to be cut off from his generations at all. So now you take dese keys and go lock up everything and wait till he come to you. Then don't you unlock nothin' until he use his strength for yo' benefit and yo' desires."

De woman thanked 'im and tole 'im, "If it wasn't for you, Lawd knows whut us po' women folks would do."

She started off but de devil halted her. "Jus' one mo' thing: don't go home braggin' 'bout yo' keys. Jus' lock up everything and say nothin' until you git asked. And then don't talk too much."

De woman went on home and did like de devil tole her. When de man come home from work she was settin' on de porch singin' some song 'bout "Peck on de wood make de bed go good."

When de man found de three doors fastened what useter stand wide open he swelled up like pine lumber after a rain. First thing he tried to break in cause he figgered his strength would overcome all obstacles. When he saw he couldn't do it, he ast de woman, "Who locked dis do'?"

She tole 'im, "Me."

"Where did you git de key from?"

"God give it to me."

33

He run up to God and said, "God, woman got me locked 'way from my vittles, my bed and my generations, and she say you give her the keys."

God said, "I did, Man, Ah give her de keys, but de devil showed her how to use 'em!"

"Well, Ole Maker, please gimme some keys jus' lak 'em so she can't git de full control."

"No, Man, what Ah give Ah give. Woman got de key."

"How kin Ah know 'bout my generations?"

"Ast de woman."

So de man come on back and submitted hisself to de woman and she opened de doors.

He wasn't satisfied but he had to give in. 'Way after while he said to de woman, "Le's us divide up. Ah'll give you half of my strength if you lemme hold de keys in my hands."

De woman thought dat over so de devil popped and tol her, "Tell 'im, naw. Let 'im keep his strength and you keep yo' keys."

So de woman wouldn't trade wid 'im and de man had to mortgage his strength to her to live. And dat's why de man makes and de woman takes. You men is still braggin' 'bout yo' strength and de women is sittin' on de keys and lettin' you blow off till she git ready to put de bridle on you.

B. Moseley looked over at Mathilda and said, "You just like a hen in de barnyard. You cackle so much you give de rooster de blues."

Mathilda looked over at him archly and quoted:

> Stepped on a pin, de pin bent
> And dat's de way de story went.

"Y'all lady people ain't smarter *than* all men folks. You got plow lines on some of us, but some of us is too smart for you. We go past you jus' like lightnin' thru de trees," Willie Sewell boasted. "And what make it so cool, we close enough to you to have a scronchous time, but never no halter on our necks.

Ah know they won't git none on dis last neck of mine."

"Oh, you kin be had," Gold retorted. "Ah mean dat ab-stifically."

"Yeah? But not wid de trace chains. Never no shack up. Ah want dis tip-in love and tip yo' hat and walk out. Ah don't want nobody to have dis dyin' love for me."

Richard Jones said: "Yeah, man. Love is a funny thing; love is a blossom. If you want yo' finger bit poke it at a possum."

Jack Oscar Jones, who had been quiet for some time, slumped way down in his chair, straightened up and said, "Ah know a speech about love."

Ruth Marshall laughed doubtfully. "Now, Jack, you can't make me b'lieve you know de first thing about no love."

"Yeah he do, too," Clara, Jack's wife defended.

"Whut do he know, then?" Ruth persisted.

"Aw, Lawd," Clara wagged her head knowingly. "You ain't got no business knowing dat. Dat's *us* business. But he know jus' as much about love as de nex' man."

"You don't say!" Johnnie Mae twitted her sister-in-law. "Blow it out, then, Jack, and tell a blind man somethin'."

"Ah'm gointer say it, then me and Zora's goin' out to Montgomery and git up a cool watermelon, ain't we, Zora?"

"If you got de price," I came back. "Ah got de car so all we need is a strong determination and we'll have melon."

"No, Zora ain't goin' nowhere wid my husband," Clara announced. "If he got anything to tell her—it's gointer be right here in front of me."

Jack laughed at Clara's feigned jealousy and recited:

SONG POEM

When the clock struck one I had just begun. Begun with Sue, begun with Sal, begun with that pretty Johnson gal.

When the clock struck two, I was through, I was through with Sue, through with Sal, through with that pretty Johnson gal.

When the clock struck three I was free, free with Sue, free with Sal, free with that pretty Johnson gal.

When the clock struck four I was at the door, at the door with Sue, at the door with Sal, at the door with that pretty Johnson gal.

When the clock struck five I was alive, alive with Sue, alive with Sal, alive with that pretty Johnson gal.

When the clock struck six I was fixed, fixed with Sue, fixed with Sal, fixed with that pretty Johnson gal.

When the clock struck seven I was even, even with Sue, even with Sal, even with that pretty Johnson gal.

When the clock struck eight I was at your gate, gate with Sue, gate with Sal, gate with that pretty Johnson gal.

When the clock struck nine I was behind, behind with Sue, behind with Sal, behind with that pretty Johnson gal.

When the clock struck ten I was in the bin, in the bin with Sue, in the bin with Sal, in the bin with that pretty Johnson gal.

When the clock struck eleven, I was in heaven, in heaven with Sue, in heaven with Sal, in heaven with that pretty Johnson gal.

When the clock struck twelve I was in hell, in hell with Sue, in hell with Sal, in hell with that pretty Johnson gal.

"Who was all dis Sue and dis Sal and dat pretty Johnson gal?" Clara demanded of Jack.

"Dat ain't for you to know. My name is West, and Ah'm so different from de rest."

"You sound like one man courtin' three gals, but Ah know a story 'bout three mens courtin' one gal," Shug commented.

"Dat's bogish,"[8] cried Bennie Lee thickly.

"Whut's bogish?" Shug demanded. She and Bennie were step-brother and sister and they had had a lawsuit over the property of his late father and her late mother, so a very little of Bennie's sugar would sweeten Shug's tea and vice versa.

"Ah don't want to lissen to no ole talk 'bout three mens

[8]Bogus.

36

after no one 'oman. It's always more'n three womens after every man."

"Well, de way Ah know de story, there was three mens after de same girl," Shug insisted. "You drunk, Bennie Lee. You done drunk so much of dis ole coon dick till you full of monkies."

"Whut you gointer do?" Bennie demanded. "Whut you gointer do?" No answer was expected to this question. It was just Bennie Lee's favorite retort. "De monkies got me, now whut you gointer do?"

"Ah ain't got you to study about, Bennie Lee. If God ain't payin' you no mo' mind than Ah is, youse in hell right now. Ah ain't talkin' to you nohow. Zora, you wanter hear dis story?"

"Sure, Shug. That's what Ah'm here for."

"Somebody's gointer bleed," Bennie Lee threatened. Nobody paid him any mind.

"God knows Ah don't wanter hear Shug tell nothin'," Bennie Lee complained.

"Ah wish yo' monkies would tell you to go hide in de hammock and forgit to tell you de way home." Shug was getting peeved.

"You better shut up befo' Ah whip yo' head to de red. Ah wish Ah was God. Ah'd turn you into a blamed hawg, and then Ah'd concrete de whole world over so you wouldn't have not one nary place to root."

"Dat's dat two-bits in change you got in yo' pocket now dat's talkin' for you. But befo' de summer's over *you'll* be rootin' lak a hawg. You already lookin' over-plus lak one now. Don't you worry 'bout me."

Bennie Lee tried to ask his well-known question but the coon dick was too strong. He mumbled down into his shirt bosom and went to sleep.

THREE

Youse in de majority, now Shug," B. Moseley said, seeing Bennie asleep. "Le's hear 'bout dat man wid three women."

Shug said:

Naw, it was three mens went to court a girl, Ah told you. Dis was a real pretty girl wid shiny black hair and coal black eyes. And all dese men wanted to marry her, so they all went and ast her pa if they could have her. He looked 'em all over, but he couldn't decide which one of 'em would make de best husband and de girl, she couldn't make up her mind, so one Sunday night when he walked into de parlor where they was all sittin' and said to 'em, "Well, all y'all want to marry my daughter and youse all good men and Ah can't decide which one will make her de best husband. So y'all be here tomorrow mornin' at daybreak and we'll have a contest and de one dat can do de quickest trick kin have de girl."

Nex' mornin' de first one got up seen it wasn't no water in de bucket to cook breakfas' wid. So he tole de girl's mama to give him de water bucket and he would go to the spring and git her some.

He took de bucket in his hand and then he found out dat de spring was ten miles off. But he said he didn't mind dat. He went on and dipped up de water and hurried on back wid it. When he got to de five-mile post he looked down into de bucket and seen dat de bottom had done dropped out. Then he recollected dat he heard somethin' fall when he dipped up de water so he turned round and run back to de spring and clapped in dat bottom before de water had time to spill.

De ole man thought dat was a pretty quick trick, but de second man says, "Wait a minute. Ah want a grubbin' hoe and a axe and a plow and a harrow." So he got everything he ast for. There was ten acres of wood lot right nex' to de house. He went out dere and chopped down all de trees, grubbed up de roots, ploughed de field, harrowed it, planted it in cow-peas, and had green peas for dinner.

De ole man says "Dat's de quickest trick. Can't nobody beat dat. No use in tryin'. He done won de girl."

De last man said, "You ain't even givin' me a chance to win de girl."

So he took his high-powered rifle and went out into de woods about seben or eight miles until he spied a deer. He took aim and fired. Then he run home, run round behind de house and set his gun down and then run back out in de woods and caught de deer and held 'im till de bullet hit 'im.

So he won de girl.

Robert Williams said:
Ah know another man wid a daughter.

The man sent his daughter off to school for seben years, den she come home all finished up. So he said to her, "Daughter, git yo' things and write me a letter to my brother!" So she did.

He says, "Head it up," and she done so.

"Now tell 'im, 'Dear Brother, our chile is done come home from school and all finished up and we is very proud of her.' "

Then he ast de girl "Is you got dat?"

She tole 'im "yeah."

"Now tell him some mo'. 'Our mule is dead but Ah got another mule and when Ah say (clucking sound of tongue and teeth) he moved from de word.'"

"Is you got dat?" he ast de girl.

"Naw suh," she tole 'im.

He waited a while and he ast her again, "You got dat down yet?"

"Naw suh, Ah ain't got it yet."

"How come you ain't got it?"

"Cause Ah can't spell (clucking sound)."

"You mean to tell me you been off to school seben years and can't spell (clucking sound)? Why Ah could spell dat myself and Ah ain't been to school a day in mah life. Well jes' say (clucking sound) he'll know what yo' mean and go on wid de letter."

Henry "Nigger" Byrd said:
I know one about a letter too.

My father owned a fas' horse—I mean a *fast* horse. We was livin' in Ocala then. Mah mother took sick and mah father come and said, "Skeet,"—he uster call me Skeet— "You oughter wire yo' sister in St. Petersburg."

"I jus' wired her," I tole him.

"Whut did you put in it?"

I tole 'im.

He says, "Dat ain't right. I'm goin' ketch it." He went out in de pasture and caught de horse and shod 'im and curried 'im and brushed 'im off good, put de saddle on 'im and got on 'im, and caught dat telegram and read it and took it on to mah sister.

Soon as he left de house, mama said, "You chillun make a fire in de stove and fix somethin' for de ole man to eat."

Befo' she could git de word out her mouf, him and mah sister rode up to de do' and said "Whoa!"

By dat time a flea ast me for a shoe-shine so I left.

Armetta said: "Nigger, I didn't know you could lie like that."

41

"I ain't lyin', Armetta. We had dat horse. We had a cow too and she was so sway-backed that she could use de bushy part of her tail for a umbrella over her head."

"Shet up, Nig!" "Seaboard" Hamilton pretended to be outraged. "Ah knowed you could sing barytone but Ah wouldn't a b'lieved de lyin' was in you if Ah didn't hear you myself. Whut makes you bore wid such a great big augur?"

Little Julius Henry, who should have been home in bed spoke up. "Mah brother John had a horse 'way back dere in slavery time."

"Let de dollars hush whilst de nickel speak," Charlies Jones derided Julius' youth. "Julius, whut make you wanta jump in a hogshead when a kag[1] will hold yuh? You hear dese hard ole coons lyin' up a nation and you stick in yo' bill."

"If his mouf is cut cross ways and he's two years ole, he kin lie good as anybody else," John French defended. "Blow it, Julius."

Julius spat out into the yard, trying to give the impression that he was skeeting tobacco juice like a man.[2]

De rooster chew t'backer, de hen dip snuff.
De biddy can't do it, but he struts his stuff.
Ole John, he was workin' for Massa and Massa had two hawses and he lakted John, so he give John one of his hawses.

When John git to workin' 'em he'd haul off and beat Massa's hawse, but he never would hit his'n. So then some white folks tole ole Massa 'bout John beatin' his hawse and never beatin' his own. So Massa tole John if he ever heard tell of him layin' a whip on his hawse agin he was gointer take and kill John's hawse dead as a nit.

John tole 'im, "Massa, if you kill my hawse, Ah'll beatcher makin' money."

One day John hit ole Massa's hawse agin. Dey went and tole Massa' bout it. He come down dere where John was

[1]Keg.
[2]This story is of European origin, but has been colored by the negro mouth.

haulin' trash, wid a great big ole knife and cut John's hawse's th'oat and he fell dead.

John jumped down off de wagon and skint his hawse, and tied de hide up on a stick and throwed it cross his shoulder, and went on down town.

Ole John was a fortune teller hisself but nobody 'round dere didn't know it. He met a man and de man ast John, "Whut's dat you got over yo' shoulder dere, John?"

"It's a fortune teller, boss."

"Make it talk some, John, and I'll give you a sack of money and a hawse and saddle, and five head of cattle."

John put de hide on de ground and pulled out de stick and hit 'cross de hawse hide and hold his head down dere to lissen.

"Dere's a man in yo' bed-room behind de bed talkin' to yo' wife."

De man went inside his house to see. When he come back out he said, "Yeah, John, you sho tellin' de truth. Make him talk some mo'."

John went to puttin' de stick back in de hide. "Naw, Massa, he's tired now."

De white man says, "Ah'll give you six head of sheeps and fo' hawses and fo' sacks of money."

John pulled out de stick and hit down on de hide and hold down his head to lissen.

"It's a man in yo' kitchen openin' yo' stove." De man went back into his house and come out agin and tole John, "Yo, fortune-teller sho is right. Here's de things Ah promised you."

John rode on past Ole Massa's house wid all his sacks of money and drivin' his sheeps and cattle, whoopin' and crackin' his whip. "Yee, whoo-pee, yee!" Crack!

Massa said, "John, where did you git all dat?"

John said, "Ah tole you if you kilt mah hawse Ah'd beatcher makin' money."

Massa said to 'im, "Reckon if Ah kilt mah hawse Ah'd make dat much money?"

"Yeah, Massa, Ah reckon so."

So ole Massa went out and kilt his hawse and went to town hollerin', "Hawse hide for sale! Hawse hide for sale!"

One man said, "Hold on dere. Ah'll give you two-bits for it to bottom some chears."

Ole Massa tole 'im, "Youse crazy!" and went on hollerin' "Hawse hide for sale!"

"Ah'll gi' you twenty cents for it to cover some chears," another man said.

"You must be stone crazy! Why, dis hide is worth five thousand dollars."

De people all laughed at 'im so he took his hawse hide and throwed it away and went and bought hisself another hawse.

Ole John, he already rich, he didn't have to work but he jus' love to fool 'round hawses so he went to drivin' hawse and buggy for Massa. And when nobody wasn't wid him, John would let his grandma ride in Massa's buggy. Dey tole ole Massa 'bout it and he said, "John, Ah hear you been had yo' grandma ridin' in mah buggy. De first time Ah ketch her in it, Ah'm gointer kill 'er."

John tole 'im, "If you kill my grandma, Ah'll beatcher makin' money."

Pretty soon some white folks tole Massa dat John was takin' his gran'ma to town in his buggy and was hittin' his hawse and showin' off. So ole Massa come out dere and cut John's gran'ma's th'oat.

So John buried his gran'ma in secret and went and got his same ole hawse hide and keered it up town agin and went 'round talkin' 'bout, "Fortune-teller, fortune-teller!"

One man tole 'im, "Why, John, make it talk some for me. Ah'll give you six head of goats, six sheeps, and a hawse and a saddle to ride 'im wid."

So John made it talk and de man was pleased so he give John more'n he promised 'im, and John went on back past Massa's house wid his stuff so ole Massa could see 'im.

Ole Massa run out and ast, "Oh, John, where did you git all dat?"

John said, "Ah tole you if you kill mah gran'ma Ah'd beatcher makin' money."

Massa said, "You reckon if Ah kill mine, Ah'll make all dat?"

"Yeah, Ah reckon so."

So Massa runned and cut his gran'ma's th'oat and went up town hollerin' "gran'ma for sale! gran'ma for sale!"

Wouldn't nobody break a breath wid him. Dey thought he was crazy. He went on back home and grabbed John and tole 'im, "You made me kill my gran'ma and my good hawse and Ah'm gointer throw you in de river."

John tole 'im, "If you throw me in de river, Ah'll beatcher makin' money."

"Naw you won't neither," Massa tole 'im. "You done made yo' last money and done yo' las' do."

He got ole John in de sack and keered 'im down to de river, but he done forgot his weights, so he went back home to git some.

While he was gone after de weights a toad frog come by dere and John seen 'im. So he hollered and said, "Mr. Hoptoad, if you open dis sack and let me out Ah'll give you a dollar."

Toad frog let 'im out, so he got a soft-shell turtle and put it in de sack wid two big ole bricks. Then ole Massa got his weights and come tied 'em on de sack and throwed it in de river.

Whilst Massa was down to de water foolin' wid dat sack, John had done got out his hawse hide and went on up town agin hollerin', "Fortune-teller! fortune-teller!"

One rich man said "Make it talk for me, John."

John pulled out de stick and hit on de hide, and put his ear down. "Uh man is in yo' smoke-house stealin' meat and another one is in yo' money-safe."

De man went inside to see and when he come back he said, "You sho kin tell de truth."

So John went by Massa's house on a new hawse, wid a sack of money tied on each side of de saddle. Ole Massa seen 'im and ast, "Oh, John, where'd you git all dat?"

"Ah tole you if you throw me in de river Ah'd beatcher makin' money."

Massa ast, "Reckon if Ah let you throw me in de river, Ah'd make all dat?"

"Yeah, Massa, Ah *know* so."

John got ole Massa in de sack and keered 'im down to de river. John didn't forgit *his* weights. He put de weights

on ole Massa and jus' befo' he throwed 'im out he said,
"Goodbye, Massa, Ah hope you find all you lookin' for."
And dat wuz de las' of ole Massa.

"Dat wuz a long tale for a li'l boy lak you," George Thomas
praised Julius.
"Ah knows a heap uh tales," Julius retorted.

Whut is de workinest pill you ever seen? Lemme tell you
whut kind of a pill it was and how much it worked.

It wuz a ole man one time and he had de rheumatism so
bad he didn't know what to do. Ah tole 'im to go to town
and git some of dem conthartic pills.[3]

He went and got de pills lak Ah tole 'im, but on his way
back he opened de box and went to lookin' at de pills. He
wuz comin' cross some new ground where dey hadn't even
started to clear up de land. He drop one of de pills but he
didn't bother to pick it up—skeered he might hurt his back
stoopin' over.

He got to de house and say, "Ole lady, look down yonder whut a big smoke! Whut is dat, nohow?"

She say, "Ah don't know."

"Well," he say. "Guess Ah better walk down dere and
see whut dat big smoke *is* down dere."

He come back. "Guess whut it is, ole lady? One of dem
conthartic pills done worked all dem roots out de ground
and got 'em burning!"

"Julius, you little but you loud. Dat's a over average lie you
tole," Shug laughed. "Lak de wind Ah seen on de East Coast.
It blowed a crooked road straight and blowed a well up out
de ground and blowed and blowed until it scattered de days
of de week so bad till Sunday didn't come till late Tuesday
evenin'."

"Shug, Whuss yuh gonna do?" Bennie Lee tried to rise to
the surface but failed and slumped back into slumber.

"A good boy, but a po' boy," somebody commented as

<hr>

[3] Compound cathartic.

John French made his mind up.

"Zora, Ah'm gointer tell one, but you be sho and tell de folks Ah tole it. Don't say Seymore said it because he took you on de all-day fishin' trip to Titusville. Don't say Seaboard Hamilton tole it 'cause he always give you a big hunk of barbecue when you go for a sandwich. Give ole John French whut's comin' to 'im."

"You gointer tell it or you gointer spend de night tellin' us you gointer tell it?" I asked.

Ah got to say a piece of litery (literary) fust to git mah wind on.
Well Ah went up on dat meat-skin
And Ah come down on dat bone
And Ah grabbed dat piece of corn-bread
And Ah made dat biscuit moan.
Once a man had two sons. One was name Jim and de other one dey call him Jack for short. Dey papa was a most rich man, so he called de boys to 'im one night and tole 'em, "Ah don't want y'all settin' 'round waitin' for me tuh die tuh git whut Ah'm gointer give yuh. Here's five hundred dollars apiece. Dat's yo' sheer of de proppity. Go put yo'selves on de ladder. Take and make men out of yourselves."

Jim took his and bought a big farm and a pair of mules and settled down.

Jack took his money and went on down de road skinnin' and winnin'. He won from so many mens till he had threbbled his money. Den he met a man says, "Come on, le's skin some." De man says "Money on de wood" and he laid down a hundred dollars.

Jack looked at de hund'ud dollars and put down five hund'ud and says, "Man, Ah ain't for no spuddin'.[4] You playin' wid yo' stuff out de winder.[5] You fat 'round de heart.[6] Bet some money."

[4]Playing for small change.

[5]Risking nothing, i.e. hat, coat and shoes out the window so that the owner can run if he loses.

[6]Scared.

De man covered Jack's money and dey went to skinnin'. Jack was dealin' and he thought he seen de other man on de turn so he said, "Five hund'ud mo' my ten spot is de bes'."

De other man covered 'im and Jack slapped down another five hund'ud and said, "Five hund'ud mo' you fall dis time."

De other man never said a word. He put down five hund'ud mo'.

Jack got to singin':

"When yo' card git-uh lucky, oh pardner
You oughter be in a rollin' game."

He flipped de card and bless God it wuz de ten spot! Jack had done fell hisself instead of de other man. He was all put out.

Says, "Well, Ah done los' all mah money so de game is through."

De other man say, "We kin still play on. Ah'll bet you all de money on de table against yo' life."

Jack agreed to play 'cause he figgered he could out-shoot and out-cut any man on de road and if de man tried to kill *him* he'd git kilt hisself. So dey shuffled agin and Jack pulled a card and it fell third in hand.

Den de man got up and he was twelve foot tall and Jack was so skeered he didn't know whut to do. De man looked down on 'im and tole 'im says, "De Devil[7] is mah name and Ah live across de deep blue sea. Ah could kill you right now, but Ah'll give yuh another chance. If you git to my house befo' de sun sets and rise agin Ah won't kill yuh, but if you don't Ah'll be compelled to take yo' life."

Den he vanished.

Jack went on down de road jus' a cryin' till he met uh ole man.

Says, "Whuss de matter, Jack?"

"Ah played skin wid de Devil for mah life and he winned and tole me if Ah ain't to his house by de time de sun sets and rise agin he's gointer take mah life, and he live way across de ocean."

[7]See glossary.

48

De ole man says, "You sho is in a bad fix, Jack. Dere ain't but one thing dat kin cross de ocean in dat time."

"Whut is dat?"

"It's uh bald eagle. She come down to de edge of de ocean every mornin' and dip herself in de sea and pick off all de dead feathers. When she dip herself de third time and pick herself she rocks herself and spread her wings and mount de sky and go straight across de deep blue sea. And every time she holler, you give her piece uh dat yearlin' or she'll eat you.

"Now if you could be dere wid a yearlin' bull and when she git thru dippin' and pick herself and rock to mount de sky and jump straddle of her back wid dat bull yearlin' you could make it."

Jack wuz dere wid de yearlin' waitin' for dat eagle to come. He wuz watchin' her from behind de bushes and seen her when she come out de water and picked off de dead feather and rocked to go on high.

He jumped on de eagle's back wid his yearlin' and de eagle was out flyin' de sun. After while she turned her head from side to side and her blazin' eyes lit up first de north den de south and she hollered, "Ah-h-h, Ah, ah! One quarter cross de ocean! Don't see nothin' but blue water, uh!"

Jack was so skeered dat instead of him givin' de eagle uh quarter of de meat, he give her de whole bull. After while she say, "Ah-h-h, ah, ah! One half way cross de ocean! Don't see nothin' but blue water!"

Jack didn't have no mo' meat so he tore off one leg and give it to her. She swallowed dat and flew on. She hollered agin, "Ah-h-h. Ah, ha! Mighty nigh cross de ocean! Don't see nothin' but blue water! Uh!"

Jack tore off one arm and give it to her and she et dat and pretty soon she lit on land and Jack jumped off and de eagle flew on off to her nest.

Jack didn't know which way de Devil lived so he ast. "Dat first big white house 'round de bend in de road," dey tole 'im.

Jack walked to de Devil's house and knocked on de do'.

"Who's dat?"

49

"One of de Devil's friends. One widout uh arm and widout uh leg."

Devil tole his wife, says: "Look behind de do' and hand dat man uh arm and leg." She give Jack de arm and leg and Jack put 'em on.

Devil says, "See you got here in time for breakfas'. But Ah got uh job for yuh befo' you eat. Ah got uh hund'ud acres uh new ground ain't never had uh brush cut on it. Ah want you to go out dere and cut down all de trees and brushes, grub up all de roots and pile 'em and burn 'em befo' dinner time. If you don't, Ah'll hafta take yo' life."

Jus' 'bout dat time de Devil's chillen come out to look at Jack and he seen he had one real pretty daughter, but Jack wuz too worried to think 'bout no girls. So he took de tools and went on out to de wood lot and went to work.

By de time he chopped down one tree he wuz tired and he knowed it would take 'im ten years to clear dat ground right, so Jack set down and went to cryin'. 'Bout dat time de Devil's pretty daughter come wid his breakfas'. "Whuss de matter, Jack?"

"Yo papa done gimme uh job he know Ah can't git through wid, and he's gonna take mah life and Ah don't wanna die."

"Eat yo' breakfas' Jack, and put yo' head in mah lap and go to sleep."

Jack done lak she tole 'im and went to sleep and when he woke up every tree was down, every bush—and de roots grubbed up and burnt. Look lak never had been a blade uh grass dere.

De Devil come out to see how Jack wuz makin' out and seen dat hundred acres cleaned off so nice and said, "Uh, huh, Ah see youse uh wise man, 'most wise as me. Now Ah got another job for yuh. Ah got uh well, uh hundred feet deep and Ah want yuh to dip it dry. Ah mean dry, Ah want it so dry till Ah kin see dust from it and den Ah want you to bring me whut you find at de bottom."

Jack took de bucket and went to de well and went to work but he seen dat de water wuz comin' in faster dan he could draw it out. So he sat down and begin to cry.

De Devil's daughter come praipsin long wid Jack's dinner and seen Jack settin' down cryin'. "Whuss de matter, Jack? Don't cry lak dat lessen you wanta make me cry too."

"Yo' pa done put me to doin' somethin' he know Ah can't never finish and if Ah don't git thru he is gonna take mah life."

"Eat yo' dinner, Jack and put yo' head in mah lap and go to sleep."

Jack done lak she tole 'im and when he woke up de well wuz so dry till red dust wuz boilin' out of it lak smoke. De girl handed 'im a ring and tole 'im "Give papa dis ring. Dat's whut he wanted. It's mama's ring and she lost it in de well de other day."

When de Devil come to see whut Jack wuz doin', Jack give 'im de ring and de Devil looked and seen all dat dust pourin' out de well. He say, "Ah see youse uh very smart man. Almos' as wise as me. All right, Ah got just one mo' job for you and if you do dat Ah'll spare yo' life and let you marry mah daughter to boot. You take dese two geeses and go up dat cocoanut palm tree and pick 'em, and bring me de geeses when you git 'em picked and bring me every feather dat come off 'em. If you lose one Ah'll have to take yo life."

Jack took de two geeses and clammed up de cocoanut palm tree and tried to pick dem geeses. But he was more'n uh hundred feet off de ground and every time he'd pull uh feather often one of dem birds, de wind would blow it away. So Jack began to cry agin. By dat time Beatrice Devil come up wid his supper. "Whuss de matter, Jack?"

"Yo' papa is bound tuh kill me. He know Ah can't pick no geeses up no palm tree, and save de feathers."

"Eat yo' supper Jack and lay down in mah lap."

When Jack woke up all both de geeses wuz picked and de girl had all de feathers even; she had done caught dem out de air dat got away from Jack. De Devil said, "Well, now you done everything Ah tole you, you kin have mah daughter. Y'all take dat ole house down de road apiece. Dat's where me and her ma got our start."

So Jack and de Devil's daughter got married and went to keepin' house.

Way in de night, Beatrice woke up and shook Jack.

51

"Jack! Jack! Wake up! Papa's comin' here to kill you. Git up and go to de barn. He got two horses dat kin jump a thousand miles at every jump. One is named Hallowed-be-thy-name and de other, Thy-kingdom-come. Go hitch 'em to dat buck board and head 'em dis way and le's go."

Jack run to de barn and harnessed de hawses and headed towards de house where his wife wuz at. When he got to de do' she jumped in and hollered, "Le's go, Jack. Papa's comin' after us!"

When de Devil got to de house to kill Jack and found out Jack wuz gone, he run to de barn to hitch up his fas' hawses. When he seen dat dey wuz gone, he hitched up his jumpin' bull dat could jump five hundred miles at every jump, and down de road, baby!

De Devil wuz drivin' dat bull! Wid every jump he'd holler, "Oh! Hallowed-be-thy-name! Thy-kingdom-come!" And every time de hawses would hear 'im call 'em they'd fall to they knees and de bull would gain on 'em.

De girl say, "Jack, he's 'bout to ketch us! Git out and drag yo' feet backwards nine steps, throw some sand over yo' shoulders and le's go!"

Jack done dat and de hawses got up and off they went, but every time they hear they master's voice they'd stop till de girl told Jack to drag his foot three times nine times and he did it and they gained so fast on de Devil dat de hawses couldn't hear 'im no mo', and dey got away.

De Devil passed uh man and he say, "Is you seen uh man in uh buck board wid uh pretty girl wid coal black hair and red eyes behind two fas' hawses?"

De man said, "No, Ah speck dey done made it to de mountain and if dey gone to de mountain you can't overtake 'em."

"Jack and his wife wuz right dere den listenin' to de Devil. When de daughter saw her pa comin' she turned herself and de hawses into goats and they wuz croppin' grass. Jack wuz so tough she couldn't turn him into nothin' so she saw a holler log and she tole 'im to go hide in it, which he did. De Devil looked all around and he seen dat log and his mind jus' tole 'im to go look in it and he went and picked de log up and said, "Ah, ha! Ah gotcher!"

Jack wuz so skeered inside dat log he begin to call on de Lawd and he said, "O Lawd, have mercy."

You know de Devil don't lak tuh hear de name uh de Lawd so he throwed down dat log and said, "Damn it! If Ah had of knowed dat God wuz in dat log Ah never would a picked it up."

So he got back in and picked up de reins and hollered to de bull, "Turn, bull, turn! Turn clean roh-hound. Turn bull tu-urn, turn clee-ean round!"

De jumpin' bull turnt so fast till he fell and broke his own neck and throwed de Devil out on his head and kilt 'im. So dat's why dey say Jack beat de Devil.

"Boy, how kin you hold all dat in yo' head?" Jack Jones asked John. "Bet if dat lie was somethin' to do yuh some good yuh couldn't remember it."

Johnnie Mae yawned wide open and Ernest seeing her called out, "Hey, there, Johnnie Mae, throw mah trunk out befo' you shet up dat place!"

This reflection upon the size of her mouth peeved Johnnie Mae no end and she and Ernest left in a red hot family argument. Then everybody else found out that they were sleepy. So in the local term everybody went to the "pad."

Lee Robinson over in the church was leading an ole spiritual, "When I come to Die," to which I listened with one ear, while I heard the parting quips of the story-tellers with the other.

Though it was after ten the street lights were still on. B. Moseley had not put out the lights because the service in the church was not over yet, so I sat on the porch for a while looking towards the heaven-rasping oaks on the back street, towards the glassy silver of Lake Sabelia. Over in the church I could hear Mrs. Laura Henderson finishing her testimony . . . "to make Heben mah home when Ah come to die. Oh, Ah'll never forget dat day when de mornin' star bust in mah heart! Ah'll never turn back! O evenin' sun, when you git on de other side, tell mah Lawd Ah'm here prayin'."

The next afternoon I sat on the porch again. The young'uns had the grassy lane that ran past the left side of the house playing the same games that I had played in the same lane years before. With the camphor tree as a base, they played "Going 'Round de Mountain." Little Hubert Alexander was in the ring. The others danced rhythmically 'round him and sang:

> Going around de mountain two by two
> Going around de mountain two by two
> Tell me who love sugar and candy.
>
> Now, show me your motion, two by two
> Show me your motion two by two
> Tell me who love sugar and candy.

I tried to write a letter but the games were too exciting. "Little Sally Walker," "Draw a bucket of water," "Sissy in de barn," and at last that most raucous, popular and most African of games, "Chirck, mah Chick, mah Craney crow." Little Harriet Staggers, the smallest girl in the game, was contending for the place of the mama hen. She fought hard, but the larger girls promptly overruled her and she had to take her place in line behind the other little biddies, two-year-old Donnie Brown, being a year younger than Harriet, was the hindmost chick.

During the hilarious uproar of the game, Charlie Jones and Bubber Mimms came up and sat on the porch with me.

"Good Lawd, Zora! How kin you stand all dat racket? Why don't you run dem chaps 'way from here?" Seeing his nieces, Laura and Melinda and his nephew, Judson, he started to chase them off home but I made him see that it was a happy accident that they had chosen the lane as a playground. That I was enjoying it more than the chaps.

That settled, Charlie asked, "Well, Zora, did we lie enough for you las' night?"

"You lied good but not enough," I answered.

"Course, Zora, you ain't at de right place to git de bes' lies. Why don't you go down 'round Bartow and Lakeland and 'round in dere—Polk County? Dat's where they really lies up a mess and dats where dey makes up all de songs and things lak dat. Ain't you never hea'd dat in Polk County de water drink lak cherry wine?"

"Seems like when Ah was a child 'round here Ah heard de folks pickin' de guitar and singin' songs to dat effect."

"Dat's right. If Ah was you, Ah'd drop down dere and see. It's liable to do you a lot uh good."

"If Ah wuz in power[8] Ah'd go 'long wid you, Zora," Bubber added wistfully. "Ah learnt all Ah know 'bout pickin' de box[9] in Polk County. But Ah ain't even got money essence. 'Tain't no mo' hawgs 'round here. Ah cain't buy no chickens. Guess Ah have tuh eat gopher."[10]

"Where you gointer git yo' gophers, Bubber?" Charlie asked. "Doc Biddy and his pa done 'bout cleaned out dis part of de State."

"Oh, Ah got a new improvement dat's gointer be a lot of help to me and Doc Biddy and all of us po' folks."

"What is it, Bubber?"

"Ah'm gointer prune a gang of soft-shells (turtles) and grow me some gophers."

The sun slid lower and lower and at last lost its grip on the western slant of the sky and dipped three times into the bloody sea—sending up crimson spray with each plunge. At last it sunk and night roosted on the tree-tops and houses.

Bubber picked the box and Charlie sang me songs of the railroad camps. Among others, he taught me verses of JOHN HENRY, the king of railroad track-laying songs which runs as follows:[11]

[8]Funds.

[9]Playing the guitar.

[10]Dry land tortoise.

[11]See glossary.

John Henry driving on the right hand side,
Steam drill driving on the left,
Says, 'fore I'll let your steam drill beat me down
I'll hammer my fool self to death,
Hammer my fool self to death.

John Henry told his Captain,
When you go to town
Please bring me back a nine pound hammer
And I'll drive your steel on down,
And I'll drive your steel on down.

John Henry told his Captain,
Man ain't nothing but a man,
And 'fore I'll let that steam drill beat me down
I'll die with this hammer in my hand,
Die with this hammer in my hand.

Captain ast John Henry,
What is that storm I hear?
He says Cap'n that ain't no storm,
'Tain't nothing but my hammer in the air,
Nothing but my hammer in the air.

John Henry told his Captain,
Bury me under the sills of the floor,
So when they get to playing good old Georgy skin,
Bet 'em fifty to a dollar more,
Fifty to a dollar more.

John Henry had a little woman,
The dress she wore was red,
Says I'm going down the track,
And she never looked back.
I'm going where John Henry fell dead,
Going where John Henry fell dead.

Who's going to shoe your pretty lil feet?
And who's going to glove your hand?
Who's going to kiss your dimpled cheek?
And who's going to be your man?
Who's going to be your man?

My father's going to shoe my pretty lil feet;
My brother's going to glove my hand;
My sister's going to kiss my dimpled cheek;
John Henry's going to be my man,
John Henry's going to be my man.

Where did you get your pretty lil dress?
The shoes you wear so fine?
I got my shoes from a railroad man,
My dress from a man in the mine,
My dress from a man in the mine.

They talked and told strong stories of Ella, Wall, East Coast
Mary, Planchita and lesser jook[12] lights around whom the
glory of Polk County surged. Saw-mill and turpentine bosses
and prison camp "cap'ns" set to music passed over the guitar
strings and Charlie's mouth and I knew I had to visit Polk
County right now.

A hasty good-bye to Eatonville's oaks and oleanders and the
wheels of the Chevvie split Orlando wide open—headed
south-west for corn (likker) and song.

[12]A fun house. Where they sing, dance, gamble, love, and compose "blues" songs
incidentally.

FOUR

Twelve miles below Kissimmee I passed under an arch that marked the Polk County line. I was in the famed Polk County.

> How often had I heard "Polk County Blues."
> "You don't know Polk County lak Ah do.
> Anybody been dere, tell you de same thing too."

The asphalt curved deeply and when it straightened out we saw a huge smoke-stack blowing smut against the sky. A big sign said, "Everglades Cypress Lumber Company, Loughman, Florida."

We had meant to keep on to Bartow or Lakeland and we debated the subject between us until we reached the opening, then I won. We went in. The little Chevrolet was all against it. The thirty odd miles that we had come, it argued, was nothing but an appetizer. Lakeland was still thirty miles away and no telling what the road held. But it sauntered on down the bark-covered road and into the quarters just as if it had really wanted to come.

We halted beside two women walking to the commissary and asked where we could get a place to stay, despite the signs all over that this was private property and that no one could enter without the consent of the company.

One of the women was named "Babe" Hill and she sent me to her mother's house to get a room. I learned later that Mrs. Allen ran the boarding-house under patronage of the company. So we put up at Mrs. Allen's.

That night the place was full of men—come to look over the new addition to the quarters. Very little was said directly to me and when I tried to be friendly there was a noticeable disposition to *fend* me off. This worried me because I saw at once that this group of several hundred Negroes from all over the South was a rich field for folk-lore, but here was I figuratively starving to death in the midst of plenty.

Babe had a son who lived at the house with his grandmother and we soon made friends. Later the sullen Babe and I got on cordial terms. I found out afterwards that during the Christmas holidays of 1926 she had shot her husband to death, had fled to Tampa where she had bobbed her hair and eluded capture for several months but had been traced thru letters to her mother and had been arrested and lodged in Bartow jail. After a few months she had been allowed to come home and the case was forgotten. Negro women *are* punished in these parts for killing men, but only if they exceed the quota. I don't remember what the quota is. Perhaps I did hear but I forgot. One woman had killed five when I left that turpentine still where she lived. The sheriff was thinking of calling on her and scolding her severely.

James Presley used to come every night and play his guitar. Mrs. Allen's temporary brother-in-law could play a good second but he didn't have a box so I used to lend him mine. They would play. The men would crowd in and buy soft drinks and woof at me, the stranger, but I knew I wasn't getting on. The ole feather-bed tactics.

Then one day after Cliffert Ulmer, Babe's son, and I had driven down to Lakeland together he felt close enough to tell me what was the trouble. They all thought I must be a revenue officer or a detective of some kind. They were accustomed to strange women dropping into the quarters, but not in shiny gray Chevrolets. They usually came plodding down the big road or counting railroad ties. The car made me look too prosperous. So they set me aside as different. And since most of them were fugitives from justice or had done plenty time, a detective was just the last thing they felt they needed on that "job."

I took occasion that night to impress the job with the fact that I was also a fugitive from justice, "bootlegging." They were hot behind me in Jacksonville and they wanted me in Miami. So I was hiding out. That sounded reasonable. Bootleggers always have cars. I was taken in.

The following Saturday was pay-day. They paid off twice a month and pay night is big doings. At least one dance at the section of the quarters known as the Pine Mill and two or three in the big Cypress Side. The company works with two kinds of lumber.

You can tell where the dances are to be held by the fires. Huge bonfires of faulty logs and slabs are lit outside the house in which the dances are held. The refreshments are parched[1] peanuts, fried rabbit, fish, chicken and chitterlings.

The only music is guitar music and the only dance is the ole square dance. James Presley is especially invited to every party to play. His pay is plenty of coon dick, and he *plays*.

Joe Willard is in great demand to call figures. He rebels occasionally because he likes to dance too.

But all of the fun isn't inside the house. A group can always be found outside about the fire, standing around and woofing and occasionally telling stories.

The biggest dance on this particular pay-night was over to the Pine Mill. James Presley and Slim assured me that they would be over there, so Cliffert Ulmer took me there. Being the reigning curiosity of the "job" lots of folks came to see what I'd do. So it was a great dance.

The guitars cried out "Polk County," "Red River" and just instrumental hits with no name, that still are played by all good

[1] Roasted.

box pickers. The dancing was hilarious to put it mildly. Babe, Lucy, Big Sweet, East Coast Mary and many other of the well-known women were there. The men swung them lustily, but nobody asked me to dance. I was just crazy to get into the dance, too. I had heard my mother speak of it and praise square dancing to the skies, but it looked as if I was doomed to be a wallflower and that was a new role for me. Even Cliffert didn't ask me to dance. It was so jolly, too. At the end of every set Joe Willard would trick the men. Instead of calling the next figure as expected he'd bawl out, "Grab yo' partners and march up to de table and treat." Some of the men did, but some would bolt for the door and stand about the fire and woof until the next set was called.

I went outside to join the woofers, since I seemed to have no standing among the dancers. Not exactly a hush fell about the fire, but a lull came. I stood there awkwardly, knowing that the too-ready laughter and aimless talk was a window-dressing for my benefit. The brother in black puts a laugh in every vacant place in his mind. His laugh has a hundred meanings. It may mean amusement, anger, grief, bewilderment, chagrin, curiosity, simple pleasure or any other of the known or undefined emotions. Clardia Thornton of Magazine Point, Alabama, was telling me about another woman taking her husband away from her. When the show-down came and he told Clardia in the presence of the other woman that he didn't want her—could never use her again, she tole me "Den, Zora, Ah wuz so outdone, Ah just opened mah mouf and laffed."

The folks around the fire laughed and boisterously shoved each other about, but I knew they were not tickled. But I soon had the answer. A pencil-shaped fellow with a big Adam's apple gave me the key.

"Ma'am, whut might be yo' entrimmins?" he asked with what was supposed to be a killing bow.

"My whut?"

"Yo entrimmins? Yo entitlum?"

The "entitlum" gave me the cue, "Oh, my name is Zora Hurston. And whut may be yours?"

More people came closer quickly.

"Mah name is Pitts and Ah'm sho glad to meet yuh. Ah asted Cliffert tuh knock me down tuh yuh but he wouldn't make me 'quainted. So Ah'm makin' mahseff 'quainted."

"Ah'm glad you did, Mr. Pitts."

"Sho nuff?" archly.

"Yeah. Ah wouldn't be sayin' it if Ah didn't mean it."

He looked me over shrewdly. "Ah see dat las' crap you shot, Miss, and Ah fade yuh."

I laughed heartily. The whole fire laughed at his quick comeback and more people came out to listen.

"Miss, you know uh heap uh dese hard heads wants to woof at you but dey skeered."

"How come, Mr. Pitts? Do I look like a bear or panther?"

"Naw, but dey say youse rich and dey ain't got de nerve to open dey mouf."

I mentally cursed the $12.74 dress from Macy's that I had on among all the $1.98 mail-order dresses. I looked about and noted the number of bungalow aprons and even the rolled down paper bags on the heads of several women. I did look different and resolved to fix all that no later than the next morning.

63

"Oh, Ah ain't got doodley squat,"[2] I countered. "Mah man brought me dis dress de las' time he went to Jacksonville. We wuz sellin' plenty stuff den and makin' good money. Wisht Ah had dat money now."

Then Pitts began woofing at me and the others stood around to see how I took it.

"Say, Miss, you know nearly all dese niggers is after you. Dat's all dey talk about out in de swamp."

"You don't say. Tell 'em to make me know it."

"Ah ain't tellin' nobody nothin'. Ah ain't puttin' out nothin' to no ole hard head but ole folks eyes and Ah ain't doin' dat till they dead. Ah talks for Number One. Second stanza: Some of 'em talkin' 'bout marryin' you and dey wouldn't know whut to do wid you if they had you. Now, dat's a fack."

"You reckon?"

"Ah know dey wouldn't. Dey'd 'spect you tuh git out de bed and fix dem some breakfus' and a bucket. Dat's 'cause dey don't know no better. Dey's thin-brainded. Now me, Ah wouldn't let you fix me no breakfus'. Ah git up and fix mah own and den, whut make it so cool, Ah'd fix *you* some and set it on de back of de cook-stove so you could git it when you wake up. Dese mens don't even know how to talk to nobody lak you. If you wuz tuh ast dese niggers somethin' dey'd answer you 'yeah' and 'naw.' Now, if you wuz some ole gator-back 'oman dey'd be tellin' you jus' right. But dat ain't de way tuh talk tuh nobody lak *you.* Now you ast *me* somethin' and see how Ah'll answer yuh."

"Mr. Pitts, are you havin' a good time?"

(In a prim falsetto) "Yes, Ma'am. See, dat's de way tuh talk tuh *you.*"

I laughed and the crowd laughed and Pitts laughed. Very successful woofing. Pitts treated me and we got on. Soon a boy came to me from Cliffert Ulmer asking me to dance. I found out that that was the social custom. The fellow that wants to broach a young woman doesn't come himself to ask. He sends

<hr/>

[2]Nothing.

his friend. Somebody came to me for Joe Willard and soon I was swamped with bids to dance. They were afraid of me before. My laughing acceptance of Pitts' woofing had put everybody at his ease.

James Presley and Slim spied noble at the orchestra. I had the chance to learn more about "John Henry" maybe. So I strolled over to James Presley and asked him if he knew how to play it.

"Ah'll play it if you sing it," he countered. So he played and I started to sing the verses I knew. They put me on the table and everybody urged me to spread my jenk,[3] so I did the best I could. Joe Willard knew two verses and sang them. Eugene Oliver knew one; Big Sweet knew one. And how James Presley can make his box cry out the accompaniment!

By the time that the song was over, before Joe Willard lifted me down from the table I knew that I was in the inner circle. I had first to convince the "job" that I was not an enemy in the person of the law; and, second, I had to prove that I was their kind. "John Henry" got me over my second hurdle.

After that my car was everybody's car. James Presley, Slim and I teamed up and we had to do "John Henry" wherever we appeared. We soon had a reputation that way. We went to Mulberry, Pierce and Lakeland.

After that I got confidential and told them all what I wanted. At first they couldn't conceive of anybody wanting to put down "lies." But when I got the idea over we held a lying contest and posted the notices at the Post Office and the commissary. I gave four prizes and some tall lying was done. The men and women enjoyed themselves and the contest broke up in a square dance with Joe Willard calling figures.

The contest was a huge success in every way. I not only collected a great deal of material but it started individuals coming to me privately to tell me stories they had no chance to tell during the contest.

Cliffert Ulmer told me that I'd get a great deal more by

[3]Have a good time.

65

going out with the swamp-gang. He said they lied a plenty while they worked. I spoke to the quarters boss and the swamp boss and both agreed that it was all right, so I strowed it all over the quarters that I was going out to the swamp with the boys next day. My own particular crowd, Cliffert, James, Joe Willard, Jim Allen and Eugene Oliver were to look out for me and see to it that I didn't get snake-bit nor 'gator-swallowed. The watchman, who sleeps out in the swamps and gets up steam in the skitter every morning before the men get to the cypress swamp, had been killed by a panther two weeks before, but they assured me that nothing like that could happen to me; not with the help I had.

Having watched some members of that swamp crew handle axes, I didn't doubt for a moment that they could do all that they said. Not only do they chop rhythmically, but they do a beautiful double twirl above their heads with the ascending axe before it begins that accurate and bird-like descent. They can hurl their axes great distances and behead moccasins or sink the blade into an alligator's skull. In fact, they seem to be able to do everything with their instrument that a blade can do. It is a magnificent sight to watch the marvelous co-ordination between the handsome black torsos and the twirling axes.

So next morning we were to be off to the woods.

It wasn't midnight dark and it wasn't day yet. When I awoke the saw-mill camp was a dawn gray. You could see the big saw-mill but you couldn't see the smoke from the chimney. You could see the congregation of shacks and the dim outlines of the scrub oaks among the houses, but you couldn't see the grey quilts of Spanish Moss that hung from the trees.

Dick Willie was the only man abroad. It was his business to be the first one out. He was the shack-rouser. Men are not supposed to over-sleep and Dick Willie gets paid to see to it that they don't. Listen to him singing as he goes down the line.

Wake up, bullies, and git on de rock. 'Tain't quite daylight but it's four o'clock.

66

Coming up the next line, he's got another song.

Wake up, Jacob, day's a breakin'. Git yo' hoe-cake a bakin' and yo' shirt tail shakin'.

What does he say when he gets to the jook and the long-house?[4] I'm fixing to tell you right now what he says. He raps on the floor of the porch with a stick and says:

"Ah ha! What make de rooster crow every morning at sun-up?

"Dat's to let de pimps and rounders know de workin' man is on his way."

About that time you see a light in every shack. Every kitchen is scorching up fat-back and hoe-cake. Nearly every skillet is full of corn-bread. But some like biscuit-bread better. Break your hoe-cake half in two. Half on the plate, half in the dinner-bucket. Throw in your black-eyed peas and fat meat left from supper and your bucket is fixed. Pour meat grease in your plate with plenty of cane syrup. Mix it and sop it with your bread. A big bowl of coffee, a drink of water from the tin dipper in the pail. Grab your dinner-bucket and hit the grit. Don't keep the straw-boss[5] waiting.

This morning when we got to the meeting place, the fore-man wasn't there. So the men squatted along the railroad track and waited.

Joe Willard was sitting with me on the end of a cross-tie when he saw Jim Presley coming in a run with his bucket and jumper-jacket.

"Hey, Jim, where the swamp boss? He ain't got here yet."

"He's ill—sick in the bed Ah hope, but Ah bet he'll git here yet."

"Aw, he ain't sick. Ah bet you a fat man he ain't," Joe said.

"How come?" somebody asked him and Joe answered:

---

[4]See glossary.

[5]The low-paid poor white section boss on a railroad; similar to swamp boss who works the gang that gets the timber to the sawmill.

"Man, he's too ugly. If a spell of sickness ever tried to slip up on him, he'd skeer it into a three weeks' spasm."

Blue Baby[6] stuck in his oar and said: "He ain't so ugly. Ye all jus' ain't seen no real ugly man. Ah seen a man so ugly till he could get behind a jimpson weed and hatch monkies."

Everybody laughed and moved closer together. Then Officer Richardson said: "Ah seen a man so ugly till they had to spread a sheet over his head at night so sleep could slip up on him."

They laughed some more, then Cliffert Ulmer said:

"Ah'm goin' to talk with my mouth wide open. Those men y'all been talkin' 'bout wasn't ugly at all. Those was pretty men. Ah knowed one so ugly till you could throw him in the Mississippi river and skim ugly for six months."

"Give Cliff de little dog," Jim Allen said. "He done tole the biggest lie."

"He ain't lyin'," Joe Martin tole them. "Ah knowed dat same man. He didn't die—he jus' uglied away."

They laughed a great big old kah kah laugh and got closer together.

"Looka here, folkses," Jim Presley exclaimed. "Wese a half hour behind schedule and no swamp boss and no log train here yet. What yo' all reckon is the matter sho' 'nough?"

"Must be something terrible when white folks get slow about putting us to work."

"Yeah," says Good Black. "You know back in slavery Ole Massa was out in de field sort of lookin' things over, when a shower of rain come up. The field hands was glad it rained so they could knock off for a while. So one slave named John says:

"More rain, more rest."

"Ole Massa says, 'What's dat you say?'

"John says, 'More rain, more grass.' "

"There goes de big whistle. We ought to be out in the woods almost."

[6]See glossary.

68

The big whistle at the saw-mill boomed and shrilled and pretty soon the log-train came racking along. No flats for logs behind the little engine. The foreman dropped off the tender as the train stopped.

"No loggin' today, boys. Got to send the train to the Everglades to fetch up the track gang and their tools."

"Lawd, Lawd, we got a day off," Joe Willard said, trying to make it sound like he was all put out about it. "Let's go back, boys. Sorry you won't git to de swamp, Zora."

"Aw, naw," the Foreman said. "Y'all had better g'wan over to the mill and see if they need you over there."

And he walked on off, chewing his tobacco and spitting his juice.

The men began to shoulder jumper-jackets and grab hold of buckets.

Allen asked: "Ain't dat a mean man? No work in the swamp and still he won't let us knock off."

"He's mean all right, but Ah done seen meaner men than him," said Handy Pitts.

"Where?"

"Oh, up in Middle Georgy. They had a straw boss and he was so mean dat when the boiler burst and blowed some of the men up in the air, he docked 'em for de time they was off de job."

Tush Hawg up and said: "Over on de East Coast Ah used to have a road boss and he was so mean and times was so hard till he laid off de hands of his watch."

Wiley said: "He's almost as bad as Joe Brown. Ah used to work in his mine and he was so mean till he wouldn't give God an honest prayer without snatching back 'Amen.' "

Ulmer says: "Joe Wiley, youse as big a liar as you is a man! Whoo-wee. Boy, you molds 'em. But lemme tell y'all a sho nuff tale 'bout Ole Massa."

"Go 'head and tell it, Cliff," shouted Eugene Oliver. "Ah love to hear tales about Ole Massa and John. John sho was one smart nigger."

So Cliff Ulmer went on.

You know befo' surrender Ole Massa had a nigger name John and John always prayed every night befo' he went to bed and his prayer was for God to come git him and take him to Heaven right away. He didn't even want to take time to die. He wanted de Lawd to come git him just like he was—boot, sock and all. He'd git down on his knees and say: "O Lawd, it's once more and again yo' humble servant is knee-bent and body-bowed—my heart beneath my knees and my knees in some lonesome valley, crying for mercy while mercy kin be found. O Lawd, Ah'm astin' you in de humblest way I know how to be *so* pleased as to come in yo' fiery chariot and take me to yo' Heben and its immortal glory. Come Lawd, you know Ah have such a hard time. Old Massa works me *so* hard, and don't gimme no time to rest. So come, Lawd, wid peace in one hand and pardon in de other and take me away from this sin-sorrowing world. Ah'm tired and Ah want to go home."

So one night Ole Massa passed by John's shack and heard him beggin' de Lawd to come git him in his fiery chariot and take him away; so he made up his mind to find out if John meant dat thing. So he goes on up to de big house and got hisself a bed sheet and come on back. He throwed de sheet over his head and knocked on de door.

John quit prayin' and ast: "Who dat?"

Ole Massa say: "It's me, John, de Lawd, done come wid my fiery chariot to take you away from this sin-sick world."

Right under de bed John had business. He told his wife: "Tell Him Ah ain't here, Liza."

At first Liza didn't say nothin' at all, but de Lawd kept right on callin' John: "Come on, John, and go to Heben wid me where you won't have to plough no mo' furrows and hoe no mo' corn. Come on, John."

Liza says: "John ain't here, Lawd, you hafta come back another time."

Lawd says: "Well, then Liza, you'll do."

Liza whispers and says: "John, come out from underneath dat bed and g'wan wid de Lawd. You been beggin' him to come git you. Now g'wan wid him."

John back under de bed not saying a mumblin' word. De Lawd out on de door step kept on callin'.

Liza says: "John, Ah thought you was so anxious to get to Heben. Come out and go on wid God."

John says: "Don't you hear him say 'You'll do'? Why don't you go wid him?"

"Ah ain't a goin' nowhere. Youse de one been whoopin' and hollerin' for him to come git you and if you don't come out from under dat bed Ah'm gointer tell God youse here."

Ole Massa makin' out he's God, says: "Come on, Liza, you'll do."

Liza says: "O, Lawd, John is right here underneath de bed."

"Come on John, and go to Heben wid me and its immortal glory."

John crept out from under de bed and went to de door and cracked it and when he seen all dat white standin' on de doorsteps he jumped back. He says: "O, Lawd, Ah can't go to Heben wid you in yo' fiery chariot in dese ole dirty britches; gimme time to put on my Sunday pants."

"All right, John, put on yo' Sunday pants."

John fooled around just as long as he could, changing them pants, but when he went back to de door, de big white glory was still standin' there. So he says agin: "O, Lawd, de Good Book says in Heben no filth is found and I got on his dirty sweaty shirt. Ah can't go wid you in dis old nasty shirt. Gimme time to put on my Sunday shirt!"

"All right, John, go put on yo' Sunday shirt."

John took and fumbled around a long time changing his shirt, and den he went back to de door, but Ole Massa was still on de door step. John didn't had nothin' else to change so he opened de door a little piece and says:

"O, Lawd, Ah'm ready to go to Heben wid you in yo' fiery chariot, but de radiance of yo' countenance is *so* bright, Ah can't come out by you. Stand back jus' a li'l way please."

Ole Massa stepped back a li'l bit.

John looked out agin and says: "O, Lawd, you know dat po' humble me is less than de dust beneath yo' shoe soles. And de radiance of yo' countenance is so bright Ah can't come out by you. Please, please, Lawd, in yo' tender mercy, stand back a li'l bit further."

Ole Massa stepped back a li'l bit mo'.

John looked out agin and he says: "O, Lawd, Heben is so high and wese so low; youse so great and Ah'm so weak and yo' strength is too much for us poor sufferin' sinners. So once mo' and agin yo' humber servant is knee-bent and body-bowed askin' you one mo' favor befo' Ah step into yo' fiery chariot to go to Heben wid you and wash in yo' glory—be so pleased in yo' tender mercy as to stand back jus' a li'l bit further."

Ole Massa stepped back a step or two mo' and out dat door John come like a streak of lightning. All across de punkin patch, thru de cotton over de pasture—John wid Ole Massa right behind him. By de time dey hit de cornfield John was way ahead of Ole Massa.

Back in de shack one of de children was cryin' and she ast Liza: "Mama, you reckon God's gointer ketch papa and carry him to Heben wid him?"

"Shet yo' mouf, talkin' foolishness!" Liza clashed at de chile. "You know de Lawd can't outrun yo' pappy—specially when he's barefooted at dat."

Kah, Kah, Kah! Everybody laughing with their mouths wide open. If the foreman had come along right then he would have been good and mad because he could tell their minds were not on work.

Joe Willard says: "Wait a minute, fellows, wese walkin' too fast. At dis rate we'll be there befo' we have time to talk some mo' about Ole Massa and John. Tell another one, Cliffert."

"Aw, naw," Eugene Oliver hollered out.

Let *me* talk some chat. Dis is de real truth 'bout Ole Massa 'cause my grandma told it to my mama and she told it to me.

During slavery time, you know, Ole Massa had a nigger named John and he was a faithful nigger and Ole Massa lakted John a lot too.

One day Ole Massa sent for John and tole him, says:

"John, somebody is stealin' my corn out de field. Every mornin' when I go out I see where they done carried off some mo' of my roastin' ears. I want you to set in de corn patch tonight and ketch whoever it is."

So John said all right and he went and hid in de field.

Pretty soon he heard somethin' breakin' corn. So John sneaked up behind him wid a short stick in his hand and hollered: "Now, break another ear of Ole Massa's corn and see what *Ah'll* do to you."

John thought it was a man all dis time, but it was a bear wid his arms full of roastin' ears. He throwed down de corn and grabbed John. And him and dat bear!

John, after while got loose and got de bear by the tail wid de bear tryin' to git to him all de time. So they run around in a circle all night long. John was so tired. But he couldn't let go of de bear's tail, do de bear would grab him in de back.

After a stretch they quit runnin' and walked. John swingin' on to de bear's tail and de bear's nose 'bout to touch him in de back.

Daybreak, Ole Massa come out to see 'bout John and he seen John and de bear walkin' 'round in de ring. So he run up and says: "Lemme take holt of 'im, John, whilst you run git help!"

John says: "All right, Massa. Now you run in quick and grab 'im just so."

Ole Massa run and grabbed holt of de bear's tail and said: "Now, John you make haste to git somebody to help us."

John staggered off and set down on de grass and went to fanning hisself wid his hat.

Ole Massa was havin' plenty trouble wid dat bear and he looked over and seen John settin' on de grass and he hollered:

"John, you better g'wan git help or else I'm gwinter turn dis bear aloose!"

John says: "Turn 'im loose, then. Dat's whut Ah tried to do all night long but Ah couldn't."

Jim Allen laughed just as loud as anybody else and then he said: "We better hurry on to work befo' de buckra[7] get in behind us."

"Don't never worry about work," says Jim Presley. "There's more work in de world than there is anything else. God made de world and de white folks made work."

"Yeah, dey made work but they didn't make us do it," Joe Willard put in. "We brought dat on ourselves."

"Oh, yes, de white folks did put us to work too," said Jim Allen.

Know how it happened? After God got thru makin' de world and de varmints and de folks, he made up a great big bundle and let it down in de middle of de road. It laid dere for thousands of years, then Ole Missus said to Ole Massa: "Go pick up dat box, Ah want to see whut's in it." Ole Massa look at de box and it look so heavy dat he says to de nigger, "Go fetch me dat big ole box out dere in de road." De nigger been stumblin' over de box a long time so he tell his wife:

"'Oman, go git dat box." So de nigger 'oman she runned to git de box. She says:

"Ah always lak to open up a big box 'cause there's nearly always something good in great big boxes." So she run and grabbed a-hold of de box and opened it up and it was full of hard work.

Dat's de reason de sister in black works harder than anybody else in de world. De white man tells de nigger to work and he takes and tells his wife.

"Aw, now, dat ain't de reason niggers is working so hard," Jim Presley objected.

Dis is de way *dat* was.
God let down two bundles 'bout five miles down de road. So de white man and de nigger raced to see who

[7]West African word meaning white people.

would git there first. Well, de nigger out-run de white man
and grabbed de biggest bundle. He was so skeered de
white man would git it away from him he fell on top of de
bundle and hollered back: "Oh, Ah got here first and dis
biggest bundle is mine." De white man says: "All right,
Ah'll take yo' leavings," and picked up de li'l tee-ninchy
bundle layin' in de road. When de nigger opened up his
bundle he found a pick and shovel and a hoe and a plow
and chop-axe and then de white man opened up his bundle
and found a writin'-pen and ink. So ever since then de nigger been out in de hot sun, usin' his tools and de white
man been sittin' up figgerin', ought's a ought, figger's a
figger; all for de white man, none for de nigger.

"Oh lemme spread my mess. Dis is Will Richardson doin'
dis lyin'."

You know Ole Massa took a nigger deer huntin' and
posted him in his place and told him, says: "Now you wait
right here and keep yo' gun reformed and ready. Ah'm
goin' 'round de hill and skeer up de deer and head him dis
way. When he come past, you shoot."
De nigger says: "Yessuh, Ah sho' will, Massa."
He set there and waited wid de gun all cocked and after
a while de deer come tearin' past him. He didn't make a
move to shoot de deer so he went on 'bout his business.
After while de white man come on 'round de hill and ast
de nigger: "Did you kill de deer?"
De nigger says: "Ah ain't seen no deer pass here yet."
Massa says: "Yes, you did. You couldn't help but see
him. He come right dis way."
Nigger says: "Well Ah sho' ain't seen none. All Ah seen
was a white man come along here wid a pack of chairs on
his head and Ah tipped my hat to him and waited for de
deer."

"Some colored folks ain't got no sense, and when Ah see
'em like dat," Ah say, "My race but not my taste."

FIVE

Y'all ever hear dat lie 'bout big talk?" cut in Joe Wiley. "Yeah we done heard it, Joe, but Ah kin hear it some 'gin. Tell it, Joe," pleaded Gene Oliver.

During slavery time two ole niggers wuz talkin' an' one said tuh de other one, "Ole Massa made me so mad yistiddy till Ah give 'im uh good cussin' out. Man, Ah called 'im everything wid uh handle on it."

De other one says, "You didn't cuss *Ole Massa,* didja? Good God! Whut did he do tuh you?"

"He didn't do *nothin',* an' man, Ah laid one cussin' on 'im! Ah'm uh man lak dis, Ah won't stan' no hunchin'. Ah betcha he won't bother *me* no mo'."

"Well, if you cussed 'im an' he didn't do nothin' tuh you, de nex' time he make me mad Ah'm goin' tuh lay uh hearin' on him."

Nex' day de nigger did somethin'. Ole Massa got in behind 'im and he turnt 'round an' give Ole Massa one good cussin' an Ole Massa had 'im took down and whipped nearly tuh death. Nex' time he saw dat other nigger he says tuh 'im. "Thought you tole me, you cussed Ole Massa out and he never opened his mouf."

"Ah did."

"Well, how come he never did nothin' tuh yuh? Ah did

77

it an' he come nigh uh killin' *me.*"

"Man, you didn't go cuss 'im tuh his face, didja?"

"Sho Ah did. Ain't dat whut you tole me you done?"

"Naw, Ah didn't say Ah cussed 'im tuh his face. You sho is crazy. Ah thought you had mo' sense than dat. When Ah cussed Ole Massa he wuz settin' on de front porch an' Ah wuz down at de big gate."

De other nigger wuz mad but he didn't let on. Way after while he 'proached de nigger dat got 'im de beatin' an' tole 'im, "Know whut Ah done tuhday?"

"Naw, whut you done? Give Ole Massa 'nother cussin'?"

"Naw, Ah ain't never goin' do dat no mo'. Ah peeped up under Ole Miss's drawers."

"Man, hush yo' mouf! You knows you ain't looked up under ole Miss's clothes!"

"Yes, Ah did too. Ah looked right up her very drawers."

"You better hush dat talk! Somebody goin' hear you and Ole Massa'll have you kilt."

"Well, Ah sho done it an' she never done nothin' neither."

"Well, whut did she say?"

"Not uh mumblin' word, an' Ah stopped and looked jus' as long as Ah wanted tuh an' went on 'bout mah business."

"Well, de nex' time Ah see her settin' out on de porch Ah'm goin' tuh look too."

"Help yo'self."

Dat very day Ole Miss wuz settin' out on de porch in de cool uh de evenin' all dressed up in her starchy white clothes. She had her legs all crossed up and de nigger walked up tuh de edge uh de porch and peeped up under Ole Miss's clothes. She took and hollored an' Ole Massa come out an' had dat nigger almost kilt alive.

When he wuz able tuh be 'bout agin he said tuh de other nigger, "Thought you tole me you peeped up under Ole Miss's drawers?"

"Ah sho did."

"Well, how come she never done nothin' tuh *you?* She got me nearly kilt."

"Man, when Ah looked under Ole Miss's drawers they

wuz hangin' out on de clothes line. You didn't go look up in 'em while she had 'em on, didja? You sho is uh fool! Ah thought you had mo' sense than dat, Ah claire Ah did. It's uh wonder he didn't kill yuh dead. Umph, umph, umph. You sho ain't got no sense atall."

"Yeah," said Black Baby, "But dat wasn't John de white folks was foolin' wid. John was too smart for Ole Massa. He never got no beatin'!"

De first colored man what was brought to dis country was name John. He didn't know nothin' mo' than you told him and he never forgot nothin' you told him either. So he was sold to a white man.

Things he didn't know he would ask about. They went to a house and John never seen a house so he asked what it was. Ole Massa tole him it was his kingdom. So dey goes on into de house and dere was the fireplace. He asked what was that. Ole Massa told him it was his flame 'vaperator.

The cat was settin' dere. He asked what it was. Ole Massa told him it was his round head.

So dey went upstairs. When he got on de stair steps he asked what dey was. Ole Massa told him it was his jacob ladder. So when they got up stairs he had a roller foot bed. John asked what was dat. Ole Massa told him it was his flowery-bed-of-ease. So dey came down and went out to de lot. He had a barn. John asked what was dat. Ole Massa told him, dat was his mound. So he had a Jack in the stable, too. John asked, "What in de world is dat?" Ole Massa said: "Dat's July, de God dam."

So de next day Ole Massa was up stairs sleep and John was smokin'. It flamed de 'vaperator and de cat was settin' dere and it got set afire. The cat goes to de barn where Ole Massa had lots of hay and fodder in de barn. So de cat set it on fire. John watched de Jack kicking up hay and fodder. He would see de hay and fodder go up and come down but he thought de Jack was eatin' de hay and fodder. So he goes upstairs and called Ole Massa and told him to get up off'n his flowery-bed-of-ease and come down on his jacob ladder. He said: "I done flamed the 'vaperator and it caught de round head and set him on fire. He's gone to de mound and set it on fire, and July the God dam is eatin' up everything he kin git his mouf on."

Massa turned over in de bed and ast, "Whut dat you say, John?"

John tole 'im agin. Massa was still sleepy so he ast John agin whut he say. John was gittin' tired so he say, "Aw, you better git up out dat bed and come on down stairs. Ah done set dat ole cat afire and he run out to de barn and set it afire and dat ole Jackass is eatin' up everything he git his mouf on."

Gene Oliver said: "Y'all hush and lemme tell this one befo' we git to de mill. This ain't no slavery time talk."

Once they tried a colored man in Mobile for stealing a goat. He was so poorly dressed, and dirty—that de judge told him, "Six months on de country road, you stink so."

A white man was standing dere and he said, "Judge, he don't stink, Ah got a nigger who smells worser than a billy goat." De judge told de man to bring him on over so he could smell him. De next day de man took de billy goat and de nigger and went to de court and sent de judge word dat de nigger and de billy goat wuz out dere and which one did he want fust.

The judge told him to bring in de goat. When he carried de goat he smelled so bad dat de judge fainted. Dey got ice water and throwed it in de Judge's face 'til he come to. He told 'em to bring in de nigger and when dey brung in de nigger de goat fainted.

Joe Wiley said: "Ah jus' got to tell this one, do Ah can't rest."

In slavery time dere was a colored man what was named John. He went along wid Ole Massa everywhere he went. He used to make out he could tell fortunes. One day him and his Old Massa was goin' along and John said, "Ole Massa, Ah kin tell fortunes." Ole Massa made out he didn't pay him no attention. But when they got to de next man's plantation Old Massa told de landlord, "I have a nigger dat kin tell fortunes." So de other man said, "Dat nigger can't tell no fortunes. I bet my plantation and all my niggers against yours dat he can't tell no fortunes."

Ole Massa says: "I'll take yo' bet. I bet everything in de world I got on John 'cause he don't lie. If he say he can tell fortunes, he can tell 'em. Bet you my plantation and all my niggers against yours and throw in de wood lot extry."

So they called Notary Public and signed up de bet. Ole Massa straddled his horse and John got on his mule and they went on home.

John was in de misery all that night for he knowed he was gointer be de cause of Ole Massa losin' all he had.

Every mornin' John useter be up and have Old Massa's saddle horse curried and saddled at de door when Ole Massa woke up. But *this* mornin' Old Massa had to git John out of de bed.

John useter always ride side by side with Massa, but on de way over to de plantation where de bet was on, he rode way behind.

So de man on de plantation had went out and caught a coon and had a big old iron wash-pot turned down over it.

There was many person there to hear John tell what was under de wash-pot.

Ole Massa brought John out and tole him, say: "John, if you tell what's under dat wash pot Ah'll make you independent, rich. If you don't, Ah'm goin' to kill you because you'll make me lose my plantation and everything I got."

John walked 'round and 'round dat pot but he couldn't git de least inklin' of what was underneath it. Drops of sweat as big as yo' fist was rollin' off of John. At last he give up and said: "Well, you got de ole coon at last."

When John said that, Ole Massa jumped in de air and cracked his heels twice befo' he hit de ground. De man that was bettin' against Ole Massa fell to his knees wid de cold sweat pourin' off him. Ole Massa said: "John, you done won another plantation fo' me. That's a coon under that pot sho 'nuff.''

So he give John a new suit of clothes and a saddle horse. And John quit tellin' fortunes after that.

Going back home Ole Massa said: "Well, John, you done made me vast rich so I goin' to Philly-Me-York and won't be back in three weeks. I leave everything in yo' charge.''

So Ole Massa and his wife got on de train and John went to de depot with 'em and seen 'em off on de train bid 'em goodbye. Then he hurried on back to de plantation. Ole Massa and Ole Miss got off at de first station and made it on back to see whut John was doin'.

John went back and told de niggers, "Massa's gone to Philly-Me-York and left everything in my charge. Ah want one of you niggers to git on a mule and ride three miles north, and another one three miles west and another one three miles south and another one three miles east. Tell everybody to come here—there's gointer be a ball here tonight. The rest of you go into the lot and kill hogs until you can walk on 'em.''

So they did. John goes in and dressed up in Ole Massa's swaller-tail clothes, put on his collar and tie; got a box of cigars and put under his arm, and one cigar in his mouth.

When the crowd come John said: "Y'all kin dance and Ah'm goin' to call figgers.''

So he got Massa's biggest rockin' chair and put it up in Massa's bed and then he got up in the bed in the chair and begin to call figgers:

"Hands up!'' "Four circle right.'' "Half back.'' "Two ladies change.'' He was puffing his cigar all de time.

'Bout this time John seen a white couple come in but they looked so trashy he figgered they was piney woods crackers, so he told 'em to g'wan out in de kitchen and git some barbecue and likker and to stay out there where they belong. So he went to callin' figgers agin. De git Fiddles[1] was raisin' cain over in de corner and John was callin' for de new set:

[1]Guitars.

"Choose yo' partners." "Couples to yo' places like horses to de traces." "Sashay all." "Sixteen hands up." "Swing Miss Sally 'round and 'round and bring her back to me!"

Just as he went to say "Four hands up," he seen Ole Massa comin' out the kitchen wipin' the dirt off his face.

Ole Massa said: "John, just look whut you done done! I'm gointer take you to that persimmon tree and break yo' neck for this—killing up all my hogs and havin' all these niggers in my house."

John ast, "Ole Massa, Ah know you gointer kill me, but can Ah have a word with my friend Jack before you kill me?"

"Yes, John, but have it quick."

So John called Jack and told him; says: "Ole Massa is gointer hang me under that persimmon tree. Now you get three matches and get in the top of the tree. Ah'm gointer pray and when you hear me ast God to let it lightning Ah want you to strike matches."

Jack went on out to the tree. Ole Massa brought John on out with the rope around his neck and put it over a limb.

"Now, John," said Massa, "have you got any last words to say?"

"Yes sir, Ah want to pray."

"Pray and pray damn quick. I'm clean out of patience with you, John."

So John knelt down. "O Lord, here Ah am at de foot of de persimmon tree. If you're gointer destroy Old Massa to-night, with his wife and chillun and everything he got, lemme see it lightnin'."

Jack up the tree, struck a match. Ole Massa caught hold of John and said: "John, don't pray no more."

John said: "Oh yes, turn me loose so Ah can pray. O Lord, here Ah am tonight callin' on Thee and Thee alone. If you are gointer destroy Ole Massa tonight, his wife and chillun and all he got, Ah want to see it lightnin' again."

Jack struck another match and Ole Massa started to run. He give John his freedom and a heap of land and stock. He run so fast that it took a express train running at the rate of ninety miles an hour and six months to bring him back, and that's how come niggers got they freedom today.

Well, we were at the mill at last, as slow as we had walked. Old Hannah[2] was climbing the road of the sky, heating up sand beds and sweating peoples. No wonder nobody wanted to work. Three fried men are not equal to one good cool one. The men stood around the door for a minute or two, then dropped down on the shady side of the building. Work was too discouraging to think about. Phew! Sun and sawdust, sweat and sand. Nobody called a meeting and voted to sit in the shade. It just happened naturally.

Jim Allen said, "Reckon we better go inside and see if they want us?"

"Oh hell, naw!" shouted Lennie Barnes. "We ain't no mill-hands nohow. Let's stay right where we is till they find us. We got plenty to do—lyin' on Ole Massa and slavery days. Lemme handle a li'l language long here wid de rest. Y'all ever hear 'bout dat nigger dat found a gold watch?"

"Yeah, Ah done heard it," said Cliff, "but go on and tell it, Lonnie, so yo' egg bag kin rest easy."[3]

"Well, once upon a time was a good ole time.
Monkey chew tobacco and spit white lime."

A colored man was walking down de road one day and he found a gold watch and chain. He didn't know what it was, so the first thing he met was a white man, so he showed the white man de watch and ast him what it was. White man said, "Lemme see it in my hand."

De colored man give it to him and de white man said, "Why this is a gold watch, and de next time you find anything kickin' in de road put in yo' pocket and sell it."

With that he put the watch in his pocket and left de colored man standing there.

So de colored man walked on down de road a piece further and walked up on a little turtle. He tied a string to it

<hr />

[2]The Sun.

[3]So you can be at ease. A hen is supposed to suffer when she has a fully developed egg in her.

and put de turtle in his pocket and let de string hang out.

So he met another colored fellow and the fellow ast him says: "Cap, what time you got?"

He pulled out de turtle and told de man, "It's a quarter past leben and kickin' lak hell for twelve."

Larkins White says: "Y'all been wearin' Ole Massa's southern can[4] out dis mornin'. Pass him over here to me and lemme handle some grammar wid him."

"You got him, Ah just hope dat straw boss don't come sidlin' 'round here," somebody said.

"Ah got to tell you 'bout Old Massa down in de piney woods."

During slavery uh nigger name Jack run off from his marster and took and hid hisself down in de piney woods.

Ole Massa hunted and hunted but he never could ketch dat nigger.

But Jack had uh good friend on de plantation dat useter slip 'im somethin' t' eat and fetch de banjo down and play 'im somethin' every day so's he could dance some. Jack wuz tryin' to make it on off de mountain where Old Massa couldn't fetch 'im back. So Ole Massa got on to dis other nigger slippin' out to Jack but he couldn't ketch 'im so he tole 'im if he lead 'im to where Jack wuz he'd give 'im a new suit uh clothes. So he said, "All right."

So he tole Old Massa to follow him and do whutever he sing. So Ole Massa said, "All right."

So dat day de nigger took Jack some dinner and de Banjo. So Jack et. Den he tole him, say: "Jack I got uh new song fuh yuh today."

"Play it and lemme dance some."

"It's about Ole Massa."

Jack said, "I don't give uh damn 'bout Ole Massa. Ah don't b'long tuh him no mo'. Play it and lemme dance."

So he started to playin'.

[4]His hips.

85

"From pine to pine, Mister Pinkney.
From pine to pine, Mister Pinkney."

Jack was justa dancin' fallin' off de log and cuttin' de pigeon
wing—(diddle dip, diddle dip—diddle dip) "from pine to pine
Mr. Pinkney."

White man coming closer all de time.
"Now take yo' time Mister Pinkney.
Now take yo' time Mister Pinkney."
(Diddle dip, diddle dip, diddle dip, diddle dip)
"Now grab 'im now Mister Pinkney
Now grab 'im now Mister Pinkney."
(Diddle dip, diddle dip, diddle dip, diddle dip)
"Now grab 'im now Mister Pinkney."

So they caught Jack and put uh hundred lashes on his back
and put him back to work.

"Now Ah tole dat one for myself, now Ah got to tell one
for my wife."
"Aw, g'wan tell de lie, Larkins, if you want to. You know
you ain't tellin' no lie for yo' wife. No mo' than de rest of us.
You lyin' cause you like it." James Presley put in. "Hurry up
so somebody else kin plough up some literary and lay-by some
alphabets."

Two mens dat didn't know how tuh count good had
been haulin' up cawn and they stopped at de cemetery wid
de last load 'cause it wuz gittin' kinda dark. They thought
they'd git thru instead uh goin' 'way tuh one of 'em's barn.
When they wuz goin' in de gate two ear uh cawn dropped
off de waggin, but they didn't stop tuh bother wid 'em, just
then. They wuz in uh big hurry tuh git home. They wuz
justa vidin' it up. "You take dis'n an Ah'll take dat'un, you
take dat'un and Ah'll take dis'un."
An ole nigger heard 'em while he wuz passin' de cemetery an' run home tuh tell ole Massa 'bout it.

"Massa, de Lawd and de devil is down in de cemetery 'vidin' up souls. Ah heard 'em. One say, 'you take that 'un an' Ah'll take dis'un'."

Ole Massa wuz sick in de easy chear, he couldn't git about by hisself, but he said, "Jack, Ah don't know whut dis foolishness is, but Ah know you lyin'."

"Naw Ah ain't neither, Ah swear it's so."

"Can't be, Jack, youse crazy."

"Naw, Ah ain't neither; if you don' believe me, come see for yo'self."

"Guess Ah better go see whut you talkin' 'bout; if you fool me, Ah'm gointer have a hundred lashes put on yo' back in de mawnin' suh."

They went on down tuh de cemetery wid Jack pushin' Massa in his rollin' chear, an' it wuz sho dark down dere too. So they couldn't see de two ears uh cawn layin' in de gate.

Sho nuff Ole Massa heard 'em sayin' "Ah'll take dis'un," and de other say, "An' Ah'll take dis'un." Ole Massa got skeered hisself but he wuzn't lettin' on, an' Jack whispered tuh 'im, "Unh hunh, didn't Ah tell you de Lawd an' de devil wuz down here 'vidin' up souls?"

They waited awhile there in de gate listenin' den they heard 'em say, "Now, we'll go git dem two at de gate."

Jack says, "Ah knows de Lawd gwine take you, and Ah ain't gwine let de devil get me—Ah'm gwine home." An' he did an' lef' Ole Massa settin' dere at de cemetery gate in his rollin' chear, but when he got home, Ole Massa had done beat 'im home and wuz settin' by de fire smokin' uh seegar."

Jim Allen began to fidget. "Don't y'all reckon we better g'wan inside? They might need us."

Lonnie Barnes shouted, "Aw naw—you sho is worrysome. You bad as white folks. You know they say a white man git in some kind of trouble, he'll fret and fret until he kill hisself. A nigger git into trouble, he'll fret a while, then g'wan to sleep."

"Yeah, dat's right, too," Eugene Oliver agreed. "Didja ever hear de white man's prayer?"

"Who in Polk County ain't heard dat?" cut in Officer Richardson.

"Well, if you know it so good, lemme hear *you* say it," Eugene snapped back.

"Oh, Ah don't know it well enough to say it. Ah jus' know it well enough to know it."

"Well, all right then, when Ah'm changing my dollars, you keep yo' pennies out."

"Ah don't know it, Eugene, say it for me," begged Peter Noble. "Don't pay Office no mind."

Well, it come a famine and all de crops was dried up and Brother John was ast to pray. He had prayed for rain last year and it had rained, so all de white folks 'sembled at they church and called on Brother John to pray agin, so he got down and prayed:

"Lord, first thing, I want you to understand that this ain't no nigger talking to you. This is a white man and I want you to hear me. Pay some attention to me. I don't worry and bother you all the time like these niggers—asking you

88

for a whole heap of things that they don't know what to do with after they git 'em—so when I do ask a favor, I want it granted. Now, Lord, we want some rain. Our crops is all burning up and we'd like a little rain. But I don't mean for you to come in a hell of a storm like you did last year—kicking up racket like niggers at a barbecue. I want you to come calm and easy. Now, another thing, Lord, I want to speak about. Don't let these niggers be as sassy as they have been in the past. Keep 'em in their places, Lord, Amen."

Larkins White burst out:

And dat put me in de mind of a nigger dat useter do a lot of prayin' up under 'simmon tree, durin' slavery time. He'd go up dere and pray to God and beg Him to kill all de white folks. Ole Massa heard about it and so de next day he got hisself a armload of sizeable rocks and went up de 'simmon tree, before de nigger got dere, and when he begin to pray and beg de Lawd to kill all de white folks, Ole Massa let one of dese rocks fall on Ole Nigger's head. It was a heavy rock and knocked de nigger over. So when he got up he looked up and said: "Lawd, I ast you to kill all de white folks, can't you tell a white man from a nigger?"

Joe Wiley says: "Y'all might as well make up yo' mind to bear wid me, 'cause Ah feel Ah got to tell a lie on Ole Massa for my mamma. Ah done lied on him enough for myself. So Ah'm gointer tell it if I bust my gall tryin'."

Ole John was a slave, you know. And there was Ole Massa and Ole Missy and de two li' children—a girl and a boy.

Well, John was workin' in de field and he seen de children out on de lake in a boat, just a hollerin'. They had done lost they oars and was 'bout to turn over. So then he went and tole Ole Massa and Ole Missy.

Well, Ole Missy, she hollered and said: "It's so sad to lose these 'cause Ah ain't never goin' to have no more chil-

89

dren." Ole Massa made her hush and they went down to de water and follered de shore on 'round till they found 'em. John pulled off his shoes and hopped in and swum out and got in de boat wid de children and brought 'em to shore.

Well, Massa and John take 'em to de house. So they was all so glad 'cause de children got saved. So Massa told 'im to make a good crop dat year and fill up de barn, and den when he lay by de crops nex' year, he was going to set him free.

So John raised so much crop dat year he filled de barn and had to put some of it in de house.

So Friday come, and Massa said, "Well, de day done come that I said I'd set you free. I hate to do it, but I don't like to make myself out a lie. I hate to git rid of a good nigger lak you."

So he went in de house and give John one of his old suits of clothes to put on. So John put it on and come in to shake hands and tell 'em goodbye. De children they cry, and Ole Missy she cry. Didn't want to see John go. So John took his bundle and put it on his stick and hung it crost his shoulder.

Well, Ole John started on down de road. Well, Ole Massa said, "John, de children love yuh."

"Yassuh."

"John, I love yuh."

"Yassuh."

"And Missy *like* yuh!"

"Yassuh."

"But 'member, John, youse a nigger."

"Yassuh."

Fur as John could hear 'im down de road he wuz hollerin', "John, Oh John! De children loves you. And I love you. De Missy *like* you."

John would holler back, "Yassuh."

"But 'member youse a nigger, tho!"

Ole Massa kept callin' 'im and his voice was pitiful. But John kept right on steppin' to Canada. He answered Ole Massa every time he called 'im, but he consumed on wid his bag.

SIX

Tookie Allen passed by the mill all dressed up in a tight shake-baby.[1] She must have thought she looked good because she was walking that way. All the men stopped talking for a while. Joe Willard hollered at her.

"Hey, Tookie, how do you like your new dress?"

Tookie made out she didn't hear, but anybody could tell that she had. That was why she had put on her new dress, and come past the mill a wringing and twisting—so she could hear the men talking about her in the dress.

"Lawd, look at Tookie switchin' it and lookin' back at it! She's done gone crazy thru de hips." Joe Willard just couldn't take his eyes off of Tookie.

"Aw, man, you done seen Tookie and her walk too much to be makin' all dat miration over it. If you can't show me nothin' better than dat, don't bring de mess up," Cliff Ulmer hooted. "Less tell some more lies on Ole Massa and John."

"John sho was a smart nigger now. He useter git de best of Ole Massa all de time," gloated Sack Daddy.

"Yeah, but some white folks is smarter than you think," put in Eugene Oliver.

[1] A dress very tight across the hips but with a full short skirt; very popular on the "jobs."

For instance now, take a man I know up in West Florida. He hired a colored man to clear off some new ground, but dat skillet blonde[2] was too lazy to work. De white man would show him what to do then he's g'wan back to de house and keep his books. Soon as he turned his back de nigger would flop down and go to sleep. When he hear somebody comin' he'd hit de log a few licks with de flat of de ax and say, "Klunk, klunk, you think Ah'm workin' but Ah ain't."

De white man heard him but he didn't say a word. Sat'-day night come and Ole Cuffee went up to de white man to git his pay. De white man stacked up his great big ole silver dollars and shook 'em in his hand and says, "Clink, clink, you think I'm gointer pay you, but I ain't."

By that time somebody saw the straw boss coming so everybody made it on into the mill. The mill boss said, "What are y'all comin' in here for? Ah ain't got enough work for my own men. Git for home."

The swamp gang shuffled on out of the mill. "Umph, umph, umph," said Black Baby. "We coulda *done* been gone if we had a knowed dat."

"Ah told y'all to come an' go inside but you wouldn't take a listen. Y'all think Ah'm an ole Fogey. Young Coon for running but old coon for cunning."

We went on back to the quarters.

When Mrs. Bertha Allen saw us coming from the mill she began to hunt up the hoe and the rake. She looked under the porch and behind the house until she got them both and placed them handy. As soon as Jim Allen hit the steps she said:

"Ah'm mighty proud y'all got a day off. Maybe Ah kin git dis yard all clean today. Jus' look at de trash and dirt! And it's so many weeds in dis yard, Ah'm liable to git snake bit at my own door."

"Tain't no use in you gittin' yo' mouf all primped up for no hoein' and rakin' out of me, Bertha. Call yo' grandson and let

[2]Very black person.

him do it. Ah'm too old for dat," said Jim testily.

"Ah'm standin' in my tracks and steppin' back on my abstract[3]—Ah ain't gointer rake up no yard. Ah'm goin' fishin',"
Cliffert Ulmer snapped back. "Grandma, you worries mo'
'bout dis place than de man dat owns it. You ain't de Everglades Cypress Lumber Comp'ny sho nuff. Youse just shacking in one of their shanties. Leave de weeds go. Somebody'll
come chop 'em some day."

"Naw, Ah ain't gointer leave 'em go! You and Jim would
wallow in dirt right up to yo' necks if it wasn't for me."

Jim threw down his jumper and his dinner bucket. "Now,
Ah'm goin' fishin' too. When Bertha starts her jawin' Ah can't
stay on de place. Her tongue is hung in de middle and works
both ways. Come on Cliff, less git de poles!"

"Speck Ah'm gointer have to make a new line for my trout
pole," Cliff said. "Dat great big ole fish Ah hooked las' time
carried my other line off in his mouth, 'member?"

"Aw, dat wasn't no trout got yo' line; dat's whut you tell us,
but dat was a log bit yo' hook dat time." Larkins White twitted.

"Yes dat was a trout, too now. Ah'm a real fisherman. Ah
ain't like y'all. Ah kin ketch fish anywhere. All Ah want to
know, is there any water. Man, Ah kin ketch fish out a water
bucket. Don't b'lieve me, just come on down to de lake. Ah'll
bet, Ah'll pull 'em all de fish out de lake befo' y'all git yo' bait
dug."

"Dat's a go," shouted Larkins. "Less go! Come on de rest
of y'all to see dis thing out. Dis boy 'bout to burst his britches
since he been chawin' tobacco reg'lar and workin' in de
swamp wid us mens."

Cliff picked up the hoe and went 'round behind the house
to dig some bait. Old Jim went inside and got the spool of No.
8 cotton and a piece of beeswax and went to twisting a trout
line. He baptized the hook in asafetida and put his hunting
knife in his pocket, met Cliffert at the gate and they were off

[3] I am standing my ground.

93

to join the others down by the jook. Big Sweet and Lucy got out their poles and joined us. It was almost like a log-rolling[4] or a barbecue. The quarters were high. The men didn't get off from work every day like this.

We proaged on thru the woods that was full of magnolia, pine, cedar, oak, cypress, hickory and many kinds of trees whose names I do not know. It is hard to know all the trees in Florida. But everywhere they were twined with climbing vines and veiled in moss.

"What's de matter, Ah don't hear no birds?" complained Eugene Oliver. "It don't seem natural."

Everybody looked up at one time like cows in a pasture.

"Oh you know how come we don't hear no birds. It's Friday and de mocking bird ain't here," said Big Sweet after a period of observation.

"What's Friday got to do with the mockin' bird?" Eugene challenged.

"Dat's exactly what Ah want to know," said Joe Wiley.

"Well," said Big Sweet. "Nobody never sees no mockin' bird on Friday. They ain't on earth dat day."

"Well, if they ain't on earth, where is they?"

"They's all gone to hell on Friday with a grain of sand in they mouth to help out they friend." She continued:

Once there was a man and he was very wicked. He useter rob and steal and he was always in a fight and killin' up people. But he was awful good to birds and mockin' birds was his favorite. This was a long time ago before de man first started to buildin' de Rocky Mountains. Well, 'way after while somebody kilt him, and being he had done lived so bad, when he died he went straight to hell.

De birds all hated it mighty bad when they seen him in hell, so they tried to git him out. But the fire was too hot so they give up—all but de mockin' birds. They come together and decided to tote sand until they squenched de

---

[4]When people used to get out logs to build a house they would get the neighbors to help. Plenty of food and drink served. Very gay time.

fire in hell. So they set a day and they all agreed on it. Every Friday they totes sand to hell. And that's how come nobody don't never see no mockin' bird[5] on Friday.

Joe Wiley chuckled. "If them mockin' birds ever speck to do dat man any good they better git some box-cars to haul dat sand. Dat one li'l grain they totin' in their bill ain't helpin' none. But anyhow it goes to show you dat animals got sense as well as peoples." Joe went on—

Now take cat-fish for instances. Ah knows a man dat useter go fishin' every Sunday. His wife begged him not to do it and his pastor strained wid him for years but it didn't do no good. He just would go ketch him a fish every Sabbath. One Sunday he went and just as soon as he got to de water he seen a great big ole cat-fish up under some water lilies pickin' his teeth with his fins. So de man baited his pole and dropped de hook right down in front of de big fish. Dat cat grabbed de hook and took out for deep water. De man held on and pretty soon dat fish pulled him in. He couldn't git out. Some folks on de way to church seen him and run down to de water but he was in too deep. So he went down de first time and when he come up he hollered—"Tell my wife." By dat time de fish pulled him under again. When he come up he hollered, "Tell my wife—" and went down again. When he come up de third time he said: "Tell my wife to fear God and cat-fish," and went down for de last time and he never come up no mo'.

"Aw, you b'lieve dat old lie?" Joe Willard growled. "Ah don't."

"Well, Ah do. Nobody ain't gointer git me to fishin' on Sunday," said Big Sweet fervently.

"How come nothin' don't happen to all dese white folks dat go fishin' on Sunday? Niggers got all de signs and white folks got all de money," retorted Joe Willard.

[5]Some say it is a jay bird.

"Yeah, but all cat-fish ain't so sensible." Joe Wiley cut in with a sly grin on his face. "One time when Ah was livin' in Plateau, Alabama—dat's right on de Alabama river you know—Ah put out some fish lines one night and went on home. Durin' de night de river fell and dat left de hooks up out de water and when Ah went there next morning a cat-fish had done jumped up after dat bait till he was washed down in sweat."

Jim Presley said, "I know you tellin' de truth, Joe, 'cause Ah saw a coach whip after a race runner one day. And de race runner was running so fast to git away from dat coach whip dat his tail got so hot it set de world on fire, and dat coach whip was running so hard to ketch him till he put de fire out wid his sweat."

Jim Allen said, "Y'all sho must not b'long to no church de way y'all tells lies. Y'all done quit tellin' 'em. Y'all done gone to moldin' 'em. But y'all want to know how come snakes got poison in they mouth and nothin' else ain't got it?"

"Yeah, tell it, Jim," urged Arthur Hopkins.

Old man Allen turned angrily upon Arthur.

"Don't you be callin' me by my first name. Ah'm old enough for yo' grand paw! You respect my gray hairs. Ah don't play wid chillun. Play wid a puppy and he'll lick yo' mouf."

"Ah didn't mean no harm."

"Dat's all right, Arthur. Ah ain't mad. Ah jus' don't play wid chillun. You go play wid Cliff and Sam and Eugene. They's yo' equal. Ah was a man when yo' daddy was born."

"Well, anyhow, Mr. Jim, please tell us how come de snakes got poison."

Well, when God made de snake he put him in de bushes to ornament de ground. But things didn't suit de snake so one day he got on de ladder and went up to see God.

"Good mawnin', God."

"How do you do, Snake?"

"Ah ain't so many, God, you put me down there on my

belly in de dust and everything trods upon me and kills off my generations. Ah ain't got no kind of protection at all."

God looked off towards immensity and thought about de subject for awhile, then he said, "Ah didn't mean for nothin' to be stompin' you snakes lak dat. You got to have some kind of a protection. Here, take dis poison and put it in yo' mouf and when they tromps on you, protect yo' self."

So de snake took de poison in his mouf and went on back.

So after awhile all de other varmints went up to God.

"Good evenin', God."

"How you makin' it, varmints?"

"God, please do somethin' 'bout dat snake. He' layin' in de bushes there wid poison in his mouf and he's strikin' everything dat shakes de bush. He's killin' up our generations. Wese skeered to walk de earth."

So God sent for de snake and tole him:

"Snake, when Ah give you dat poison, Ah didn't mean for you to be hittin' and killin' everything dat shake de bush. I give you dat poison and tole you to protect yo'self when they tromples on you. But you killin' everything dat moves. Ah didn't mean for you to do dat."

De snake say, "Lawd, you know Ah'm down here in de dust. Ah ain't got no claws to fight wid, and Ah ain't got no feets to git me out de way. All Ah kin see is feets comin' to tromple me. Ah can't tell who my enemy is and who is my friend. You gimme dis protection in my mouf and Ah uses it."

God thought it over for a while then he says:

"Well, snake, I don't want yo' generations all stomped out and I don't want you killin' everything else dat moves. Here take dis bell and tie it to yo' tail. When you hear feets comin' you ring yo' bell and if it's yo' friend, he'll be keerful. If it's yo' enemy, it's you and him."

So dat's how de snake got his poison and dat's how come he got rattles.

Biddy, biddy, bend my story is end.

Turn loose de rooster and hold de hen.

"Don't tell no mo' 'bout no snakes—specially when we walkin' in all dis tall grass," pleaded Presley. "Ah speck Ah'm gointer be seein' 'em in my sleep tonight. Lawd, Ah'm skeered of snakes."

"Who ain't?" cut in Cliff Ulmer. "It sho is gittin' hot. Ah'll be glad when we git to de lake so Ah kin find myself some shade."

"Man, youse two miles from dat lake yet, and otherwise it ain't hot today," said Joe Wiley. "He ain't seen it hot, is he Will House?"

"Naw, Joe, when me and you was hoboing down in Texas it was so hot till we saw old stumps and logs crawlin' off in de shade."

Eugene Oliver said, "Aw dat wasn't hot. Ah seen it so hot till two cakes of ice left the ice house and went down the street and fainted."

Arthur Hopkins put in: "Ah knowed two men who went to Tampa all dressed up in new blue serge suits, and it was so hot dat when de train pulled into Tampa two blue suits got off de train. De men had done melted out of 'em."

Will House said, "Dat wasn't hot. Dat was chilly weather. Me and Joe Wiley went fishin' and it was so hot dat before we got to de water, we met de fish, coming swimming up de road in dust."

"Dat's a fact, too," added Joe Wiley. "Ah remember dat day well. It was so hot dat Ah struck a match to light my pipe and set de lake afire. Burnt half of it, den took de water dat was left and put out de fire."

Joe Willard said "Hush! Don't Ah hear a noise?"

Eugene and Cliffert shouted together, "Yeah—went down to de river—

> Heard a mighty racket
> Nothing but de bull frog
> Pullin' off his jacket!"

"Dat ain't what Ah hea'd," said Joe.

"Well, whut did you hear?"

"Ah see a chigger[6] over in de fence corner wid a splinter in his foot and a seed tick is pickin' it out wid a fence rail and de chigger is hollerin', 'Lawd, have mercy.'"

"Dat brings me to de boll-weevil," said Larkins White. "A boll-weevil flew onto de steerin' wheel of a white man's car and says, 'Mister, lemme drive yo' car.'

"De white man says, 'You can't drive no car.'

"Boll-weevil says: 'Oh yeah, Ah kin. Ah drove in five thousand cars last year and Ah'm going to drive in ten thousand dis year.'

"A man told a tale on de boll-weevil agin. Says he heard a terrible racket and noise down in de field, went down to see whut it was and whut you reckon? It was Ole Man Boll-Weevil whippin' li' Willie Boll-Weevil 'cause he couldn't carry two rows at a time."

Will House said, "Ah know a lie on a black gnat. Me and my buddy Joe Wiley was ramshackin' Georgy over when we come to a loggin' camp. So bein' out of work we ast for a job. So de man puts us on and give us some oxes to drive. Ah had a six-yoke team and Joe was drivin' a twelve-yoke team. As we was comin' thru de woods we heard somethin' hummin' and we didn't know what it was. So we got hungry and went in a place to eat and when we come out a gnat had done et up de six-yoke team and de twelve-yoke team, and was sittin' up on de wagon pickin' his teeth wid a ox-horn and cryin' for somethin' to eat."

"Yeah," put in Joe Wiley, "we seen a man tie his cow and calf out to pasture and a mosquito come along and et up de cow and was ringin' de bell for de calf."

"Dat wasn't no full-grown mosquito at dat," said Eugene Oliver, "Ah was travellin' in Texas and laid down and went to sleep. De skeeters bit me so hard till Ah seen a ole iron

[6]A young flea.

wash-pot, so Ah crawled under it and turned it down over me good so de skeeters couldn't git to me. But you know dem skeeters bored right thru dat iron pot. So I up wid a hatchet and bradded their bills into de pot. So they flew on off 'cross Galveston bay wid de wash pot on their bills."

"Look," said Black Baby, "on de Indian River we went to bed and heard de mosquitoes singin' like bull alligators. So we got under four blankets. Shucks! dat wasn't nothin'. Dem mosquitoes just screwed off dem short bills, reached back in they hip-pocket and took out they long bills and screwed 'em on and come right on through dem blankets and got us."

"Is dat de biggest mosquito you all ever seen? Shucks! Dey was li'l baby mosquitoes! One day my ole man took some men and went out into de woods to cut some fence posts. And a big rain come up so they went up under a great big ole tree. It was so big it would take six men to meet around it. De other men set down on de roots but my ole man stood up and leaned against de tree. Well, sir, a big old skeeter come up on de other side of dat tree and bored right thru it and got blood out of my ole man's back. Dat made him so mad till he up wid his ax and bradded dat mosquito's bill into dat tree. By dat time de rain stopped and they all went home.

"Next day when they come out, dat mosquito had done cleaned up ten acres dying. And two or three weeks after dat my ole man got enough bones from dat skeeter to fence in dat ten acres."

Everybody liked to hear about the mosquito. They laughed all over themselves.

"Yeah," said Sack Daddy, "you sho is tellin' de truth 'bout dat big old mosquito 'cause my ole man bought dat same piece of land and raised a crop of pumpkins on it and lemme tell y'all right now—mosquito dust is de finest fertilizer in de world. Dat land was so rich and we raised pumpkins so big dat we et five miles up in one of 'em and five miles down and ten miles acrost one and we ain't never found out how far it went. But my ole man was buildin' a scaffold inside so we could cut de pumpkin meat without so much trouble, when he dropped his hammer. He tole me, he says, 'Son, Ah done dropped my hammer. Go git it for me.' Well, Ah went down in de pump-kin and begin to hunt dat hammer. Ah was foolin' 'round in there all day, when I met a man and he ast me what Ah was lookin' for. Ah tole him my ole man had done dropped his hammer and sent me to find it for him. De man tole me Ah might as well give it up for a lost cause, he had been lookin' for a double mule-team and a wagon that had got lost in there for three weeks and he hadn't found no trace of 'em yet. So Ah stepped on a pin, de pin bent and dat's de way de story went."

"Dat was rich land but my ole man had some rich land too," put in Will House. "My ole man planted cucumbers and he went along droppin' de seeds and befo' he could git out de way he'd have ripe cucumbers in his pockets. What is the richest land you ever seen?"

"Well," replied Joe Wiley, "my ole man had some land dat was so rich dat our mule died and we buried him down in our bottom-land and de next mornin' he had done sprouted li'l jackasses."

"Aw, dat land wasn't so rich," objected Ulmer. "My ole man had some land and it was so rich dat he drove a stob[7] in de ground at de end of a corn-row for a landmark and next morning there was ten ears of corn on de corn stalk and four ears growin' on de stob."

"Dat lan' y'all talkin' 'bout might do, if you give it plenty commercial-nal[8] but my ole man wouldn't farm no po' land like dat," said Joe Wiley. "Now, one year we was kinda late puttin' in our crops. Everybody else had corn a foot high when papa said, 'Well, chillun, Ah reckon we better plant some corn.' So Ah was droppin' and my brother was hillin' up behind me. We had done planted 'bout a dozen rows when Ah looked back and seen de corn comin' up. Ah didn't want it to grow too fast 'cause it would make all fodder and no

[7]Stake.
[8]Commercial fertilizer.

101

roastin' ears so Ah hollered to my brother to sit down on some of it to stunt de growth. So he did, and de next day he dropped me back a note—says: "passed thru Heben yesterday at twelve o'clock sellin' roastin' ears to de angels."

"Yeah," says Larkins White, "dat was some pretty rich ground, but whut is de poorest ground you ever seen?"

Arthur Hopkins spoke right up and said:

"Ah seen some land so poor dat it took nine partridges to holler 'Bob White.' "

"Dat was rich land, boy," declared Larkins. "Ah seen land so poor dat de people come together and 'cided dat it was too poor to raise anything on, so they give it to de church, so de congregation built de church and called a pastor and held de meetin'. But de land was so poor they had to wire up to Jacksonville for ten sacks of commercial-nal before dey could raise a tune on dat land."

The laughter was halted by the sound of a woodpecker against a cypress. Lonnie Barnes up with his gun to kill it, but Lucy stopped him.

"What you want to kill dat ole thing for? He ain't fitten to eat. Save dat shot and powder to kill me a rabbit. Ah sho would love a nice tender cotton-tail. Slim Ellis brought me a great big ole fat ham off a rabbit last night, and Ah lakted dat."

"Ah kin shoot you a rabbit just as good as Slim kin," Lonnie protested. "Ah wasn't gointer kill no ole tough peckerwood for you to eat, baby. Ah was goin' to shoot dat red-head for his meanness. You know de peckerwood come pretty nigh drownin' de whole world once."

"How was dat?"

Well, you know when de Flood was and dey had two of everything in de ark—well, Ole Nora[9] didn't take on no trees, so de woodpecker set 'round and set 'round for a week or so then he felt like he just had to peck himself some wood. So he begin to peck on de Ark. Ole Nora

[9]Noah.

come to him and tole him, "Don't peck on de Ark. If you peck a hole in it, we'll all drown."

Woodpecker says: "But Ah'm hungry for some wood to peck."

Ole Nora says, "Ah don't keer how hongry you gits don't you peck on dis ark no mo. You want to drown everybody and everything?"

So de woodpecker would sneak 'round behind Ole Nora's back and peck every chance he got. He'd hide hisself way down in de hold where he thought nobody could find him and peck and peck. So one day Ole Nora come caught him at it. He never opened his mouth to dat woodpecker. He just hauled off and give dat peckerwood a cold head-whipping wid a sledge hammer, and dat's why a peckerwood got a red head today—'cause Ole Nora bloodied it wid dat hammer. Dat's how come Ah feel like shootin' every one of 'em Ah see. Tryin' to drown *me* before Ah was born.

"A whole lot went on on dat ole Ark," Larkins White commented. "Dat's where de possum lost de hair off his tail."

"Now don't you tell me no possum ever had no hair on dat slick tail of his'n," said Black Baby, " 'cause Ah know better."

Yes, he did have hair on his tail one time. Yes, indeed. De possum had a bushy tail wid long silk hair on it. Why, it useter be one of de prettiest sights you ever seen. De possum struttin' 'round wid his great big ole plumey tail. Dat was 'way back in de olden times before de big flood.

But de possum was lazy—jus' like he is today. He sleep too much. You see Ole Nora had a son name Ham and he loved to be playin' music all de time. He had a banjo and a fiddle and maybe a guitar too. But de rain come up so sudden he didn't have time to put 'em on de ark. So when rain kept comin' down he fretted a lot 'cause he didn't have nothin' to play. So he found a ole cigar box and made hisself a banjo, but he didn't have no strings for it. So he seen de possum stretched out sleeping wid his tail all spread 'round. So Ham slipped up and shaved de possum's tail and made de strings for his banjo out de hairs. When dat possum woke up from his nap, Ham was playin' his tail hairs down to de bricks and dat's why de possum ain't got no hair on his tail today. Losin' his pretty tail sorta broke de possum's spirit too. He ain't never been de same since. Dat's how come he always actin' shame-faced. He know his tail ain't whut it useter be; and de possum feel mighty bad about it.

"A lot of things ain't whut they useter be," observed Jim Presley. "Now take de 'gator for instance. He been changed 'round powerful since he been made."

"Yeah," cut in Eugene Oliver, "He useter have a nice tongue so he could talk like a nat'chal man, but Brer Dog caused de 'gator to lose his tongue, and dat's how come he hate de dog today."

"Brer 'Gator didn't fall out wid Brer Dog 'bout no tongue," retorted Presley.

Brer Dog done de 'gator a dirty trick 'bout his mouth. You know God made de dog and the 'gator without no mouth. So they seen everybody else had a mouth so they made it up to git theirselves a mouth like de other varmints. So they agreed to cut one 'nothers' mouth, and each one said dat when de other one tole 'em to stop cuttin' they would. So Brer Dog got his mouth first. Brer 'Gator took de razor and cut. Brer Dog tole him, "Stop," which he did. Den Brer Dog took de razor and begin to cut Brer 'Gator a mouth. When his mouth was big as he wanted it, Brer 'Gator says, "Stop, Brer Dog. Dat'll do, I thank you, please." But Brer Dog kept right on cuttin' till he ruint Brer 'Gator's face. Brer 'Gator was a very handsome gent'-man befo' Brer Dog done him that a way, and everytime he look in de lookin' glass he cry like a baby over de dis-figgerment of his face. And dat's how come de 'gator hate de dog.

"My people, my people," lamented Oliver. "They just will talk whut they don't know."

"Go on Oliver."

De 'gator didn't fall out wid de dog 'bout no mouth cuttin' scrape. You know all de animals was havin' a ball down in de pine woods, and so they all chipped in for refreshments and then they didn't have no music for de dance. So all de animals what could 'greed to furnish music. So de dog said he'd be de trumpet in de band, and de horse and de frog and de mockin' bird and all said they'd be there and help out all they could. But they didn't have no bass drum, till somebody said, "Whut's de matter wid Brer 'Gator, why he don't play de bass drum for us?" Dey called Brer 'Gator but he wasn't at de meetin' so de varmints depitized Brer Dog to go call on Brer 'Gator and see if he wouldn't furnish de drum music for de dance. Which he did.

"Good evenin', Brer 'Gator."

"My compliments, Brer Dog, how you makin' out? Ah'm always glad when folks visit me. Whut you want?"

"Well Brer 'Gator, de varmints is holdin' a big convention tonight in de piney woods and we want you to furnish us a little bit of yo' drum music."

"It's like this, Brer Dog, tell de other animals dat Ah'm mighty proud they wants me and de compliments run all over me, but my wife is po'ly and my chillun is down sick. But Ah'll lend you my drum if you know anybody kin play it, and know how to take keer of it too!"

"Oh, Ah'll do *dat,* Brer 'Gator. You just put it in my keer. You don't have to worry 'bout dat atall."

So de dog took Brer 'Gator's tongue to de ball dat night and they beat it for a drum. De varmints lakted de bass drum so well till they didn't play nothin' else hardly. So by daybreak it was wore clean out. Brer Dog didn't want to go tell Brer 'Gator they had done wore his tongue out so he hid from Brer 'Gator. Course de 'gator don't like it 'bout his tongue so he's de sworn enemy of de dog.

Big Sweet says, "Dat's de first time Ah ever heard 'bout de dawg wearin' out de 'gator's tongue, but Ah do know he useter be a pretty varmint. He was pure white all over wid red and yeller stripes around his neck. He was pretty like dat 'till he met up wid Brer Rabbit. Kah, kah, kah! Ah have to laugh everytime Ah think how sharp dat ole rabbit rascal is."

"Yeah," said Sam Hopkins. "At night time, at de right time; Ah've always understood it's de habit of de rabbit to dance in de wood."

"When Ah'm shellin' my corn; you keep out yo' nubbins, Sam," Big Sweet snapped as she spat her snuff.

Ah'm tellin' dis lie on de 'gator. Well, de 'gator was a pretty white varmint wid coal black eyes. He useter swim in de water, but he never did bog up in de mud lak he do now. When he come out de water he useter lay up on de clean grass so he wouldn't dirty hisself all up.

So one day he was layin' up on de grass in a marsh sunnin' hisself and sleepin' when Brer Rabbit come bustin' cross de marsh and run right over Brer 'Gator before he stopped. Brer 'Gator woke up and seen who it was trompin' all over him and trackin' up his pretty white hide. So he seen Brer Rabbit, so he ast him, "Brer Rabbit, what you mean by runnin' all cross me and messin' up my clothes lak dis?"

Brer Rabbit was up behind a clump of bushes peerin' out to see what was after him. So he tole de 'gator, says: "Ah

106

ain't got time to see what Ah'm runnin' over nor under. Ah got trouble behind me."

'Gator ast, "Whut is trouble? Ah ain't never heard tell of dat befo'."

Brer Rabbit says, "You ain't never heard tell of trouble?"

Brer 'Gator tole him, "No."

Rabbit says: "All right, you jus' stay right where you at and Ah'll show you whut trouble is."

He peered 'round to see if de coast was clear and loped off, and Brer 'Gator washed Brer Rabbit's foot tracks off his hide and went on back to sleep agin.

Brer Rabbit went on off and lit him a li'dard knot[10] and come on back. He sat dat marsh afire on every side. All around Brer 'Gator de fire was burnin' in flames of fire. De 'gator woke up and pitched out to run, but every which a way he run de fire met him.

He seen Brer Rabbit sittin' up on de high ground jus' killin' hisself laughin'. So he hollered and ast him:

"Brer Rabbit, whut's all dis goin' on?"

"Dat's trouble, Brer 'Gator, dat's trouble youse in."

De 'gator run from side to side, round and round. Way after while he broke thru and hit de water "ker ploogum!" He got all cooled off but he had done got smoked all up befo' he got to de water, and his eyes is all red from de smoke. And dat's how come a 'gator is black today—cause de rabbit took advantage of him lak dat.

---

[10]Lightwood, fat pine. So called because it is frequently used as a torch.

SEVEN

J oe Wiley said, " 'Tain't nothin' cute as a rabbit. When
they come cuter than him, they got to have 'cute indiges-
tion." He cleared his throat and continued:

Dat's de reason de dog is mad wid de rabbit[1]
now—'cause he fooled de dog.
   You know they useter call on de same girl. De rabbit
useter g'wan up to de house and cross his legs on de porch
and court de girl. Brer Dog, he'd come in de gate wid his
banjo under his arm.
   "Good evenin', Miss Saphronie."
   "My compliments, Brer Dog, come have a chair on de
pe-azza."
   "No thank you ma'am, Miss Saphronie. B'lieve Ah'll set
out here under de Chinaberry tree."
   So he'd set out dere and pick de banjo and sing all 'bout:

If Miss Fronie was a gal of mine
She wouldn't do nothin' but starch and iron.

   So de girl wouldn't pay no mind to Brer Rabbit at all.
She'd be listenin' to Brer Dog sing. Every time he'd stop

[1]See glossary.

109

she'd holler out dere to him, "Wont you favor us wid another piece, Brer Dog? Ah sho do love singin' especially when they got a good voice and picks de banjo at de same time."

Brer Rabbit saw he wasn't makin' no time wid Miss Saphronie so he waylaid Brer Dog down in de piney woods one day and says:

"Brer Dog, you sho is got a mellow voice. You can sing. Wisht Ah could sing like dat, den maybe Miss Fronie would pay me some mind."

"Gawan, Brer Rabbit, you makin' great 'miration at nothin'. Ah can whoop a little, but Ah really do wish Ah could sing enough to suit Miss Fronie."

"Well, dat's de very point Ah'm comin' out on. Ah know a way to make yo' voice sweeter."

"How? Brer Rabbit, how?"

"Ah knows a way."

"Hurry up and tell me, Brer Rabbit. Don't keep me waitin' like dis. Make haste."

"Ah got to see inside yo' throat first. Lemme see dat and Ah can tell you exactly what to do so you can sing more better."

Brer Dog stretched his mouth wide open and the rabbit peered way down inside. Brer Dog had his mouth latched back to de last notch and his eyes shut. So Brer Rabbit pulled out his razor and split Brer Dog's tongue and tore out across de mountain wid de dog right in behind him. Him and him! Brer Rabbit had done ruint Brer Dog's voice, but he ain't had time to stop at Miss Fronie's nor nowhere else 'cause dat dog is so mad he won't give him time.

"Yeah," said Cliff.

De dog is sho hot after him. Run dem doggone rabbits so that they sent word to de dogs dat they want peace. So they had a convention. De rabbit took de floor and said they was tired of runnin', and dodgin' all de time, and they asted de dogs to please leave rabbits alone and run some-

110

thin' else. So de dogs put it to a vote and 'greed to leave off runnin' rabbits.

So after de big meetin' Brer Dog invites de rabbit over to his house to have dinner wid him.

He started on thru de woods wid Brer Dog but every now and then he'd stop and scratch his ear and listen. He stop right in his tracks. Dog say:

"Aw, come on Brer Rabbit, you too suscautious. Come on."

Kept dat up till they come to de branch just 'fore they got to Brer Dog's house. Just as Brer Rabbit started to step out on de foot-log, he heard some dogs barkin' way down de creek. He heard de old hound say, "How o-l-d is he?" and the young dogs answer him: "Twenty-one or two, twenty-one or two!" So Brer Rabbit say, "Excuse me, but Ah don't reckon Ah better go home wid you today, Brer Dog."

"Aw, come on, Brer Rabbit, you always gitten scared for nothin'. Come on."

"Ah hear dogs barkin', Brer Dog."

"Naw, you don't, Brer Rabbit."

"Yes, Ah do. Ah know, dat's dogs barkin'."

"S'posin' it is, it don't make no difference. Ain't we done held a convention and passed a law dogs run no mo' rabbits? Don't pay no 'tention to every li'l bit of barkin' you hear."

Rabbit scratch his ear and say,

"Yeah, but all de dogs ain't been to no convention, and anyhow some of dese fool dogs ain't got no better sense than to run all over dat law and break it up. De rabbits didn't go to school much and he didn't learn but three letter, and that's trust no mistake. Run every time de bush shake."

So he raced on home without breakin' another breath wid de dog.

"Dat's right," cut in Larkins White. "De Rabbits run from everything. They held a meetin' and decided. They say, 'Le's all go drown ourselves 'cause ain't nothin' skeered of us.' So it was agreed.

111

"They all started to de water in a body fast as time could wheel and roll. When they was crossin' de marsh jus' befo' they got to de sea, a frog hollered, 'Quit it, quit it!' So they say, 'Somethin' is 'fraid of us, so we won't drown ourselves.' So they all turnt 'round and went home."

"Dat's as bad as dat goat Ah seen back in South Carolina. We was on de tobacco truck goin' after plants when we passed a goat long side de road. He was jus' chewin' and he looked up and ast, 'Whose truck is dat?' Nobody answered him. When we come on back Ah said, 'Mr. Rush Pinkney's, why?' De goat says, 'Oh nothin',' and kept right on chewin'."

"Ow, Big Sweet! gimme dat lyin' goat! You know damn well dat goat ain't broke a breath wid you and nobody else," scolded Jim Allen.

"But a goat's got plenty sense, ugly as he is," said Arthur Hopkins.

Ah know my ole man had a goat and one Sunday mornin' he got mama to wash his shirt so't would be clean for him to wear to church. It was a pretty red silk shirt and my ole man was crazy about it.

So my ole lady washed it and hung it out to dry so she could iron it befo' church time. Our goat spied pa's shirt hangin' on de line and et it up tiddy umpty.

My ole man was so mad wid dat goat 'bout his shirt till he grabbed him and tied him on de railroad track so de train could run over him and kill him.

But dat old goat was smart. When he seen dat train bearin' down on him, he coughed up dat red shirt and waved de train down.

Dad Boykin said: "No ef and ands about it. A goat is a smart varmint, but my feets sho is tired."

"Dat *was* a long two miles," Jim Allen added. "Ah see de lake now, and Ah sho am glad."

"Doggone it!" said Lonnie Barnes, "here we is almost at de lake and Ah ain't got myself no game yet. But maybe Ah'll

112

have mo' luck on de way back."

"Yeah," Lucy remarked dryly, "dat gun you totin' ain't doin' you much good! Might just as well left it home."

"He act just like dat nigger did in slavery time wid Ole Massa's gun," laughed Willie Roberts.

"How as dat?"

Well, you know John was Ole Massa's pet nigger. He give John de best of everything and John thought Ole Massa was made outa gold. So one day Massa decided he wanted a piece of deer meat to eat so he called John and some more of his niggers together and told 'em:

"Now Ah want y'all to go git me a deer today. Ah'm goin' to give John my new gun and Ah want de rest of y'all go 'round and skeer up de deer and head him towards John, and he will shoot him wid de gun." When de others got there they said, "Did you git him, John?"

He said, "Naw, Ah didn't."

They said, "Well how come you didn't? He come right dead down de hill towards you."

"Y'all crazy! You think Ah'm gointer sprain Massa's brand new gun shootin' up hill wid it?"

"Dat's put me in de mind of a gun my ole man had," said Gene Oliver. "He shot a man wid it one time and de bullet worked him twice befo' it kilt him and three times after. If you hold it high, it would sweep de sky; if you hold it level, it'd kill de devil."

"Oh Gene, stop yo' lyin'! You don't stop lyin' and gone to flyin'."

"Dat ain't no lie, dat's a fact. One night I fired it myself," said Pitts.

"It's a wonder you didn't shoot it off dat time when de quarters boss was hot behind you."

"Let dat ride! Ah didn't want to kill dat ole cracker. But one night Ah heard somethin' stumblin' 'round our woodpile, so Ah grabbed de gun, stepped to de back door and fired it at de woodpile, and went on back to bed. All night long Ah heard somethin' goin' 'round and 'round de house hummin' like a nest of hornets. When daybreak come Ah found out what it was. What you reckon? It was dat bullet. De night was so dark it was runnin' 'round de house waitin' for daylight so it could find out which was the way to go!''

"Dat was a mighty gun yo' pa had," agreed Larkins, "but Ah had a gun dat would lay dat one in the shade. It could shoot so far till Ah had to put salt down de barrel so de game Ah kilt wid it would keep till Ah got to it.''

"Larkins—" Jim Allen started to protest.

"Mr. Allen, dat ain't no lie. Dat's a fack. Dat gun was so bad dat all Ah need to do was walk out in de woods wid it to skeer all de varmints. Ah went huntin' one day and saw three thousand ducks in a pond. Jus' as Ah levelled dis gun to fire, de weather turned cold and de water in de lake froze solid and them ducks flew off wid de lake froze to their feets.''

"Larkins, s'posin' you was to die right now, where would you land?—jus' as straight to hell as a martin to his gourd. Whew! you sho kin lie. You'd pass slap thru hell proper. Jus' a bouncin' and a jumpin' and go clear to Ginny Gall, and dat's four miles south of West Hell; you better stop yo' lyin', man.''

"Dat ain't no lie, man. You jus' ain't seen no real guns and no good shootin'.''

"Ah don't want to see none. Less fish. Here we is at de lake. You can't talk and ketch fish too. You'll skeer all de fish away.''

"Aw, nobody ain't even got a hook baited yet. Leave Larkins lie till we git set!" suggested Joe Wiley. "You gittin' old, Jim, when you can't stand good lyin'. It's jus' like sound doctrine. Everybody can't stand it.''

"Who gittin' old? Not me! Ah laks de lies. All I said is yo' talkin' skeers off all de trouts and sheepheads. Ah can't eat no lies.''

"Aw, gran'pa, don't be so astorperious! We all wants to hear Larkins' tale. I'm goin' ketch you some fish. We ain't off lak dis often. Tomorrow we'll be back in de swamp 'mong de cypress knees, de 'gators, and de moccasins, and strainin' wid de swamp boss," pleaded Cliff. "Go head on, and talk, Larkins, God ain't gonna bother you."

"Well," says Larkins:

A man had a wife and a whole passle of young 'uns, and they didn't have nothin' to eat.

He told his ole lady, "Well, Ah got a load of ammunition in my gun, so Ah'm gointer go out in de woods and see what Ah kin bring back for us to eat."

His wife said: "That's right, go see can't you kill us somethin'—if 'tain't nothin' but a squirrel."

He went on huntin' wid his gun. It was one of dese muzzle-loads. He knowed he didn't have but one load of ammunition so he was very careful not to stumble and let his gun go off by accident.

He had done walked more'n three miles from home and he ain't saw anything to shoot at. He got worried. Then all of a sudden he spied some wild turkeys settin' up in a tree on a limb. He started to shoot at 'em, when he looked over in de pond and seen a passle of wild ducks; and down at de edge of de pond he saw a great big deer. He heard some noise behind him and he looked 'round and seen some partiges.

He wanted all of 'em and he didn't know how he could get 'em. So he stood and he thought and he thought. Then he decided what to do.

He took aim, but he didn't shoot at de turkeys. He shot de limb de turkeys was settin' on and de ball split dat limb and let all dem turkeys' feets dropped right down thru de crack and de split limb shet up on 'em and helt 'em right dere. De ball went on over and fell into de pond and kilt all dem ducks. De gun had too heavy a charge in her, so it bust and de barrel flew over and kilt dat deer. De stock kicked de man in de breast and he fell backwards and smothered all dem partiges.

Well, he drug his deer up under de tree and got his

ducks out de pond and piled them up wid de turkeys and so forth. He seen he couldn't tote all dat game so he went on home to git his mule and wagon.

Soon as he come in de gate his wife said:

"Where is de game you was gointer bring back? you musta lost yo' gun, you ain't got it."

He told his wife, "Ah wears de longest pants in dis house. You leave me tend to my business and you mind yours. Jus' you put on de pot and be ready. Plenty rations is comin'."

He took his team on back in de woods wid him and loaded up de wagon. He wouldn't git up on de wagon his-self because he figgered his mule had enough to pull without him.

Just as he got his game all loaded on de wagon, it commenced to rain but he walked on beside of the mule pattin' him and tellin' him to "come up," till they got home.

When he got home his wife says: "De pot is boilin'. Where is de game you tole me about?"

He looked back and seen his wagon wasn't behind de mule where it ought to have been. Far as he could see— nothin' but them leather traces, but no wagon.

Then he knowed de rain had done made dem traces stretch, and de wagon hadn't moved from where he loaded it.

So he told his wife, "De game will be here. Don't you worry."

So he just took de mule out and stabled him and wrapped dem traces 'round de gate post and went on in de house.

De next day it was dry and de sun was hot and it shrunk up dem traces, and about twelve o'clock they brought dat wagon home, "Cluck-cluck, cluck-cluck," right on up to de gate.

In spite of the laughter and talk, Cliff had landed two perch already, so Jim Allen laughed with the rest.

"Now," he said, beaming upon the fish his grandson had hooked, "I'm goin' to tell y'all about de hawk and de buzzard.

You know de hawk and de buzzard was settin' up in a pine tree one day, so de hawk says: "How you get yo' livin', Brer Buzzard?"

"Oh Ah'm makin' out pretty good, Brer Hawk. Ah waits on de salvation of de Lawd."

Hawk says, "Humph, Ah don't wait on de mercy of nobody. Ah takes mine."

"Ah bet, Ah'll live to pick yo' bones, Brer Hawk."

"Aw naw, you won't, Brer Buzzard. Watch me git my livin'."

He seen a sparrer sittin' on a dead limb of a tree and he sailed off and dived down at dat sparrer. De end of de limb was stickin' out and he run his breast right up on de sharp point and hung dere. De sparrer flew on off.

After while he got so weak he knowed he was gointer die. So de buzzard flew past just so—flyin' slow you know, and said, "Un hunh, Brer Hawk, Ah told you Ah was gointer live to pick yo' bones. Ah waits on de salvation of de Lawd." And dat's de way it is wid some of you young colts."

"Heh, heh, heh! Y'all talkin' 'bout me being old. Ah betcher Ah'll be here when a many of y'all is gone."

Joe Wiley said: "Less table discussion 'bout dyin' and open up de house for new business.

Y'all want to know how come they always use raw-hide on mule, so Ah'm gointer tell you. Whenever they make a whip they gointer have raw-hide on it, if it ain't nothin' but de tip.

A man had a mule you know and he had a ox too. So he used to work 'em together.

Both of 'em used to get real tired befo' knockin' off time but dat ole ox had mo' sense than de mule, so he played off sick.

Every day de mule would go out and work by hisself and de ox stayed in de stable. Every night when de mule come in, he'd ast, "Whut did Massa say 'bout me today?"

De mule would say, "Oh nothin'," or maybe he'd say,

117

"Ah heard him say how sorry he was you was sick and couldn't work."

De ox would laugh and go on to sleep.

One day de mule got tired, so he said, "Massa dat ox ain't sick. 'Tain't a thing de matter wid him. He's jus' playin' off sick. Ah'm tired of doin' all dis work by myself."

So dat night when he got in de stable, de ox ast him. "What did Ole Massa say 'bout me today?"

Mule told him, "Ah didn't hear him say a thing, but Ah saw him talkin' to de butcher man."

So de ox jumped up and said, "Ah'm well. Tell Ole Massa Ah'll be to work tomorrow."

But de next mornin' bright and soon de butcher come led him off.

So he said to de mule, "If you hadn't of told Massa on me, Ah wouldn't be goin' where Ah am. They're gointer kill me, but Ah'll always be war on yo' back."

And that's why they use raw-hide on mule's back—on account of dat mule and dat ox."

"Oh, well, if we gointer go way back there and tell how everything started," said Ulmer, "Ah might just as well tell how come we got gophers."

"Pay 'tention to yo' pole, Cliff," Jim Allen scolded. "You gittin' a bite. You got 'im! A trout too! If dat fool ain't lucky wid fish!"

Old Man Jim strung the trout expertly. "Now, Cliff, you kin do all de talkin' you want, just as long as you ketch me some fish Ah don't keer."

"Well," began Cliff:

God was sittin' down by de sea makin' sea fishes. He made de whale and throwed dat in and it swum off. He made a shark and throwed it in and then he made mullets and shad-fish and cats and trouts and they all swum on off.

De Devil was standin' behind him lookin' over his shoulder.

Way after while, God made a turtle and throwed it in de

118

water and it swum on off. Devil says, "Ah kin make one of those things."

God said, "No, you can't neither."

Devil told him, "Aw, Ah kin so make one of those things. 'Tain't nothin' to make nohow. Who couldn't do dat? Ah jus' can't blow de breath of life into it, but Ah sho kin make a turtle."

God said: "Devil, Ah know you can't make none, but if you think you kin make one go 'head and make it and Ah'll blow de breath of life into it for you."

You see, God was sittin' down by de sea, makin' de fish outa sea-mud. But de Devil went on up de hill so God couldn't watch him workin', and made his outa high land dirt. God waited nearly all day befo' de Devil come back wid his turtle.

As soon as God seen it, He said, "Devil, dat ain't no turtle you done made."

Devil flew hot right off. "Dat ain't no turtle? Who say dat ain't no turtle? Sho it's a turtle."

God shook his head, says, "Dat sho *ain't* no turtle, but Ah'll blow de breath of life into it like Ah promised."

Devil stood Him down dat dat was a turtle.

So God blowed de breath of life into what de Devil had done made, and throwed him into de water. He swum out. God throwed him in again. He come on out. Throwed him in de third time and he come out de third time.

God says: "See, Ah told you dat wasn't no turtle."

"Yes, suh, dat *is* a turtle."

"Devil, don't you know dat all turtles loves de water? Don't you see whut you done made won't stay in there?"

Devil said, "Ah don't keer, dat's a turtle, Ah keep a 'tellin' you."

God disputed him down dat it wasn't no turtle. Devil looked it over and scratched his head. Then he says, "Well, anyhow it will go for one." And that's why we have gophers!

"Dat gopher had good sense. He know he was a dry-land turtle so he didn't try to mix wid de rest. Take for instance de time they had de gopher up in court.

"De gopher come in and looked all around de place. De judge was a turtle, de lawyers was turtles, de witnesses was turtles and they had turtles for jurymen.

"So de gopher ast de judge to excuse his case and let him come back some other time. De judge ast him how come he wanted to put off his case and de gopher looked all around de room and said, 'Blood is thicker than water,' and escused hisself from de place.

"Yeah," said Floyd Thomas, "but even God ain't satisfied wid some of de things He makes and changes 'em Hisself."

Jim Presley wanted to know what God ever changed, to Floyd's knowledge.

Well, He made butterflies after de world wuz all finished and thru. You know de Lawd seen so much bare ground till He got sick and tired lookin' at it. So God tole 'em to fetch 'im his prunin' shears and trimmed up de trees and made grass and flowers and throwed 'em all over de clearin's and dey growed dere from memorial days.

Way after while de flowers said, "Wese put heah to keep de world comp'ny but wese lonesome ourselves." So God said, "A world is somethin' ain't never finished. Soon's you make one thing you got to make somethin' else to go wid it. Gimme dem li'l tee-ninchy shears."

So he went 'round clippin' li'l pieces offa everything—de sky, de trees, de flowers, de earth, de varmints and every one of dem li'l clippin's flew off. When folks seen all them li'l scraps fallin' from God's scissors and flutterin' they called 'em flutter-bys. But you know how it is wid de brother in black. He got a big mouf and a stambling tongue. So he got it all mixed up and said, "butter-fly" and folks been calling 'em dat ever since. Dat's how come we got butterflies of every color and kind and dat's why dey hangs 'round de flowers. Dey wuz made to keep de flowers company.

"Watch out, Cliffert!" yelled Jim Allen. "A 'gator must be on yo' hook! Look at it! It's dived like a duck."

"Aw, 'tain't nothin' but a gar fish on it. Ah kin tell by his bite!" said Cliff.

"You pull him up and see!" Jim commanded.

Cliff hauled away and landed a large gar on the grass.

"See, Ah told you, Gran'pa. Don't you worry. Ah'm gointer ketch you mo' fish than you kin eat. Plenty for Mama and Gran'ma too. Less take dis gar-fish home to de cat."

"Yeah," said Jim Presley. "Y' take de cat a fish, too. They love it better than God loves Gabriel—and dat's His best angel."

"He sho do and dat's how cats got into a mess of trouble—'bout eatin' fish," added Jim Presley.

"How was dat? I done forgot if Ah ever knowed."

"If, if, if," mocked Jim Allen. "Office Richardson, youse always iffin'! If a frog had wings he wouldn't bump his rump so much."

"Gran'pa is right in wid de cats," Cliff teased. "He's so skeered he ain't gointer git all de fish he kin eat, he's just like a watch-dog when de folks is at de table. He'll bite anybody then. Think they cheatin' 'im outa his vittles."

Jim Presley spat in the lake and began:

Once upon a time was a good ole time—monkey chew tobacco and spit white lime.

Well, this was a man dat had a wife and five chillun, and a dog and a cat.

Well, de hongry times caught 'em. Hard times everywhere. Nobody didn't have no mo' then jus' enough to keep 'em alive. First they had a long dry spell dat parched up de crops, then de river rose and drowned out everything. You could count anybody's ribs. De white folks all got faces look lak blue-John[2] and de niggers had de white mouf.[3]

So dis man laid in de bed one night and consulted wid his piller. Dat means he talked it over wid his wife. And he

[2]Skimmed milk.

[3]A very hungry person is supposed to look ashy-gray around the mouth.

121

told her, "Tomorrow less git our pole and go to de lake and see kin we ketch a mess of fish. Dat's our last chance. De fish done got so skeerce and educated they's hard to ketch, but we kin try."

They was at de lake bright and soon de next day. De man took de fishin' pole hisself 'cause he was skeered to trust his wife er de chillun wid it. It was they last chance to git some grub.

So de man fished all day long till he caught seven fishes. Not no great big trouts nor mud-cats but li'l perches and brims. So he tole 'em, "Now, Ah got a fish apiece for all of us, but Ah'm gointer keep on till Ah ketch one apiece for our dog and our cat."

So he fished on till sundown and caught a fish for the dog and de cat, and then they went on home and cooked de fish.

After de fish was all cooked and ready de woman said: "We got to have some drinkin' water. Less go down to de spring to git some. You better come help me tote it 'cause Ah feel too weak to bring it by myself."

So de husband got de water bucket off de shelf and went to de spring wid his wife. But 'fore he went, he told de chillun, "Now, y'all watch out and keep de cat off de fish. She'll steal it sho if she kin."

De chillun tole him, "Yessuh," but they got to foolin' 'round and playin' and forgot all about de cat, and she jumped up on de table and et all de fish but one. She was so full she jus' couldn't hold another mouthful without bustin' wide open.

When de old folks come back and seen what de cat had done they bust out cryin'. They knowed dat one li'l fish divided up wouldn't save they lives. They knowed they had to starve to death. De man looked at de cat and he knowed dat one mo' fish would kill her so he said, "Ah'm gointer make her greedy gut kill her." So he made de cat eat dat other fish and de man and his wife and chillun and de dog and cat all died.

De cat died first so's he was already in Heben when de rest of de family got there. So when God put de man's soul on de scales to weigh it, de cat come up and was lookin' at

122

de man, and de man was lookin' at de cat.

God seen how they eye-balled one 'nother so He ast de man, "Man, what is it between you and dis cat?"

So de man said, "God, dat cat's got all our nine lives in her belly." And he told God all about de fish.

God looked hard at dat cat for a hundred years, but it seem lak a minute.

Then he said: "Gabriel, Peter, Rayfield, John and Michael, all y'all ketch dat cat, and throw him outa Heben."

So they did and he was fallin' for nine days, and there ain't been no cats in Heben since. But he still got dem nine lives in his belly and you got to kill him nine times befo' he'll stay dead.

> Stepped on a pin, de pin bent
> And dat's de way de story went.

"Dat may be so, Presley," commented Jim Allen, "but if Ah ketch one messin' 'round *my* fish, Ah bet Ah kin knock dat man and woman and dem five chillun, de dog *and* de cat outa any cat Ah ever seen wid one lick."

"Dat's one something, Ah ain't never gointer kill," announced Willard forcefully. "It's dead bad luck."

"Me neither," assented Sack Daddy. "Everybody know it's nine years hard luck. Ah shot a man once up in West Florida, killed him dead for bull-dozin' me in a skin game, and got clean away. Ah got down in de phosphate mines around Mulberry and was doin' fine till Ah shacked up wid a woman dat had a great big ole black cat wid a white star in his bosom. He had a habit of jumpin' up on de bed all durin' de night time. One night Ah woke up and he was on my chest wid his nose right to mine, suckin' my breath.

"Ah got so mad Ah grabbed dat sucker by de tail and bust his brains out aginst a stanchion. My woman cried and carried on 'bout de cat and she tole me Ah was gointer have bad luck. Man, you know it wasn't two weeks befo' Sheriff Joe Brown laid his hand on my shoulder and tole me, 'Le's go.' Ah made five years for dat at Raiford. Killin' cats is bad luck."

"Talkin' 'bout dogs," put in Gene Oliver, "they got plenty sense. Nobody can't fool dogs much."

"And speakin' 'bout hams," cut in Big Sweet meaningly, "if Joe Willard don't stay out of dat bunk he was in last night, Ah'm gointer sprinkle some salt down his back and sugar-cure *his* hams."

Joe snatched his pole out of the water with a jerk and glared at Big Sweet, who stood sidewise looking at him most pointedly.

"Aw, woman, quit tryin' to signify."[4]

"Ah kin signify all Ah please, Mr. Nappy-chin, so long as Ah know what Ah'm talkin' about."

"See dat?" Joe appealed to the other men. "We git a day off and figger we kin ketch some fish and enjoy ourselves, but naw, some wimmins got to drag behind us, even to de lake."

"You didn't figger Ah was draggin' behind you when you was bringin' dat Sears and Roebuck catalogue over to my house and beggin' me to choose my ruthers.[5] Lemme tell *you* something, *any* time Ah shack up wid any man Ah gives myself de privilege to go wherever he might be, night or day. Ah got de law in my mouth."

"Lawd, ain't she specifyin'!" sniggered Wiley.

"Oh, Big Sweet does dat," agreed Richardson. "Ah knowed she had somethin' up her sleeve when she got Lucy and come along."

"Lawd," Willard said bitterly. "My people, my people," as de monkey said. "You fool wid Aunt Hagar's[6] chillun and they'll sho distriminate you and put yo' name in de streets."

Jim Allen commented: "Well, you know what they say—a man can cackerlate his life till he git mixed up wid a woman or git straddle of a cow."

Big Sweet turned viciously upon the old man. "Who you

---

[4]To show off.

[5]Make a choice.

[6]Negroes are in similie children of Hagar; white folks, of Sarah.

callin' a cow, fool? Ah know you ain't namin' *my* mama's daughter no cow."

"Now all y'all heard what Ah said. Ah ain't called nobody no cow," Jim defended himself. "Dat's just an old time by-word 'bout no man kin tell what's gointer happen when he gits mixed up wid a woman or set straddle of a cow."

"I done heard my gran'paw say dem very words many and many a time," chimed in Larkins. "There's a whole heap of them kinda by-words. Like for instance:

" 'Ole coon for cunnin', young coon for runnin',' and 'Ah can't dance, but Ah know good moves.' They all got a hidden meanin', jus' like de Bible. Everybody can't understand what they mean. Most people is thin-brained. They's born wid they feet under de moon. Some folks is born wid they feet on de sun and they kin seek out de inside meanin' of words."

"Fack is, it's a story 'bout a man sittin' straddle of a cow," Jim Allen went on.

A man and his wife had a boy and they thought so much of him that they sent him off to college. At de end of seven years, he schooled out and come home and de old man and his ma was real proud to have de only boy 'round there dat was book-learnt.

So de next mornin' after he come home, de ma was milkin' de cows and had one young cow dat had never been to de pail befo' and she used to kick every time anybody milked her.

She was actin' extry bad dat mornin' so de woman called her husband and ast him to come help her wid de cow. So he went out and tried to hold her, but she kept on rearin' and pitchin' and kickin' over de milk pail, so he said to his wife: "We don't need to strain wid dis cow. We got a son inside that's been to school for seben years and done learnt everything. He'll know jus' what to do wid a kickin' cow. Ah'll go call him."

So he called de boy and told him.

De boy come on out to de cow-lot and looked everything over. Den he said, "Mama, cow-kickin' is all a matter of scientific principle. You see before a cow can kick she has to hump herself up in the back. So all we need to do is to take the hump out the cow's back."

His paw said, "Son, Ah don't see how you gointer do dat. But 'course you been off to college and you know a heap mo' than me and yo' ma ever will know. Go 'head and take de hump outa de heifer. We'd be mighty much obliged."

De son put on his gold eye glasses and studied de cow from head to foot. Then he said, "All we need to keep this animal from humping is a weight on her back."

"What kinda weight do she need, son?"

"Oh, any kind of a weight, jus' so it's heavy enough, papa," de son told him. "It's all in mathematics."

"Where we gointer git any weight lak dat, son?"

"Why don't you get up there, papa? You're just about the weight we need."

"Son, you been off to school a long time, and maybe you done forgot how hard it is for anybody to sit on a cow, and Ah'm gittin' old, you know."

"But, papa, I can fix that part, too. I'll tie your feet together under her belly so she can't throw you. You just get on up there."

"All right, son, if you say so, Ah'll git straddle of dis cow. You know more'n Ah do, Ah reckon."

So they tied de cow up short to a tree and de ole man got on by de hardest,[7] and de boy passed a rope under her belly and tied his papa on. De old lady tried to milk de cow but she was buckin' and rearin' so till de ole man felt he couldn't stand it no mo'. So he hollered to de boy, "Cut de rope, son, cut de rope! Ah want to git down."

Instead of de boy cuttin' loose his papa's feet he cut de rope dat had de cow tied to de tree and she lit out 'cross de wood wid de ole man's feet tied under de cow. Wasn't no way for him to git off.

De cow went bustin' on down de back-road wid de ole man till they met a sister he knowed. She was surprised to

7With great difficulty.

126

see de man on de cow, so she ast: "My lawd, Brother So-
and-so, where you goin'?"

He tole her, "Only God and dis cow knows."

"Wonder what de swamp boss is studyin' 'bout whilst we
out here fishin'?" Oliver wondered.

"Nobody don't know and here's one dat don't keer," Cliff
Ulmer volunteered. "Ah done caught me a nice mess of fish
and Ah'm gointer bust dat jook wide open tonight.

"Ah was over there last night and maybe de boys didn't get
off lyin'! Somebody tole one on de snail.

"You know de snail's wife took sick and sent him for de
doctor.

"She was real low ill-sick and rolled from one side of de bed
to de other. She was groanin', 'Lawd knows Ah got so much
misery Ah hope de Doctor'll soon git here to me.'

"After seben years she heard a scufflin' at de door. She was
real happy so she ast, 'Is dat you baby, done come back wid
de doctor? Ah'm so glad!'

"He says, 'Don't try to rush me—Ah ain't gone yet.' He
had been seben years gettin' to de door."

"Yeah, Ah was over there too," said Larkins White, "and
somebody else tole a lie on de snail. A snail was crossin' de
road for seben years. Just as he got across a tree fell and barely
missed him 'bout a inch or two. If he had a been where he was
six months before it would er kilt him. De snail looked back
at de tree and tole de people, 'See, it pays to be fast.' "

"Look at de wind risin'!" Willard exclaimed.

"We ain't no hogs, Joe, we can't see no wind."

"You kin see it, if you squirt some sow milk in yo' eyes. Ah
seen it one time," Jim Allen announced.

"How did it look, gran'pa? Dat's a sight Ah sho would love
to see," cried Cliff.

"Naw, you wouldn't, son. De wind is blood red and when
you see it comin' it look lak a bloody ocean rushin' down on
you from every side. It ain't got no sides and no top. Youse
jus' drownin' in blood and can't help yo'self. When Ah was

a li'l chap dey tole me if Ah put hawg milk in mah eyes Ah could see de wind, and—"

"Why they say 'hawg milk'? Can't you try some cow milk?" Cliffert asked.

"De hawg is de onliest thing God ever made whut kin see de wind. Ain't you never seen uh sow take a good look in one direction and go tuh makin' up a good warm nest? She see great winds a comin' a whole day off."

"Well, how didja quit seein' de wind, gran'pa?"

"De sow milk wore outa mah eyes gradual lak, but Ah seen dat wind fo' more'n a week. Dey had to blindfold me tuh keep me from runnin' wild."

Cliff Ulmer said:

De wind is a woman, and de water is a woman too. They useter talk together a whole heap. Mrs. Wind useter go set down by de ocean and talk and patch and crochet.

They was jus' like all lady people. They loved to talk about their chillun, and brag on 'em.

Mrs. Water useter say, "Look at *my* chillun! Ah got de biggest and de littlest in de world. All kinds of chillun. Every color in de world, and every shape!"

De wind lady bragged louder than de water woman: "Oh, but Ah got mo' different chilluns than anybody in de world. They flies, they walks, they swims, they sings, they talks, they cries. They got all de colors from de sun. Lawd, my chillun sho is a pleasure. 'Tain't nobody got no babies like mine."

Mrs. Water got tired of hearin' 'bout Mrs. Wind's chillun so she got so she hated 'em.

One day a whole passle of her chillun come to Mrs. Wind and says: "Mama, wese thirsty. Kin we go git us a cool drink of water?"

She says, "Yeah chillun. Run on over to Mrs. Water and hurry right back soon."

When them chillun went to squinch they thirst Mrs. Water grabbed 'em all and drowned 'em.

When her chillun didn't come home, de wind woman got

worried. So she went on down to de water and ast for her babies.

"Good evenin' Mis' Water, you see my chillun today?"

De water woman tole her, "No-oo-oo."

Mrs. Wind knew her chillun had come down to Mrs. Water's house, so she passed over de ocean callin' her chillun, and every time she call de white feathers would come up on top of de water. And dat's how come we got white caps on waves. It's de feathers comin' up when de wind woman calls her lost babies.

When you see a storm on de water, it's de wind and de water fightin' over dem chillun.

" 'Bout dat time a flea wanted to get a hair cut, so Ah left."

EIGHT

Y'all been tellin' and lyin' 'bout all dese varmints but you ain't yet spoke about de high chief boss of all de world which is de lion," Sack Daddy commented.

"He's de King of de Beasts, but he ain't no King of de World, now Sack," Dad Boykin spoke up. "He *thought* he was de King till John give him a straightenin'."

"Don't put dat lie out!" Sack Daddy contended. "De lion won't stand no straightenin'."

"Course I 'gree wid you dat everybody can't show de lion no deep point, but John showed it to him. Oh, yeah, John not only straightened him out, he showed dat ole lion where in."

"When did he do all of dis, Dad? Ah ain't never heard tell of it." Dad spoke up:

Oh, dis was way befo' yo' time. Ah don't recolleck myself. De old folks told me about John and de lion. Well, John was ridin' long one day straddle of his horse when de grizzly bear come pranchin' out in de middle of de road and hollered: "Hold on a minute! They tell me you goin' 'round strowin' it dat youse de King of de World."

John stopped his horse: "Whoa! Yeah, Ah'm de King of

de World, don't you b'lieve it?" John told him.

"Naw, you ain't no King. Ah'm de King of de World. You can't be no King till you whip me. Git down and fight."

John hit de ground and de fight started. First, John grabbed him a rough-dried brick and started to work de fat offa de bear's head. De bear just fumbled 'round till he got a good holt, then he begin to squeeze and squeeze. John knowed he couldn't stand dat much longer, do he'd be jus' another man wid his breath done give out. So he reached into his pocket and got out his razor and slipped it between dat bear's ribs. De bear turnt loose and reeled on over in de bushes to lay down. He had enough of dat fight.

John got back on his horse and rode on off.

De lion smelt de bear's blood and come runnin' to where de grizzly was layin' and started to lappin' his blood.

De bear was skeered de lion was gointer eat him while he was all cut and bleedin' nearly to death, so he hollered and said: *"Please* don't touch me, Brer Lion. Ah done met de King of de World and he done cut me all up."

De lion got his bristles all up and clashed down at de bear: "Don't you lay there and tell me you done met de King of de World and not be talkin' 'bout me! Ah'll tear you to pieces!"

"Oh, don't tetch me, Brer Lion! Please lemme alone so Ah kin git well."

"Well, don't you call nobody no King of de World but me."

"But Brer Lion, Ah done *met* de King sho' nuff. Wait till you see him and you'll say Ah'm right."

"Naw, Ah won't, neither. Show him to me and Ah'll show you how much King he is."

"All right, Brer Lion, you jus' have a seat right behind dese bushes. He'll be by here befo' long."

Lion squatted down by de bear and waited. Fust person he saw goin' up de road was a old man. Lion jumped up and ast de bear, "Is dat him?"

132

Bear say, "Naw, dat's Uncle Yistiddy, he's a useter-be!"

After while a li'l boy passed down de road. De lion seen him and jumped up agin. "Is dat him?" he ast de bear.

Bear told him, "Naw, dat's li'l tomorrow, he's a gointer-be, you jus' lay quiet. Ah'll let you know when he gits here."

Sho nuff after while here come John on his horse but he had done got his gun. Lion jumped up agin and ast, "Is dat him?"

Bear say: "Yeah, dat's him! Dat's de King of de World."

Lion reared up and cracked his tail back and forwards like a bull-whip. He 'lowed, "You wait till Ah git thru wid him and you won't be callin' him no King no mo'."

He took and galloped out in de middle of de road right in front of John's horse and laid his years back. His tail was crackin' like torpedoes.

"Stop!" de lion hollered at John. "They tell me you goes for de King of de World!"

John looked him dead in de ball of his eye and told him, "Yeah, Ah'm de King. Don't you like it, don't you take it. Here's mah collar, come and shake it!"

De lion and John eye-balled one another for a minute or two, den de lion sprung on John.

Talk about fightin'! Man, you ain't seen no sich fightin' and wrasslin' since de mornin' stars sung together. De lion clawed and bit John and John bit him right back.

Way after while John got to his rifle and he up wid de muzzle right in ole lion's face and pulled de trigger. Long, slim black feller, snatch 'er back and hear 'er beller! Dog damn! Dat was too much for de lion. He turnt go of John and wheeled to run to de woods. John levelled down on him agin and let him have another load, right in his hind-quarters.

Dat ole lion give John de book; de bookity book.[1] He hauled de fast mail back into de woods where de bear was laid up.

"Move over," he told de bear. "Ah wanta lay down too."

[1]Sound word meaning running.

"How come?" de bear ast him.

"Ah done met de King of de World, and he done ruint me."

"Brer Lion, how you know you done met de King?"

" 'Cause he made lightnin' in my face and thunder in my hips. Ah know Ah done met de King, move over."

"Dad, dat lie of your'n done brought up a high wind," said Jim Allen, measuring the weather with his eye. "Look a li'l bit like rain."

"Tain't gonna rain, but de wind's too high for fish to bite. Le's go back," suggested Presley. "All them that caught fish got fish. All them that didn't got another chance."

Everybody began to gather up things. The bait cans were kicked over so that the worms could find homes. The strings of fish were tied to pole ends. When Joe Wiley went to pull up his string of fish, he found a water moccasin stealin' them and the men made a great ceremony of killin' it. Then they started away from the water. Cliff had a long string of fish.

"Look, Gran'pa" he said, "Ah reckon you satisfied, ain't you?"

"Sho Ah'm satisfied, Ah must *is* got cat blood in me 'cause Ah never gits tired of fish. Ah knows how to eat 'em too, and dat's somethin' everybody don't know."

"Oh, anybody can eat fish," said Joe Willard.

"Yeah," Jim conceded grudgingly, "they kin eat it, but they can't git de real refreshment out de meat like they oughter."

"If you kin git any mo' refreshment off a fish bone than me, you must be got two necks and a gang of bellies," said Larkins.

"You see," went on Jim, "y'all ain't got into de techincal apex of de business. When y'all see a great big platter of fried fish y'all jus' grab hold of a fish and bite him any which way, and dat's wrong."

"Dat's good enough for me!" declared Willard emphatically. "Anywhere and any place Ah ketch a fish Ah'm ready to bite him 'ceptin' he's raw."

"Me too."

"See dat?" Jim cried, exasperated. "You young folks is just like a passle of crows in a corn patch. Everybody talkin' at one time. Ain't nary one of you tried to learn how to eat a fish right."

"How you eat 'em, Mr. Allen?" Gene Oliver asked to pacify him.

"Well, after yo' hands is washed and de blessin' is said, you look at de fried fish, but you don't grab it. First thing you chooses a piece of corn-bread for yo' plate whilst youse lookin' de platter over for a nice fat perch or maybe it's trout. Nobody wid any manners or home-raisin' don't take de fork and turn over every fish in de dish in order to pick de best one. You does dat wid yo' eye whilst youse choosin' yo' pone bread. Now, then, take yo' fork and stick straight at de fish you done choosed, and if somebody ast you to take two, you say 'No ma'am, Ah thank you. This un will do for right now.'

"You see if you got too many fishes on yo' plate at once, folkses, you can't lay 'em out proper. So you take one fish at de time. Then you turn him over and take yo' fork and start at de tail, liff de meat all off de bone clear up to de head, 'thout misplacin' a bone. You eats dat wid some bread. Not a whole heap of bread—just enough to keep you from swallerin' de fish befo' you enjoy de consequences. When you thru on dat side of de fish turn him over and do de same on de other side. Don't eat de heads. Shove 'em to one side till you thru wid all de fish from de platter, den when there ain't no mo' fish wid sides to 'em, you reach back and pull dem heads befo' you and start at de back of de fish neck and eat right on thru to his jaw-bones.

"Now then, if it's summer time, go set on de porch and rest yo'self in de cool. If it's winter time, go git in front of de fireplace and warm yo'self—now Ah done tole you right. A whole heap of people talks about fish-eatin' but Ah done tole you real."

"He's tellin' you right," agreed Dad Boykin. "Ah'm older than he is, 'cause Ah was eighty-one las' November, and Ah was eatin' fish befo' Jim was born, but Ah never did get de gennywine schoolin' till Jim showed me. But Ah teached him somethin' too, didn't Ah, Jim?"

"Yeah, Dad, yo' showed me how to warm myself."

There was a great burst of laughter from the young men, but the two old men scowled upon them.

"You see," Dad said bitingly. "You young poots won't lissen to nothin'! Not a one of you knows how to warm hisself right and youse so hard-headed you don't want to be teached. Any fool kin lam hisself up in a chimbley corner and cook his shins, but when it comes right down to de entrimmins, youse as ig'nant as a hog up under a acorn tree—he eats and grunts and never look up to see where de acorns is comin' from."

"Dad, *please* such, teach us how to warm ourselves," begged Cliff. "We all wants to know."

"Oh, y'all done wasted too much time, almost back in de quarters now, and de crowd will be scatterin'."

"Dat's all right, Dad," urged Joe Willard soothingly. "We ain't goin' nowhere till we been teached by you."

"Well, then, Ah'll tell y'all somethin'. De real way to git warm is first to git a good rockin' chear and draw it up to de fire. Don't flop yo'self down in it lak a cow in de pasture. Draw it right up in de center of de fireplace 'cause dat's de best. Some folks love to pile into de chimbley corner 'cause they's lazy and feared somebody gointer step on they foots. They don't want to have no trouble shiftin' 'em back and forth. But de center is de best place, so take dat. You even might have to push and shove a li'l bit to git dere, but dat's all right, go' head.

"When you git yo' chear all set where you wants it, then you walk up to de mantel piece and turn yo' back to de fire—dat's

136

to knock de breezes offen yo' back. You know, all de time youse outside in de weather, li'l breezes and winds is jumpin' on yo' back and crawlin' down yo' neck, to hide. They'll stay right there if you don't do somethin' to git shet of 'em. They don't lak fires, so when you turn yo' back to de fire, de inflamed atmosphere goes up under yo' coat-tails and runs dem winds and breezes out from up dere. Sometimes, lessen you drive 'em off, they goes to bed wid you. Ain't y'all never been so you couldn't git warm don't keer how much kivver you put on?"

"Many's de time I been lak dat."

"Well," went on Dad, "Dat because some stray breezes had done rode you to bed. Now dat brings up to de second claw of de subjick. You done got rid of de back breezes, so you git in yo' chear and pull off yo' shoes and set in yo' sock feet. Now, don't set there all spraddle-legged and let de heat just hit you any which way, put yo' feet right close together so dat both yo' big toes is side by side. Then you shove 'em up close to de fire and let 'em git good and hot. Ah know it don't look lak it but dem toes'll warm you all over. You see when Ah was studyin' doctor Ah found out dat you got a leader dat runs from yo' big toe straight to yo' heart, and when you git dem toes hot youse hot all over."

"Yeah, Ah b'lieve youse right, Dad, 'bout dat warmin' business, but Ah wisht somebody'd tell us how to git cool right now."

The party was back in the camp. Everybody began to head for his own shack.

"See you tonight at de jook," Jim Presley called to Willard. "Don't you and Big Sweet put on no roll now. Ah hate to see men and wimmin folks fightin'."

"Me too," said Wiley emphatically. "If a man kin whip his woman and whip her good; all right, but when they don't do nothin' but fight, it makes my stomach turn."

"Well," said Big Sweet crisply. "If Joe Willard try to take dese few fishes he done caught where he shacked up last night,

Ah'm gointer take my Tampa switch-blade knife, and Ah'm goin' 'round de hambone lookin' for meat."

"Aw, is *dat* so?" Joe challenged her.

"Ah been baptized, papa, and Ah wouldn't mislead you," Big Sweet told him to his teeth.

"Hey, hey!" Gene Oliver exclaimed. "Big Moose done come down from de mountain. Ah'm gointer be at dat jook tonight to see what Big Sweet and Ella Wall gointer talk about."

"Me too. De time is done come where big britches gointer fit li'l Willie,"[2] Joe Wiley declared significantly.

"Oh, wese all gointer be there," Larkins said. "Say, Big Sweet, don't let de 'gator beat you to de pond,[3] do he'll give you mo' trouble than de day is long."

So everybody got for home.

Back in the quarters the sun was setting. Plenty women over the cook-pot scorching up supper. Lots of them were already thru cooking, with the pots shoved to the back of the stove while they put on fresh things and went out in front of the house to see and be seen.

The fishermen began scraping fish and hot grease began to pop in happy houses. All but the Allen's. Mrs. Allen wouldn't have a thing to do with our fish because Mr. Allen and Cliffert had made her mad about the yard. So I fried the fish. She wouldn't touch a bite, but Mr. Allen, Cliffert and I pitched into it. Mr. Allen might have eaten by the rules but Cliffert and I went at it rough-and-tumble with no holds barred.

But we did sit down on the front porch to rest after the fish was eaten.

The men were still coming into the quarters from various parts of the "job." The children played "Shoo-round," and "Chick-mah-Chick" until Mrs. Williams called her four year

[2]Things have come to critical pass.

[3]Don't be out-done; or don't be too slow.

138

old Frankie and put her to sleep by rocking her and singing "Mister Frog."

It wasn't black dark, but night was peeping around the corner. The quarters were getting alive. Woofing, threats and brags up and down the line.

Three figures in the dusk-dark detached themselves from the railroad track and came walking into the quarters. A tall black grim-faced man with a rusty black reticule, followed by two women.

Everybody thought he was a bootlegger and yelled orders to him to that effect. He paid no attention, but set down his bag slowly, opened it still slower and took out a dog-eared Bible and opened it. The crowd quieted down. They knew he was a travelling preacher, a "stump-knocker" in the language of the "job."

Some fell silent to listen. Others sucked their teeth and either went back into their houses or went on to the jook.

When he had a reasonable amount of attention he nodded to the woman at his left and she raised "Death comes a Creepin'" and the crowd helped out. At the end the preacher began:[4]

You all done been over in Pentecost (got to feeling
spiritual by singing) and now we going to talk about de
woman that was taken from man. I take my text from
Genesis two and twenty-one (Gen. 2:21)

Behold de Rib!
Now, my beloved,
Behold means to look and see.
Look at dis woman God done made,
But first thing, ah hah!
Ah wants you to gaze upon God's previous works.
Almighty and arisen God, hah!
Peace-giving and prayer-hearing God,

[4]See glossary.

139

High-riding and strong armded God
Walking acrost his globe creation, hah!

Wid de blue elements for a helmet
And a wall of fire round his feet
He wakes de sun every morning from his fiery bed
Wid de breath of his smile
And commands de moon wid his eyes.
And Oh—
Wid de eye of Faith
I can see him
Standing out on de eaves of ether
Breathing clouds from out his nostrils,
Blowing storms from 'tween his lips
I can see!
Him seize de mighty axe of his proving power
And smite the stubborn-standing space,
And laid it wide open in a mighty gash—
Making a place to hold de world
I can see him—
Molding de world out of thought and power
And whirling it out on its eternal track,

Ah hah, my strong armded God!
He set de blood red eye of de sun in de sky
And told it,
Wait, wait! Wait there till Shiloh come
I can see!
Him mold de mighty mountains
And melting de skies into seas.
Oh, Behold, and look and see! hah
We see in de beginning
He made de bestes every one after its kind,
De birds that fly de trackless air,
De fishes dat swim de mighty deep—
Male and fee-male, hah!
Then he took of de dust of de earth
And made man in his own image.
And man was alone,
Even de lion had a mate
So God shook his head
And a thousand million diamonds
Flew out from his glittering crown
And studded de evening sky and made de stars.
So God put Adam into a deep sleep
And took out a bone, ah hah!
And it is said that it was a rib.
Behold de rib!
A bone out of a man's side.
He put de man to sleep and made wo-man,
And men and women been sleeping together ever since.
Behold de rib!
Brothers, if God
Had taken dat bone out of man's head
He would have meant for woman to rule, hah
If he had taken a bone out of his foot,
He would have meant for us to dominize and rule.
He could have made her out of back-bone
And then she would have been behind us.
But, no, God Amighty, he took de bone out of his side
So dat places de woman beside us;
Hah! God knowed his own mind.
Behold de rib!

And now I leave dis thought wid you,
Let us all go marchin' up to de gates of Glory.
Tramp! tramp! tramp!
In step wid de host dat John saw.
Male and female like God made us
Side by side.
Oh, behold de rib!
And less all set down in Glory together
Right round his glorified throne
And praise his name forever.
                    Amen.

At the end of the sermon the woman on the preacher's left raised, "Been a Listenin' All de Night Long," and the preacher descended from his fiery cloud and lifted the collection in his hat. The singers switched to, "You Can't Hide, Sinners, You Can't Hide." The sparse contribution taken, the trio drifted back into the darkness of the railroad, walking towards Kissimmee.

NINE

The little drama of religion over, the "job" reverted to the business of amusing itself. Everybody making it to the jook hurriedly or slowly as the spirit moved.

Big Sweet came by and we went over together. I didn't go with Cliffert because it would mean that I'd be considered his property more or less and the other men would keep away from me, and being let alone is no way to collect folk-lore.

The jook was in full play when we walked in. The piano was throbbing like a stringed drum and the couples slow-dragging about the floor were urging the player on to new lows. "Jook, Johnnie, Ah know you kin spank dat ole pe-anner." "Jook it Johnnie!"[1] "Throw it in de alley!"[2]

The Florida-flip game was roaring away at the left. Four men playing skin game with small piles of loose change.[3]

"High, Jack, game," one side called.

"Low and not ashamed," from the other.

Another deal.

Dealer: (to play at left) "Whut yuh say?"

Player: "Beggin'."

---

[1] Play the piano in the manner of the jook or "blues."

[2] Get low down.

[3] See glossary.

Dealer: "Git up off yo' knees. Go 'head and tell 'em Ah sent you." (I give you one point.)

Dealer: "Pull off, partner."

A frenzied slapping of cards on the table. "Ha! we caught little britches!" (low) "Pull off again!"

"Can't. Ain't seen de deck but one time."

"Aw shucks. Ah got de wrong sign from you. Ah thought you had de king."

"Nope, Ah can't ketch a thing. Ah can't even ketch nobody lookin' at me."

The opponents grin knowingly and one of them sticks the Jack up on his forehead and gloats, "De Jack's a gentleman." It is now the highest card out.

A furious play to the end of the hand and the dealer cries: "Gone from three. Jus' like Jeff Crowder's eye" (out).

"Out!" cries the outraged opponents. "Out yo' head! Out wid whut!"

"We played high, low, game!"

"Take dat game right out yo' mouf. We got twenty by tens."

"Le's go to school." (Let's count game.)

One player slyly picks up the deck and tries to mix it with his cards.

"Aw naw, put down dat deck! You can't count it on me."

"Aw, you tryin' to bully de game, but if you ain't prepared to back yo' crap wid hot lead, don't bring de mess up."

Joe Wiley was on the floor in the crap game. He called me to come stand by him and give him luck. Big Sweet left me there and went on over to the skin game.

Somebody had squeezed the alcohol out of several cans of Sterno and added sugar, water and boiled-off spirits of nitre and called it wine. It was dealt out with the utmost secrecy. The quarters boss had a way of standing around in the dark and listening and he didn't allow a drop of likker on the job. Paynights used to mean two or three killings but this boss had ended the murders abruptly. And one caught with likker was sent down to Bartow to the jail and bound over to the Big

Court. So it had come to the place where "low" wine was about all the quarters could get and the drinker was taking two terrible risks at that—arrest and death.

But there was enough spirits about for things to keep lively. The crap game was frothy. Office had the dice when I walked up. He was shivering the dice and sliding them out expertly.

"Hah! good dice is findin' de money! Six is mah point."

"Whut's yo' come bet?" Blue asked.

"Two bits."

"Two bits you don't six."

Office picked up the dice stealthily, shook them, or rather failed to shake them craftily and slid them out. Blue stopped them. Office threw three times and three times Blue stopped them. Office took out his switch-blade knife and glared at Blue.

"Nigger, don't you stop mah dice befo' dey point."

"You chokin' dem dice. Shake and lemme hear de music."

I wanted to get into the game in a small way but Big Sweet was high balling[4] me to come over to the skin game. I went over to see what she wanted and was given her purse to hold. She wanted to play and she wanted a free hand. It was the liveliest and most intense game in the place. I got all worked up myself watching the falling cards.

A saddle-colored fellow called "Texas Red" was fighting the wine inside him by trying to tenor "Ol' Pal, Why Don't You Answer Me," while he hung over the game watching it. His nasal tones offended Big Sweet, who turned and asked him, "Did somebody hit yuh tuh start yuh? 'Cause if dey did Ah'm goin' ter hit yuh to stop yuh." Texas and Big Sweet did what is locally known as "eye-balling" each other. His eyes fell lower. Her knife was already open, so he strolled on off.

There had been a new deal. Everybody was getting a fresh card.

Dealer: "You want a card, Big Sweet?"

Big Sweet: "Yeah, Ah wanta scoop one in de rough."

[4]Waving ahead. A railroad term.

Dealer: "Aw right, yo' card is gointer cost you a dollar. Put yo' money on de wood and make de bet go good and then agin, put yo' money in sight and save a fight."

She drew a card from the deck and put it face up beside her, with a dollar bill.

Dealer: "Heah, Hardy, heah's a good card—a queen." He tossed the card to Hardy.

Hardy: "Aw naw, Ah don't play dem gals till way late in de night."

Dealer: "Well take de ace and go to wee-shoppy-tony and dat means East Hell. Ah'm gointer ketch you anyhow."

Hardy: "When you ketch me, you damn sho will ketch a man dat's caught a many one. Ah'm playin' up a nation."

Dealer: "Put down! You all owe de bet a dime. Damn sitters rob St. Peter, rob St. Paul."

Larkins: "Dat nigger is gointer top somebody. He's got a cub.[5] Ah ain't goin' in dat damn steel trap."

Dealer: "Aw naw, Ah ain't! You sap-sucker!" (To Hardy) "You owe de bet a dime if you never pay it."

The dealer starts down the deck, and the singing goes with it. Christopher Jenkins' deep baritone is something to remember.

"Let de deal go down, boys.[6]
Let de deal go down.
When yo' card gits lucky, oh padner;
You ought to be in a rollin' game."

Each line punctuated by "hah!" and a falling card.

Larkins: "Ah'm dead on de turn."

Dealer: "Ah heard you buddy."

"Ain't had no money, oh padner!"

(To Larkins) "You head-pecked shorty, drive up to de cryin'

---

[5]He has arranged the cards so he can deal winning cards to himself and losing cards to others.

[6]See appendix.

146

post and hitch up. You want another card?"

Larkins: "Shuffle and deal and ain't stop fallin' yet." (He means he stays in the game so he takes another hand.)

Dealer: "Put down dat chicken-change quarter you got in yo' hand."

The singing goes on—

"Ah'm goin' back to de Bama,
Won't be worried wid you."

(To Hardy) "De nine" (card dealer holds) "is de best. Is you got air nickel to cry?"

"Let de deal go down, boys;
Let de deal go down."

Big Sweet: "De four" (card she holds) "says a dollar mo'."

Dealer: "Oh hell and brothers! Ah'm strictly a two-bit man."

Big Sweet (arrogantly): "You full of dat ole ism blood. Fat covered yo' heart. Youse skeered to bet. Gamblin' wid yo' stuff out de window."[7]

Dealer: "Dollar mo'."

Hardy: "Hell broke loose in Georgy!"

Big Sweet: "Ah mean to carry y'all to Palatka and bring yuh back by de way of Winter Park."

Hardy: "Big Sweet, Ah don't b'lieve Ah'll see yo' raise."

Big Sweet: "Oh g'wan and bet. You got mo' sense than me. Look at dem damn kidneys all over yo' head."

"Ain't had no trouble, Lawd padner
Till Ah stop by here."

Dealer: "Take it and cry, children." (His card falls.) "Dey sent me out by de way of Sandusky. Lemme see kin Ah find me a clean card."

[7]Risking nothing. Ready to run.

Big Sweet: "Ah caught you guilty lyin'! Make a bet and tell a lie about it."

Hardy: "He done cocked a face card. Look out we don't ketch *you* guilty."

Big Sweet: "He got de cards in his hand."

> "Let de deal go down, boys,
> Let de deal go down."

Hardy: "Dat's me. Ah thought dat card was in Bee-luther-hatchee!"[8]

Dealer: "Tell de truth and stay in de church! Ah'm from down in Ginny-Gall where they eat cow-belly, skin and all. Big Sweet, everybody done fell but you. You must be setting on roots."

Big Sweet: "Nope, Ah got my Joe Moore in my hair."[9]

Dealer: "Well, Ah got de cards. I can cheat if I want to and beat you anyway."

Big Sweet: "You mess wid dem cards and see if Ah don't fill you full of looky-deres."

Hardy: "Whut a looky-dere?"

Big Sweet: "A knot on yo' head so big till when you go down de street everybody will point at it and say 'Looky-dere.' "

Dealer: (His card falls.) "Ah'm hot as seven hells."

Big Sweet: "Ah played de last card. Ah don't tell lies all de time. Now, you rich son of a bitch, pay off."

Larkins: "God! She must be sittin' on roots! Luck is a fortune."

Big Sweet raked in the money and passed it to me. She was about to place another bet when we heard a lot of noise outside. Everybody looked at the door at one time.

"Dat *must* be de Mulberry crowd. Nobody else wouldn't keep dat much noise. Ella Wall strowin' it."

---

[8]A mythical place, like "ginny gall."

[9]A piece of gamblers lucky hoodoo.

"She's plenty propaganda, all right."

Ella Wall flung a loud laugh back over her shoulder as she flourished in. Everybody looked at her, then they looked at Big Sweet. Big Sweet looked at Ella, but she seemed not to mind. The air was as tight as a fiddle string.

Ella wrung her hips to the Florida-flip game. Big Sweet stayed on at the skin game but didn't play. Joe Willard, knowing the imminence of forthright action, suddenly got deep into the crap game.

Lucy came in the door with a bright gloat in her eyes and went straight to Ella. So far as speaking was concerned she didn't see Big Sweet, but she did flirt past the skin game once, overcome with merriment.

"Dat li'l narrer contracted piece uh meatskin gointer make me stomp her right now!" Big Sweet exploded. "De two-faced heifer! Been hangin' 'round me so she kin tote news to Ella. If she don't look out she'll have on her last clean dress befo' de crack of day."

"Ah'm surprised at Lucy," I agreed. "Ah thought you all were de *best* of friends."

"She mad 'cause Ah dared her to jump *you*. She don't lak Slim always playing JOHN HENRY for you. She would have done cut you to death if Ah hadn't of took and told her."

"Ah can see she doesn't like it, but—"

"Neb' mind 'bout ole Lucy. She know Ah backs yo' fallin'. She know if she scratch yo' skin Ah'll kill her so dead till she can't fall. They'll have to push her over. Ella Wall look lak she tryin' to make me kill her too, flourishin' dat ole knife 'round. But she oughter know de man dat made one, made two. She better not vary, do Ah'll be all over her jus' lak gravy over rice."

Lucy and Ella were alternately shoo-shooing[10] to each other and guffawing. Then Ella would say something to the whole table and laugh.

Over at the Florida-flip game somebody began to sing that

[10]Whispering.

jook tribute to Ella Wall which has been sung in every jook
and on every "job" in South Florida:

> Go to Ella Wall
> Oh, go to Ella Wall
> If you want good boody[11]
> Oh, go to Ella Wall
>
> Oh, she's long and tall
> Oh, she's long and tall
> And she rocks her rider
> From uh wall to wall
>
> Oh, go to Ella Wall
> Take yo' trunk and all—

"Tell 'em 'bout me!" Ella Wall snapped her fingers and
revolved her hips with her hands.

"I'm raggedy, but right; patchey but tight; stringy, but I *will*
hang on."

"Look at her puttin' out her brags." Big Sweet nudged me.
"Loud-talkin' de place. But countin' from yo' little finger back
to the thumb; if she start anything Ah got her some."

I knew that Big Sweet didn't mind fighting; didn't mind
killing and didn't too much mind dying. I began to worry a
bit. Ella kept on hurling slurs. So I said, "Come on, Big Sweet,
we got to go to home."

"Nope, Ah ain't got to do nothin' but die and stay black.
Ah stays right here till de jook close if anybody else stay. You
look and see how much in dat pocket book."

I looked. "Forty-one dollars and sixty-three cents."

"Just you hold on to it. Ah don't want a thing in mah hands
but dis knife."

Big Sweet turned to scoop a card in the rough. Just at that
moment Ella chose to yell over, "Hey, bigger-than-me!" at
Big Sweet. She whirled around angrily and asked me, "Didn't
dat storm-buzzard throw a slam at me?"

[11]Sex.

150

"Naw, she was hollerin' at somebody else," I lied to keep the peace.

Nothing happening, Ella shouted, " 'Tain't nothin' to her. She ain't hit me yet."

Big Sweet heard that and threw in her cards and faced about. "If anything start, Little-Bit, you run out de door like a streak uh lightning and get in yo' car. They gointer try to hurt you too."

I thought of all I had to live for and turned cold at the thought of dying in a violent manner in a sordid saw-mill camp. But for my very life I knew I couldn't leave Big Sweet even if the fight came. She had been too faithful to me. So I assured her that I wasn't going unless she did. My only weapons were my teeth and toe-nails.

Ella crowded her luck. She yelled out, "Lucy, go tell Mr. Lots-of-Papa Joe Willard Ah say come here. Jus' tell 'im his weakness want 'im. He know who dat is."

Lucy started across. Ella stood up akimbo, but everybody knew she was prepared to back her brag with cold steel in some form, or she wouldn't have been there talking like she was.

A click beside me and I knew that the spring blade knife that Big Sweet carried was open.

"Stop right where you is, Lucy," Big Sweet ordered, "lessen you want to see yo' Jesus."

"Gwan Lucy," Ella Wall called out, " 'tain't nothin' stoppin' yuh. See nothin', say nothin'."

Big Sweet turned to Ella. "Maybe Ah ain't nothin'. But Ah say Lucy ain't gointer tell Joe Willard nothin'. What you sendin' her for? Why don't you go yo'self? Dere he is."

"Well, Ah kin go, now," Ella countered.

Big Sweet took a step forward that would put her right in Ella's path in case she tried to cross the room. "Ah can't hear what you say for yo' damn teeth rattlin'. Come on!"

Then the only thing that could have stopped the killing happened. The Quarters Boss stepped in the door with a .45

in his hand and another on his hip. Expect he had been eavesdropping as usual.

"What's the matter here, y'all? Big Sweet, what you mean tuh do wid that knife?"

"Ahm jus' 'bout tuh send God two niggers. Come in here bull-dozin' me."

The Quarters Boss looked all around and pointed at Ella. "What tha hell *you* doin' in here wid weapons? You don't belong on this job nohow. Git the hell outa here and that quick. This place is for people that works on this job. Git! Somebody'll be in Barton jail in twenty minutes."

"You don't need tuh run her off, Cap'n," Big Sweet said. "Ah can git her tuh go. Jus' you stand back and gimme lief. She done stepped on mah starter and Ahm rearin' tuh go. If God'll send me uh pistol Ah'll send 'im uh man!"

"You ain't gonna kill nobody right under mah nose," the Quarters Boss snorted. "Gimme that knife you got dere, Big Sweet."

"Naw suh! Nobody gits *mah* knife. Ah bought it for dat storm-buzzard over dere and Ah means tuh use it on her, too. As long as uh mule go bareheaded she better not part her lips tuh me. Do Ah'll kill her, law or no law. Don't you touch me, white folks!"

"Aw she ain't so bad!" Ella sneered as she wrung her hips towards the door. "She didn't kill Jesse James."

"Git on 'way from here!" the Boss yelled behind her. "Lessen yuh wanna make time in Barton jail. Git off these premises and that quick! Gimme that knife!" He took the knife and gave Ella a shove. She moved sullenly behind her crowd away from the door, mumbling threats. He followed and stayed outside until the car pulled off. Then he stuck his head back inside and said, "Now you behave yo'self, Big Sweet. Ah don't wanna hafta jail yuh."

Soon as he was gone the mob got around Big Sweet. "You wuz noble!" Joe Willard told her, "You wuz uh whole woman and half uh man. You made dat cracker stand off a *you.*"

"Who wouldn't?" said Presley. "She got loaded muscles.

152

You notice he don't tackle Big Sweet lak he do de rest round here. Dats cause she ain't got uh bit better sense then tuh make 'im kill her."

"Dats right," Big Sweet admitted, "and de nex' time Joe tell his Mulberry woman tuh come here bulldozin' *me*, Ahm gointer beat 'im to death grabbin' at 'im."

Joe Willard affected supreme innocence. "Will you lissen at dis 'oman? Ah ain't sent fuh nobody. Y'all see Ah didn't never go where she wuz, didn't yuh? Come on Big Sweet, less go home. How 'bout uh li'l keerless love? Ahm all ravalled out from de strain."

Joe and Big Sweet went home together and that was that.

When the quarters boss had gone, I saw Box-Car Daddy creeping back in the door. I didn't see him leave the place so I asked him where he had been.

"Had to step off a li'l piece," he told me with an effort at nonchalance.

"He always steps off whenever he see dat Quarters Boss, and he doing right, too," someone said.

"How come?" I asked. "Nobody else don't run."

Everybody laughed but nobody told me a thing. But after a while Box-Car began to sing a new song and I liked the swing of it.

"What's dat you singing, Box-Car?" I asked.

"'Ah'm Gointer Loose dis Right-hand Shackle from 'Round my Leg.' Dat's a chain-gang song. Thought everybody knowed dat."

"Nope, never heard it. Ain't never been to de gang. How did you learn it?"

"Working on de gang."

"Whut you doin' on de gang, Box-Car? You look like a good boy, but a poor boy."

"Oh, dey put me under arrest one day for vacancy in Bartow. When de judge found out Ah had a job of work. He took and searched me and when he found out Ah had a deck of cards on me, he charged me wid totin' concealed cards, and attempt to gamble, and gimme three months. Then dey made out another charge 'ginst me. 'Cused me of highway shufflin', and attempt to gamble. You know dese white folks sho hates tuh turn a nigger loose, if every dey git dey hands on 'im. And dis very quarters boss was Cap'n on de gang where Ah wuz. Me and him ain't never gointer set hawses."[12] So he went on singing:

All day long, you heard me moan
Don't you tell my Cap'n which way I gone
Ah'm gointer lose dis right hand shackle from 'round my leg.

You work me late, you work me soon
Some time you work me by de light of de moon
Ah'm gointer lose dis right hand shackle from 'round my leg.

I learned several other songs. Thanks to James Presley and Slim; and Gene Oliver and his sister brought me many additional tales.

But the very next pay-night when I went to a dance at the Pine Mill, Lucy tried to steal me. That is the local term for an attack by stealth. Big Sweet saved me and urged me to stay on, assuring me that she could always defend me, but I shivered at the thought of dying with a knife in my back, or having my face mutilated. At any rate, I had made a very fine and full collection on the Saw-Mill Camp, so I felt no regrets at shoving off.

The last night at Loughman was very merry. We had a party at Mrs. Allen's. James Presley and Slim with their boxes; Joe Willard calling figures in his best mood. Because it was a special occasion and because I was urged, I actually took a sip of low-wine and found out how very low it was. The dancing stopped and I was hilariously toted off to bed and the party moved to my bedroom. We had had a rain flood early in the afternoon and a medium size rattlesnake had come in out of the wet. I had thrown away a pile of worn out stockings and he was asleep upon them there in the corner by the washstand.

[12]Never going to get along. As two horses pull together.

The boys wanted to kill it, but I begged them not to hurt my lowly brother. He rattled away for a while, but when everybody got around the bed on the far end of the room and got quiet, he moved in the manner of an hour-hand to a crack where the floor and wall had separated, and popped out of sight.

Cliffert told me the last Loughman story around midnight.

"Zora, did yuh ever hear 'bout Jack and de Devil buckin' 'ginst one 'nother to see which one was de strongest?"

"Naw. Ah done heard a lot about de Devil and dat Jack, but not dat tale *you* know. Tell it."

Jack and de Devil wuz settin' down under a tree one day arguin' 'bout who was de strongest. De Devil got tired of talkin' and went and picked up a mule. Jack went and picked up de same mule. De Devil run to a great big old oak tree and pulled it up by de roots. Jack grabbed holt of one jus' as big and pulled it up. De Devil broke a anchor cable. Jack took it and broke it agin.

So de Devil says, "Shucks! Dis ain't no sho nuff trial. Dis is chillun foolishness. Meet me out in dat hund'ed acre clearin' tomorrow mornin' at nine o'clock and we'll see who kin throw mah hammer de furtherest. De one do dat is de strongest."

Jack says, "Dat suits me."

So nex' mawnin' de Devil wuz dere on time wid his hammer. It wuz bigger'n de white folks church house in Winter Park. A whole heap uh folks had done come out tuh see which one would win.

Jack wuz late. He come gallopin' up on hawseback and reined in de hawse so short till he reared up his hind legs.

Jack jumped off and says: "Wese all heah, le's go. Who goin' first?"

De Devil tole 'im, "Me. Everybody stand back and gimme room."

So he throwed de hammer and it went so high till it went clean outa sight. Devil tole 'em, "Iss Tuesday now. Y'all go home and come back Thursday mornin' at nine. It won't fall till then."

Sho 'nuff de hammer fell on Thursday mornin' at nine o'clock and knocked out a hole big as Polk County.

Dey lifted de hammer out de hole and levelled it and it wuz Jack's time to throw.

Jack took his time and walked 'round de hammer to de handle and took holt of it and throwed his head back and looked up at de sky.

"Look out, Rayfield! Move over, Gabriel! You better stand 'way back, Jesus! Ah'm fixin' to throw." He meant Heaven.

Devil run up to 'im, says, "Hold on dere a minute! Don't you throw mah damn hammer up dere! Ah left a whole lot uh mah tools up dere when dey put me out and Ah ain't got 'em back yet. Don't you *throw* mah hammer up dere!''

TEN

So I left most of my things at Loughman and ran down in the phosphate country around Mulberry. Around Mulberry, Pierce and Lakeland, I collected a mass of children's tales and games. The company operating the mines at Pierce maintains very excellent living conditions in their quarters. The cottages are on clean, tree-lined streets. There is a good hospital and a nine-months school. They will not employ a boy under seventeen so that the parents are not tempted to put minors to work. There is a cheerful community center with a large green-covered table for crap games under a shady oak.

We held a lying contest out under the trees in the night time, some sitting, some standing, everybody in a jolly mood. Mack C. Ford proved to be a mighty story teller before the Lord.

I found out about creation from him. The tail of the porpoise is on crosswise and he explains the mystery of that.

"Zora, did you ever see a porpoise?"

"Yep. Many times."

"Didja ever notice his tail?"

"Don't b'lieve Ah did. He moves so fast till Ah don't remember much except seeing him turning somersault and shootin' up and down de Indian River like lightnin' thru de trees.''

Well, it's on crossways. Every other fish got his tail on straight but de porpoise. His is on crossways and bent down lak dis. (He bent down the fingers of his left hand sharply from the knuckles.)

De reason for dat is, God made de world and de sky and de birds and animals and de fishes. He finished off de stars and de trees.

Den He made a gold track clear 'round de world and greased it, and called de sun to Him and says, "Now Sun, Ah done made everything but Time and Ah want you to make dat. Ah made dat gold track for you to run on and Ah want you to git on it and go 'round de world jus' as fas' as you kin stave it and de time it take you to go and come Ah'm gointer call it 'day' and 'night.' "

De porpoise was standin' 'round and heard God when He spoke to de sun. So he says, "B'lieve Ah'll take dat trip around de world myself."

So de sun lit out and de porpoise took out. Him and him! 'Round de world—lickety split!

So de porpoise beat de sun 'round de world by a hour and three minutes.

When God seen dat He shook His head and says, "Unh, unh! Dis ain't gointer do. Ah never meant for nothin' to be faster than de sun."

So He took out behind dat porpoise and run him for three days and nights befo' He overtook him. But when he *did* ketch dat ole porpoise He grabbed him by de tail and snatched it off and set it back on crossways to slow him up. He can't beat de sun no mo' but he's de next fastest thing in de world.

Everybody laughed one of those blow-out laughs, so Mack Ford said, "Mah lyin' done got good tuh me, so Ahm gointer tell yuh how come de dawg hates de cat."

De dog and de cat used to live next door to one 'nother and both of 'em loved ham. Every time they git a chance they'd buy a slice of ham.

One time both of 'em got holt of a li'l extry change so de dog said to de cat, "Sis Cat, we both got a li'l money, and it would be fine if bofe of us could buy a ham apiece. But neither one of us ain't got enough money to buy a whole ham by ourselves. Why don't we put our money together and buy us a ham together?"

"Aw right, Brer Dawg. T'morrer begin' Sat'day, le's we go to town and git ourselves a ham."

So de next day they went to town and bought de ham. They didn't have no convenience so they had to walk and tote it. De dawg toted it first and he said as he walked up de road wid de ham over his shoulder, "Ours! Ours! Ours! Our ham!"

After while it was de cat's time to tote de meat. She said, "My ham, my ham, my ham." Dawg heard her but he didn't say nothin'.

When de dawg took it agin he says, "Ours, ours, our ham!" Cat toted it and says, "My ham, my ham."

Dawg says, "Sis Cat, how come you keep on sayin' 'My ham' when you totes our meat. Ah always say, 'Our ham.'"

De Cat didn't turn him no answer, but every time she toted de ham she'd say "My ham" and every time de dawg toted it he'd say "Ours."

When they was almost home, de cat was carryin' de ham and all of a sudden she sprung up a tree and set up there eatin' up de ham. De dawg did all he could to stop her, but he couldn't clim' and so he couldn't do nothin' but bark. But he tole de cat, "You up dat tree eatin' all de ham, and Ah can't git to you. But when you come down ahm gointer make you take dis Indian River for uh dusty road."

"Didja ever pass off much time round de railroad camps, Zora?" asked Mr. Ford.

159

"Ah been round dere some."

"Ah wuz jus' fixin' tuh tell yuh if you ain't been there you missed some good singin', well ez some good lyin'. Ever hear dat song bout 'Gointer See my Long-haired Babe'?"[1]

"Naw, but ah sho wisht ah had. Can you sing it?"

"Sho can and then ahm gointer do it too, and that one bout 'Oh Lulu, oh Gal.'"

"Ah know you want to hear some more stories, don't you? Ah know ah feels lak tellin' some."

"Unh hunh," I agreed.

"Don't you know dat's one word de Devil made up?"

"Nope, Ah had never heard about it. It's a mighty useful word Ah know for lazy folks like me."

"Yes, everybody says 'unh hunh' and Ah'll tell you why." He cleared his throat and continued:

Ole Devil looked around hell one day and seen his place was short of help so he thought he'd run up to Heben and kidnap some angels to keep things runnin' tell he got reinforcements from Miami.

Well, he slipped up on a great crowd of angels on de outskirts of Heben and stuffed a couple of thousand in his mouth, a few hundred under each arm and wrapped his tail 'round another thousand and darted off towards hell.

When he was flyin' low over de earth lookin' for a place to land, a man looked up and seen de Devil and ast 'im, "Ole Devil, Ah see you got a load of angels. Is you goin' back for mo'?"

Devil opened his mouth and tole 'im, "Yeah," and all de li'l angels flew out of his mouf and went on back to Heben. While he was tryin' to ketch 'em he lost all de others. So he went back after another load.

He was flyin' low agin and de same man seen him and says, "Ole Devil, Ah see you got another load uh angels."

[1]See appendix.

160

Devil nodded his head and said "unh hunh," and dat's
why we say it today.

"Dat's a fine story. Tell me some more."
"Ah'm gointer tell you all about Big Sixteen and High
Walker and Bloody Bones but first Ah want to ask you a
question."
"All right, go ahead and ask me."
"Zora, why do you think dese li'l slim women was put on
earth?"
"Couldn't tell you to save my life."
"Well, dese slim ones was put here to beautify de world."
"De big ones musta been put here for de same reason."
"Ah, naw, Zora. Ah don't agree wid you there."
"Well then, what *was* they put here for?"
"To show dese slim girls how far they kin stretch without
bustin'."
Everybody out under the trees laughed except Good Bread.
She took in a whole lot of breath and added to herself. Then
she rolled her eyes and said, "Mack Ford, Ah don't come in
yo' conversation atall. You jus' leave me out yo' mouf. And
furthermo' Ah don't crack."
"Nobody ain't called yo' name, Good Bread, Ah wuz jus'
passin' uh joke."
"Oh yes you wuz hintin' at me."
"Aw, nobody ain't studyin' 'bout yuh. Jus' cause you done
set round and growed ruffles round yo' hips nobody can't
mention fat 'thout you makin' out they talkin' bout you. Ah
wuzn't personatin' yuh, but if de cap fit yuh, wear it."
"G'wan Mack, you knows dat a very little uh yo' sugar
sweetens mah tea. Don't git *me* started."
"G'wan start something if dats de way yuh feel. You kin be
stopped. Now you tryin' to make somebody believe you so
bad till you have tuh tote uh pistol tah bed tuh keep from
gettin' in uh fight wid yo' self! You got mo' poison in yuh than
dat snake dat wuz so poison tell he bit de railroad track and
killed de train, hunh?"

161

"Don't y'all break dis lyin' contest up in no fight," Christopher Jenkins said.

Mah Honey laughed scornfully. "Aw, tain't gointer be no fight. Good Bread jus' feel lak bull woofin' uh little t'night. Her likker told her tuh pick uh fight but let Mack make uh break at her now, and there'll hafta be some good runnin' done befo' dat fight come off. Tain't nothin' tuh her. She know she ugly. She look lak de devil ground up in pieces."

Good Bread jumped up with her pocket knife out. "Who y'all tryin tuh double teen? Trying tuh run de hawg over de wrong one now."

"Aw set down Good Bread, and put dat froe back in yo' pocket. Somebody's liable tuh take dat ole piece uh knife you got and wear it out round yo' own neck."

"Dats what Ah say," Christopher put in. "She always tryin' tuh loud talk somebody. Ah hates women wid men's overalls on anyhow."

"Let her holler all she wants tuh," Ford added off-hand. "Dis is uh holler day. She kin whoop lak de Seaboard and squall lak de A.C.L. Nobody don't keer, long as she don't put her hand on me. Sho as she do dat Ahm gointer light her shuck for her."

Good Bread got to her feet importantly as if she was going to do something. For a fraction of a second I held my breath in fear. Nobody else paid it the least bit of mind. Good Bread flounced on off.

"Ahm glad she gone," said Mah Honey. "She always pickin' fights and gittin beat. Dat 'oman hates peace and agreement." He looked after her a moment then yelled after her. "Hey, lady, you got all you' bust in de back!" Everybody laughed and Mah Honey went on. "She so mad now she'll stay way and let Mack tell Zora some lies. Gwan, Mack, you got de business."

"Aw, Ah feel lak singin'," Mack Ford said.

"Well nobody don't feel lak hearin' yuh, so g'wan tell dat lie on Big Sixteen. Ah never gits tired uh dat one."

"You ruther hear uh story, Zora?"

"Yeah, g'wan tell it. Dats jus' what Ah'm here for."
"Well alright then:

It was slavery time, Zora, when Big Sixteen was a man.
They called 'im Sixteen 'cause dat was de number of de
shoe he wore. He was big and strong and Ole Massa
looked to him to do everything.

One day Ole Massa said, "Big Sixteen, Ah b'lieve Ah
want you to move dem sills Ah had hewed out down in de
swamp."

"I yassuh, Massa."

Big Sixteen went down in de swamp and picked up dem
12 × 12's and brought 'em on up to de house and stack
'em. No one man ain't never toted a 12 × 12 befo' nor
since.

So Ole Massa said one day, "Go fetch in de mules. Ah
want to look 'em over."

Big Sixteen went on down to de pasture and caught dem
mules by de bridle but they was contrary and balky and he
tore de bridles to pieces pullin' on 'em, so he picked one
of 'em up under each arm and brought 'em up to Old
Massa.

He says, "Big Sixteen, if you kin tote a pair of balky
mules, you kin do anything. You kin ketch de Devil."

"Yassuh, Ah kin, if you git me a nine-pound hammer
and a pick and shovel!"

Ole Massa got Sixteen de things he ast for and tole 'im
to go ahead and bring him de Devil.

Big Sixteen went out in front of de house and went to
diggin'. He was diggin' nearly a month befo' he got where
he wanted. Then he took his hammer and went and
knocked on de Devil's door. Devil answered de door hisself.

"Who dat out dere?"

"It's Big Sixteen."

"What you want?"

"Wanta have a word wid you for a minute."

Soon as de Devil poked his head out de door, Sixteen
lammed him over de head wid dat hammer and picked 'im

up and carried 'im back to Old Massa.

Ole Massa looked at de dead Devil and hollered, "Take dat ugly thing 'way from here, quick! Ah didn't think you'd ketch de Devil sho 'nuff."

So Sixteen picked up de Devil and throwed 'im back down de hole.

Way after while, Big Sixteen died and went up to Heben. But Peter looked at him and tole 'im to g'wan 'way from dere. He was too powerful. He might git outa order and there wouldn't be nobody to handle 'im. But he had to go somewhere so he went on to hell.

Soon as he got to de gate de Devil's children was playin' in de yard and they seen 'im and run to de house, says, "Mama, mama! Dat man's out dere dat kilt papa!"

So she called 'im in de house and shet de door. When Sixteen got dere she handed 'im a li'l piece of fire and said, "You ain't comin' in here. Here, take dis hot coal and g'wan off and start you a hell uh yo' own."

So when you see a Jack O'Lantern in de woods at night you know it's Big Sixteen wid his piece of fire lookin' for a place to go.

"Give us somethin' to wet our goozles wid, and you kin git some lies, Zora," Jenkins prompted. I stood treats.

"Now g'wan, Mack, and lie some more," I said, and he remarked:

"De mosquitoes mighty bad right now, but down there on de East Coast they used to 'em. Know why we got so many skeeters heah and why we have so many storms?"

"Naw, but Ah'd love to know," I answered eagerly.

Well, one Christmas time, God was goin' to Palatka. De Devil was in de neighborhood too and seen God goin' long de big road, so he jumped behind a stump and hid. Not dat he was skeered uh God, but he wanted to git a Christmas present outa God but he didn't wanta give God nothin'.

So he squatted down behind dis stump till God come along and then he jumped up and said, "Christmas gift!"

164

God just looked back over his shoulder and said, "Take de East Coast," and kept on walkin'. And dat's why we got storms and skeeters—it's de Devil's property.

I should mention it is a custom in the deep South for the children to go out Christmas morning "catching" people by saying "Christmas gift." The one who says it first gets a present from the other. The adults usually prepare for this by providing plenty of hard candy, nuts, coconuts, fruits and the like. They never try to catch the neighbors' children but let themselves be caught.

"Ah know one mo' story on de devil. Reckon Ah'll tell it now.

"One day de Devil was walkin' along when he met Raw Head."

"Who is Raw Head?" I interrupted to ask. "Ah been hearin' his name called all my life, but never did find out who he was."

"Why, Zora! Ah thought everybody knowed who Raw Head was. Why he was a man dat was more'n a man. He was big and strong like Big Sixteen and he was two-headed. He knowed all de words dat Moses used to make. God give 'im de power to bring de ten plagues and part de Red Sea. He had done seen de Smokey Mountain and de Burnin' Bush. And his head didn't have no hair on it, and it sweated blood all de time. Dat's why he was named Raw Head."[2] Then Mr. Ford told the following story:

As Ah started to say, de Devil met Raw Head and they passed de time of day. Neither one wasn't skeered of de other, so they talked about de work they been doin'.

Raw Head said he had done turnt a man into a ground puppy. Devil said he been havin' a good time breakin' up couples. All over de world de Devil had husbands and wives fightin' and partin'.

[2] He was a conjure doctor. They are always referred to as "two-headed doctors," i.e. twice as much sense.

Tol 'im says, "Devil, youse my cousin and Ah know you got mo' power than me, but Ah know one couple you can't part. They lives cross de big creek in my district, and Ah done everything Ah could but nothin' can't come between 'em."

Devil says, "Dat's because de right one ain't tried yet. Ah kin part any two people. Jus' like Ah kin throw 'em together. You show 'em to me and Ah betcha half of hell Ah'll have 'em fightin' and partin' befo' Sunday."

So de Devil went to where dis couple lived and took up 'round de house.

He done everything he could but they wouldn't fight and they wouldn't part. Devil was real outdone. He had never had such a tussle since they throwed him outer Heben, and it was Friday. He seen he was 'bout to lose half of his kingdom and have to go back on his brag.

He was 'bout to give up and go somewhere else dat night when he met a woman as barefooted as a yard-dog. They spoke and she says, "You don't look so good. You been down sick?"

Devil told her, "Naw, but Ah been tryin' to break up dat lovin' couple up de road a piece there, but Ah can't do it."

De woman says, "Aw shucks, is dat all? Tell you whut: Ah ain't never had a pair of shoes in my life and if you promise to give me a pair of shoes tonight Ah'll part 'em for you."

"If you part 'em you get de shoes, and good ones at dat. But you got to do it first."

"Don't you worry 'bout dat, you jus' meet me at dat sweet-gum tree on de edge of de swamp tomorrer evenin' and bring de shoes."

Next mornin' she got up soon and went past de place to see where de man was workin' at. He was plowin' way off from de house. So she spoke to 'im nice and polite and went on up to de house where de wife was.

De wife asted her in and give her a chair. She took her seat and begin to praise everything on de place. It was de prettiest house she ever seen. It was de bes' lookin' yard in dat part of the state. Dat was de finest dawg she ever laid eyes on. *Nobody* never had no cat as good as dat one was.

De wife thanked her for all her compliments and give her a pound of butter.

De woman told her, "Everything you got is pretty, but youse de prettiest of all."

De wife is crazy 'bout her husband and she can't stand to see him left out so she say, "My husband is prettier than Ah ever dared to be."

"Oh, yeah, he's pretty too. Almost as pretty as you. De only thing dat spoil his looks is dat long flesh-mole on his neck. Now if dat was off he'd be de prettiest man in de world."

De wife says, "Ah thinks he's already de prettiest man in de world, but if anything will make 'im *mo'* prettier still, Ah will too gladly do it."

"Well, then, you better cut dat big ole mole offa his neck."

"How kin Ah do dat? He skeered to cut it off. Say he might bleed to death."

"Aw naw, he won't neither. He won't lose more'n a drop of blood if you cut it off right quick wid a sharp razor and then wipe cob-web on de place. It's a pity he won't let you do it 'cause it sho do spoil his looks."

"If Ah knowed jus' how to do it, Ah sho would, 'cause Ah love him so and he is too pretty a man to be spoilt by a mole."

"Why don't you take de razor to bed wid you tonight. Then when he gets to sleep, you chop it off right quick and fix it lak Ah told you. He'll thank you for it next day."

De wife thanked de woman and give her a settin' of eggs and de woman told her good-bye and went on down to de field where de husband was plowin', and sidled up to him. "Good mornin' suh, you sho is a hard-workin' man."

"Yes ma'am, Ah works hard but Ah loves to work so Ah kin do for my wife. She's all Ah got."

"Yeah, and she sho got a man when she got you. 'Tain't many mens dat will hit from sun to sun for a woman."

The man said, "Sho ain't. But ain't no man got no wife as good as mine."

De woman spit on de ground and said, "It's good for a

167

person's mind to be satisfied. But lovin' a person don't make them love you. And youse a pitiful case."

"Why you say dat? Ain't I got de prettiest wife in de world. And what make it so cool, she's de sweetest wife God ever made."

"All Ah got to say is 'Watch out.'"

"Watch out for what? My wife don't need no watchin'. She's pretty, it's true, but Ah don't have to watch her."

"Somebody else done found out she pretty too and she's gointer gid rid of *you*. You better keep a close watch on her and when you go to bed tonight, make out you sleep and see if she don't try to cut yo' throat wid a razor!"

"Git off dis place—lyin' on my wife?"

De woman hid in de bushes outside de fence row and watched. Sho nuff, pretty soon he knocked off and went on towards de house. When he got dere he searched all over de place to see if anybody was there besides his wife. He didn't find nothin' but he watched everybody dat passed de gate, and he didn't say nothin' to his wife.

Dat night he got in bed right after supper and laid there wid his eyes shut. De wife went and got his razor and slipped it to bed wid her. When she thought he was good and sleep she got de cob-web in one hand and de razor in de other and leaned over him to cut his mole off. He had de cover up 'round his neck and soon as she started to ease it back he opened his eyes and grabbed her and took de razor.

"Unh, hunh! Ah was told you was goin' to cut my throat, but Ah didn't b'lieve it. From now on, we ain't no mo' husband and wife."

He dressed and left her cryin' in de bed.

De woman run on down to de sweet-gum tree to git her shoes. De Devil come brought 'em but he took and cut a long sapling and tied de shoe to de end of it and held 'em out to de woman and told her, "You parted 'em all right. Here's de shoes I promised you. But anybody dat kin create mo' disturbance than me is too dangerous. Ah don't want 'em round me. Here, take yo' shoes." And soon as she took 'em he vanished.

Horace Sharp said, "You lemme tell one now, Mack; you been talkin' all night. Tell yuh bout de farmer courtin' a girl.

Well, the startin' of it is, a farmer was courtin' a girl and after he decided to marry her, they married and started home. So when he passed a nice farm he said to the girl: "You see dat nice farm over yonder?" She said, "Yes." He said: "Well, all of these are mine." (Strokes his whiskers.)

Well, they traveled on further and they saw a herd of cattle and he said, "See dat nice herd of cattle?" She said. "Yes." "Well, all of these are mine." He smoothed his whiskers again.

So he traveled on a piece further and come to a big plantation with a big nice house on it, and he said: "All of these are mine."

So he traveled on further. He said, "See dat nice bunch of sheep?" She said, "Yes." "Well, all of these are mine."

Traveled on further. Come across a nice bunch of hogs and he said: "See dat nice bunch of hogs?" "Yes." "Well, all of these are mine."

So the last go 'round he got home and drove up to a dirty li'l shack and told her to get out and come in.

She says, "You got all those nice houses and want me to come in there? I couldn't afford to come in here. *Why you told me a story.* I'm going back home."

He says, "Why no, I didn't tell you a story. Everytime I showed you those things I said 'all of these were mine' and Ah wuz talkin' bout my whiskers." So the girl jumped out of the wagon and out for home she went.

Goat fell down and skint his chin
Great God A'mighty how de goat did grin.

"You do pretty good, Horace," Mah Honey drawled, "but how come you want to stick in yo' bill when Mack is talkin'? Dat story you told ain't doodly squat."

"Less see *you* tell one better'n dat one, then," Horace slashed back.

"Oh Ah can't tell none worth listenin' tuh and you can't neither. Only difference in us is Ah know Ah can't and you

169

don't. Dat lie you told is po' ez owl harkey. Gwan tell some mo' Mack. Maybe somebody'll come long and help yuh out after while."

"Ah thought Horace's story wuz jus' alright," Lessie Lee Hudson said. "Can't eve'ybody talk de same."

"Course it wuz!" Horace yelled, "it wuz alright wid everybody 'ceptin Mah Honey. He's a nigger wid white folks' head—let *him* tell it. He make out he know every chink in China."

"What you gointer do?" Mah Honey asked. "Ah kin tell yuh fo' yuh part yo' lips. You ain't gointer do nothin' but mildew."

Somebody came along singing, "You Won't Do," and everybody looked round at one time like cows in a pasture. "Here come A.D. He kin lie good too. Hurry up, A.D. and help Mack out!"

"What Mack doin'?"

"Lyin' up a breeze."

"Awright, lemme git in dis shag-lag. Who lied last?"

"Mack. Youse next."

"Who all know what uh squinch owl[3] is?" Frazier lit out.

"Man, who you reckon it is, *don't* know what dat bad luck thing is?" Christopher Jenkins asked. "Sign uh death every time you hear one hollerin round yo' house. Ah shoots every one Ah kin find."

"You kin stop 'em without shootin' 'em. Jus' tie uh loose knot in uh string and every time he holler you pull de knot uh lil bit tighter. Dat chokes 'im. Keep on you choke 'im tuh death. Go out doors nex' mawnin and look ahround you'll find uh dead owl round dere somewhere." Said Mah Honey.

"All you need tuh do is turn somethin' wrong side outuds, pull off yo' coat and turn it or else you kin turn uh pocket," Carrie Jones added. "Me, Ah always pull off uh stockin' and turn it. Dat always drives 'im off."

"Throw some salt on de lamp or stick uh rusty fork in de

[3]Screech owl, sometimes known as a shivering owl.

170

floor will do de same thing. In fact its de best of all; Ah mean
de salt in de lamp. Nothin' evil can't stand salt, let alone
burnin' salt."

"Lemme tell y'all how come we got squinch owls and then
y'all kin talk all yuh please bout how tuh kill 'em and drive 'em
off de house top in de night time," said A.D.

Yuh know Ole Marster had uh ole maid sister that never
been married. You know how stringy white folks necks gits
when dey gits ole. Well hers had done got that-a-way and
more special cause she never been married.

Her name wuz Miss Pheenie and Ole Marster had uh
daughter so there wuz young mens round de parlor and de
porch. All in de sittin' chairs and in de hammock under de
trees. So Miss Pheenie useter stand round and peer at 'em
and grin lak uh possum—wishin' she could git courted and
married.

So one devilish young buck, he seen de feelin' in her so
he 'gin tuh make manners wid her and last thing he done,
he told her says, "If you go set up on de roof uh de house
all night Ah'll marry yuh in de mawnin'."

It wuz uh bitter cold night. De wind searchin' lak de police. So she clambed up dere and set straddle of de highest
part cause she couldn't stick nowhere's else. And she
couldn't help but shake and shiver. And everytime de clock
would strike de hour she'd say, "C-o-o-o-l-d on de
housetop, but uh young man in de mawnin'." She kept dat
up till de clock struck four, when she tumbled down, froze
tuh death. But de very next night after they buried her, she
took de shape of uh owl and wuz back dere shivverin' and
cryin'. And dats how come us got squinch owls.

"Dat sho waz uh true lie, A.D.," Carrie said. "Ah sho is
wished many de time dat Miss Pheenie had uh stayed off de
top uh dat house."

"Ah knows one 'bout uh witch woman," A.D. went on.
"Ah'll tell dat one too, whilst Ah got mah wind."

"Naw, Ah don't wanta hear bout no witches ridin' nobody," Baby-face Turl objected. "Ah been near rode tuh death in mah time. Can't bear tuh hear tell of it."

"Well then Ah kin tell yuh bout dat talkin' mule.

Ole feller one time had uh mule. His name wuz Bill. Every mornin' de man go tuh ketch 'im he say, "Come 'round, Bill!"

So one mornin' he slept late, so he decided while he wuz drinkin' some coffee he'd send his son tuh ketch Ole Bill.

Told 'im say, "Go down dere, boy, and bring me dat mule up here."

Boy, he sich a fast Aleck, he grabbed de bridle and went on down tuh de lot tuh ketch ole Bill.

He say, "Come round, Bill!"

De mule looked round at 'im. He told de mule, "Tain't no use you rollin' yo' eyes at *me*. Pa want yuh dis mawnin'. Come on round and stick yo' head in dis bridle."

Mule kept on lookin' at 'im and said, "Every mornin' it's 'Come round, Bill! Come round, Bill!' Don't hardly git no night rest befo' it's 'Come round, Bill!' "

De boy throwed down dat bridle and flew back tuh de house and told his Pa, "Dat mule is talkin'."

"Ah g'wan, boy, tellin' yo' lies! G'wan ketch dat mule."

"Naw suh, Pa, dat mule's done gone tuh talkin'. You hatta ketch dat mule yo' ownself. Ah ain't gwine."

Ole man looked at ole lady and say, "See whut uh lie dat boy is tellin'?"

So he gits out and goes on down after de mule his-self. When he got down dere he hollered, "Come round, Bill!"

Ole mule looked round and says, "Every mornin' it's come round, Bill!"

De old man had uh little fice dog useter foller 'im every-where he go, so he lit out wid de lil fice right behind 'im. So he told de ole lady, "De boy ain't told much of uh lie. Dat mule *is* talkin'. Ah never heered uh mule talk befo'."

Lil fice say, "Me neither."

De ole man got skeered agin. Right through de woods he went wid de fice right behind 'im. He nearly run hisself tuh death. He stopped and commenced blowin' and says, "Ahm so tired Ah don't know whut tuh do."

Lil dog run and set down in front of 'im and went to hasslin'[4] and says, "Me too."

Dat man is runnin' yet.

Everybody agreed that the old man did right by running, only some thought they could have bettered his record both for speed and distance.

"What make you love tuh tell dem skeery lies, A.D.?" Clarence Beale asked.

Lessie Lee snuggled up to Clarence with the eyes of Eve and said, "He skeers me too, Clarence. Less me and you hug up together." Clarence grabbed her and wrapped her up tight.

"Youse jus' all right, A.D. If you know another one skeerier than dat one, Ah'll give yuh five dollars tuh tell it. And then Ah'm gointer git de job uh keepin' de boogers offa Lessie Lee tuhnight. G'wan tell it."

"Yeah man!" Christopher Jenkins chimed in. "All dese frail eels gittin' skittish. Tell some mo' A.D. Skeer Carrie right up on me!"

So A.D. told another one.

This wuz uh man. His name was High Walker. He walked into a boneyard with skull-heads and other bones. So he would call them, "Rise up bloody bones and shake yo'self." And de bones would rise up and come together, and shake theirselves and part and lay back down. Then he would say to hisself, "High Walker," and de bones would say, "Be walkin'."

When he'd git off a little way he'd look back over his

---

[4]Panting.

shoulder and shake hisself and say, "High Walker and bloody bones," and de bones would shake theirselves. Therefore he knowed he had power.

So uh man sold hisself to de high chief devil. He give 'im his whole soul and body tuh do ez he pleased wid it. He went out in uh drift uh woods[5] and laid down flat on his back beyond all dese skull heads and bloody bones and said, "Go 'way Lawd, and come here Devil and do as you please wid me. Cause Ah want tuh do everything in de world dats wrong and never do nothing right."

And he dried up and died away on doin' wrong. His meat all left his bones and de bones all wuz separated.

And at dat time High Walker walked upon his skull head and kicked and kicked it on ahead of him a many and a many times and said tuh it, "Rise up and shake yo'self. High Walker is here."

Ole skull head wouldn't say nothin'. He looked back over his shoulder cause he heard some noises behind him and said, "Bloody bones you won't say nothin' yet. Rise tuh de power in de flesh."

Den de skull head said, "My mouf brought me here and if you don't mind, you'n will bring you here."

High Walker went on back to his white folks and told de white man dat a dry skull head wuz talkin' in de drift today. White man say he didn't believe it.

"Well, if you don't believe it, come go wid me and Ah'll prove it. And if it don't speak, you kin chop mah head off right where it at."

So de white man and High Walker went back in de drift tuh find dis ole skull head. So when he walked up tuh it, he begin tuh kick and kick de ole skull head, but it wouldn't say nothin'. High Walker looked at de white man and seen 'im whettin' his knife. Whettin' it hard and de sound of it said rick-de-rick, rick-de-rick, rick-de-rick! So High Walker kicked and kicked dat ole skull head and called it many and many uh time, but it never said nothin'. So de white man cut off High Walker's head.

[5]10,000 "faces" in the turpentine woods, i.e. tree trunks that have been cut on one side to make the sap run from which turpentine is made.

And de ole dry skull head said, "See dat now! Ah told you dat mouf brought me here and if you didn't mind out it'd bring you here."

So de bloody bones riz up and shook they selves seben times and de white man got skeered and said, "What you mean by dis?"

De bloody bones say, "We got High Walker and we all bloody bones now in de drift together."

The next day was Thursday and I got a letter from Big Sweet saying I must be back at Loughman by Saturday because that was pay night and Thelma and Cliffert were getting married and big doings would be going on.

Friday I arrived in Loughman. Thelma and Cliffert got married on Saturday and everybody that wasn't mad put out to give them a big time.

The biggest crowd was over at the Pine Mill where Jim Presley was playing so I wanted to go there. Big Sweet didn't want to go there much. At least that is what she told everybody, but she told me to go on. She might be over later. She gave me some advice about looking out for myself.

"Don't let nobody bring yuh nothin' tuh eat and drink, and don't let 'em send it neither. They liable tuh put uh spider in yo' dumplin'. Don't let nobody git yuh intuh no fuss, cause you can't do dis kind uh fightin'. You don't know no better'n tuh go face tuh face tuh fight. Lucy and dem ain't gointer fight nobody lak dat. They think it make 'em look big tuh cut yuh. Ah done went tuh her and put mah foot up on her door step and told her dat if she tetch yuh Ah'll gently chain-gang fuh her, but she don't aim tuh lemme ketch her. She mean tuh slip up on yuh sometime and hit yuh uh back hand lick wid her knife and turn her hand over right quick and hit yuh forward wid it and pull it down. Then she aims tuh run cross back yards and jump fences so fast till me and de law neither can't find her."

"Well, Big Sweet, if it's like dat, Ah speck Ah better not go out unless you be wid me," I told her.

"Oh yeah, you go on. You come here tuh see and lissen and Ah means fuh yuh tuh do it. Jus' watch out. Ah could give yuh uh knife tuh tote but dat wouldn't do you no good. You don't know how tuh handle it. Ah got two round here. One real good one Ah got down in Tampa, and one ole froe.[6] But you jus' gwan over dere and mind what Ah tell yuh. Ahm liable tuh be dere tuhreckly mahself. And don't git biggity wid nobody and let yuh head start more than yo' rump kin stand."

I promised sincerely and took Cliffert and Thelma in the car with me to the Pine Mill.

A new man had come from Groveland, where another big sawmill was located, and he was standing behind Jim Presley and Slim, singing new songs, and I was so glad that I had come. It didn't take me long to learn some new ones and I forgot all about Lucy.

Way after midnight Big Sweet came in. The place was hot by then. Everything was done got loud. The music, the dancing, the laughing, and nobody could say a thing even over the card games unless they made it sound something like singing. Heard one woman playing Coon Can sing out:

> Give mah man mah money, tuh play Coon Can
> He lost all mah money but he played his hand.

In a little while I heard her again:

> Befo' Ah'll lose mah rider's change
> Ah'll spread short deuces and tab de game.

Big Sweet nodded me over in a corner and said, "Ah done strowed it over on de other side dat Ahm gone home tuh bed. Jus' wanta see whut might come off."

"Lucy ain't been here atall," I told her. "Believe she skeered you might kill her sho 'nuff."

[6]A damaged pocket knife.

176

"She know Ah will lessen she kill me first. Ah hates uh two-facedted heifer lak her. And Ah ain't skeered tuh see Mah Jesus neither cause de Bible say God loves uh plain sinner and he's married tuh de backslider. Ah got jus' as good uh chance at Heben as anybody else. So have yo' correct amount uh fun. Ahm settin' right over dere in dat skin game."

Heard somebody at the Florida Flip game say, "Ahm gone—jus' lak uh turkey through de corn. Deal!"

Heard somebody else in the game say, "Beggin'" and the dealer told him, "Eat acorns."[7]

Heard Blue Baby ask Box-Car, "Who is dat new nigger over dere by de refreshments? God Amighty, ugly got de mug on him wid four wheel brakes."

"He's de new skitter man.[8] He sho' ain't nobody's pretty baby. Bet he have tuh slip up on de dipper tuh git uh drink uh water. B'lieve Ah'll holler at 'im. 'Hey Ugly, who made you? Don't start tuh lyin' on God now.'"

A general laugh followed this. Box-Car, a little proud of his crack, grabbed Blue Baby. "Come on less go over dere and marry Cliff and Thelma all over agin. Hey Cliff, you and Thelma git up on de floor and raise yo' right hand. Y'all ain't been hitched right till Box-Car git thew widja." The couple bashfully stood up.

"Join hands. Alright Cliff, Ahm de preacher—

> Here's yo' woman, here's de ring,
> Here's de banana, here's de skin
> Now you married, go—

A huge burst of laughter drowned out Box Car's voice and when the laugh died out, I could hear Nunkie, "reading the deck" where the flip game used to be. Calling the names of the cards and laying them down rhythmically and dramatically as he read:

[7] I give you one point.
[8] A panther had killed the other one a week earlier.

177

Ace means the first time that Ah met you, Deuce means
there was nobody there but us two, Trey means the third
party, Charlie was his name, Four spot means the fourth
time you tried dat same ole game, Five spot is five years
you played me for a clown, Six spot, six feet of earth when
de deal goes down, Now, Ahm holdin' de seben spot for
each day in de week, Eight spot, eight hours you sheba-ed
wid yo' sheik, Nine spot means nine hours Ah work hard
every day, Ten spot de tenth of every month Ah brought
you home mah pay, De Jack is Three Card Charlie who
played me for a goat, De Queen, dat's you, pretty mama,
also tryin' tuh cut mah throat, De King, dat hot papa
Nunkie, and he's gointer wear de crown, So be keerful
y'all ain't broke when de deal goes down.

Nunkie looked around belligerently on the last sentence
and Joe Willard jumped up and pulled at Big Sweet.
"Play some music, Jim, y'all over dere, and less dance some
mo'. Nunkie wants tuh pick uh fight wid Who Flung. Play us
uh slow drag. Come on Big Sweet, less me and you have uh
schronchuns dance."
"Dance wid Zora, honey, Ah don't choose tuh move from
where Ahm at. Ah ain't mad wid nobody, baby, jus' wanta set
and look on uh while yet."
Heard the new singing man climbing up on

Tell me, tell me where de blood red river ru-u-un
Oh tell me where de blood red river run
From mah back door, straight to de risin' sun.

Heard Slim's bass strings under the singing throbbing like
all Africa and Jim Presley's melody crying like repentance as
four or five couples took the floor. Doing the slow drag, doing
the schronch. Joe Willard doing a traveling buck and wing
towards where I stood against the wall facing the open door.
Just about that time Lucy hopped up in the doorway with
an open knife in her hands. She saw me first thing. Maybe she
had been outside peeping a long time and there I was leaning

178

against the wall right close to Slim. One door in the place and Lucy standing in it.

"Stop dat music," she yelled without moving. "Don't vip another vop till Ah say so! Ah means tuh turn dis place out right now. Ah got de law in mah mouf."

So she started walking hippily straight at me. She knew I couldn't get out easily because she had me barred and she knew not many people will risk running into a knife blade to stop a fight. So she didn't have to run. I didn't move but I was running in my skin. I could hear the blade already crying in my flesh. I was sick and weak. But a flash from the corner about ten feet off and Lucy had something else to think about besides me. Big Sweet was flying at her with an open blade and now it was Lucy's time to try to make it to the door. Big Sweet kicked her somewhere about the knees and she fell. A doubled back razor flew thru the air very close to Big Sweet's head. Crip, the new skitter man, had hurled it. It whizzed past Big Sweet and stuck in the wall; then Joe Willard went for Crip. Jim Presley punched me violently and said, "Run you chile! Run and ride! Dis is gointer be uh nasty ditch. Lucy been feedin' Crip under rations tuh git him tuh help her. Run clean off dis job! Some uh dese folks goin' tuh judgment and some goin' tuh jail. Come on, less run!"

Slim stuck out the guitar to keep two struggling men from blocking my way. Lucy was screaming. Crip had hold of Big Sweet's clothes in the back and Joe was slugging him loose. Curses, oaths, cries and the whole place was in motion. Blood was on the floor. I fell out of the door over a man lying on the steps, who either fell himself trying to run or got knocked down. I don't know. I was in the car in a second and in high just too quick. Jim and Slim helped me throw my bags into the car and I saw the sun rising as I approached Crescent City.

PART II

HOODOO

ONE

Winter passed and caterpillars began to cross the road again. I had spent a year in gathering and culling over folk-tales. I loved it, but I had to bear in mind that there was a limit to the money to be spent on the project, and as yet, I had done nothing about hoodoo.

So I slept a night, and the next morning I headed my toenails toward Louisiana and New Orleans in particular.

New Orleans is now and has ever been the hoodoo capital of America. Great names in rites that vie with those of Hayti in deeds that keep alive the powers of Africa.

Hoodoo, or Voodoo, as pronounced by the whites, is burning with a flame in America, with all the intensity of a suppressed religion. It has its thousands of secret adherents. It adapts itself like Christianity to its locale, reclaiming some of its borrowed characteristics to itself, such as fire-worship as signified in the Christian church by the altar and the candles and the belief in the power of water to sanctify as in baptism.

Belief in magic is older than writing. So nobody knows how it started.

The way we tell it, hoodoo started way back there before everything. Six days of magic spells and mighty words and the world with its elements above and below was made. And now, God is leaning back taking a seventh day rest. When the eighth day comes around, He'll start to making new again.

Man wasn't made until around half-past five on the sixth day, so he can't know how anything was done. Kingdoms crushed and crumbled whilst man went gazing up into the sky and down into the hollows of the earth trying to catch God working with His hands so he could find out His secrets and learn how to accomplish and do. But no man yet has seen God's hand, nor yet His finger-nails. All they could know was that God made everything to pass and perish except stones. God made stones for memory. He builds a mountain Himself when He wants things not forgot. Then His voice is heard in rumbling judgment.

Moses was the first man who ever learned God's power-compelling words and it took him forty years to learn ten words. So he made ten plagues and ten commandments. But God gave him His rod for a present, and showed him the back part of His glory. Then too, Moses could walk out of the sight of man. But Moses never would have stood before the Burning Bush, if he had not married Jethro's daughter. Jethro was a great hoodoo man. Jethro could tell Moses could carry power as soon as he saw him. In fact he felt him coming. Therefore, he took Moses and crowned him and taught him. So Moses passed on beyond Jethro with his rod. He lifted it up and tore a nation out of Pharaoh's side, and Pharaoh couldn't help himself. Moses talked with the snake that lives in a hole right under God's foot-rest. Moses had fire in his head and a cloud in his mouth. The snake had told him God's making words. The words of doing and the words of obedience. Many a man thinks he is making something when he's only changing things around. But God let Moses make. And then Moses had so much power he made the eight winged angels split open a mountain to bury him in, and shut up the hole behind them.

And ever since the days of Moses, kings have been toting rods for a sign of power. But it's mostly sham-polish because no king has ever had the power of even one of Moses' ten words. Because Moses made a nation and a book, a thousand million leaves of ordinary men's writing couldn't tell what Moses said.

Then when the moon had dragged a thousand tides behind her, Solomon was a man. So Sheba, from her country where she was, felt him carrying power and therefore she came to talk with Solomon and hear him.

The Queen of Sheba was an Ethiopian just like Jethro, with power unequal to man. She didn't have to deny herself to give gold to Solomon. She had gold-making words. But she was thirsty, and the country where she lived was dry to her mouth. So she listened to her talking ring and went to see Solomon, and the fountain in his garden quenched her thirst.

So she made Solomon wise and gave him her talking ring. And Solomon built a room with a secret door and everyday he shut himself inside and listened to his ring. So he wrote down the ring-talk in books.

That's what the old ones said in ancient times and we talk it again.

It was way back there—the old folks told it—that Raw-Head-And-Bloody-Bones had reached down and laid hold of the taproot that points to the center of the world. And they talked about High Walker too. But they talked in people's language and nobody knew them but the old folks.

Nobody knows for sure how many thousands in America are warmed by the fire of hoodoo, because the worship is bound in secrecy. It is not the accepted theology of the Nation and so believers conceal their faith. Brother from sister, husband from wife. Nobody can say where it begins or ends. Mouths don't empty themselves unless the ears are sympathetic and knowing.

That is why these voodoo ritualistic orgies of Broadway and popular fiction are so laughable. The profound silence of the initiated remains what it is. Hoodoo is not drum beating and dancing. There are no moon-worshippers among the Negroes in America.

I was once talking to Mrs. Rachel Silas of Sanford, Florida, so I asked her where I could find a good hoodoo doctor.

"Do you believe in dat ole fogeyism, chile? Ah don't see how nobody could do none of dat work, do you?" She laughed unnecessarily. "Ah been hearin' 'bout dat mess ever since Ah been big enough tuh know mahself, but shucks! Ah don't believe nobody kin do me no harm lessen they git somethin' in mah mouth."

"Don't fool yourself," I answered with assurance. "People can do things to you. I done seen things happen."

"Sho nuff? Well, well, well! Maybe things *kin* be done tuh harm yuh, cause Ah done heard *good* folks—folks dat ought to know—say dat it sho is a fact. Anyhow Ah figger it pays tuh be keerful."

"Oh yeah, Mrs. Rachel, Ah've seen a woman full of scorpions."

"Oh it kin be done, honey, no effs and ands 'bout de thing. There's things that kin be done. Ah seen uh' 'oman wid uh gopher in her belly. You could see 'm movin' 'round in her. And once every day he'd turn hisself clear over and then you could hear her hollerin' for more'n a mile. Dat hard shell would be cuttin' her insides. Way after 'while she took down ill sick from it and died. Ah knowed de man dat done dat trick. Dat wuz done in uh dish of hoppin-john."[1]

Mrs. Viney White, a neighbor, was sitting there so she spoke. "Ah knowed into dat mahself. It wuz done over her breaking de leg of one of his hens dat wuz scratchin' up her garden. When she took down sick Ah went to see her and Ah told her folks right then dat somebody had done throwed at her, but they didn't b'lieve in nothin'. Went and got a Medical doctor, and they can't do them kind of cases no good at all. Fact is it makes it worser." She stopped short and nodded her head apprehensively towards the window. Rachel nodded her head knowingly. "She out dere now, tryin' tuh eavesdrop."

"Who you talkin' 'bout?" I asked.

[1]Peas and rice cooked together.

"De one dat does all de underhand work 'round here. She even threw at *me* once, but she can't do nothin'. Ah totes mah Big John de Conquerer[2] wid me. And Ah sprinkles mustard seed 'round my door every night before Ah goes tuh bed."

"Yeah, and another thing," Mrs. Rachel said, "Ah keeps her offa me too. She tries tuh come in dis yard so she kin put something down for me too, but air Lawd, Ah got something buried at dat gate dat she can't cross. She done been dere several times, but she can't cross."

"Ah'd git her tuh go if ah wuz you, Rachel," Mrs. Viney said.

"Wisht ah knowed how. Ah'd sho do it."

"You throw salt behind her, everytime she go out of her gate. Do dat nine times and Ah bet she'll move so fast she won't even know where she's going. Somebody salted a woman over in Georgetown and she done moved so much she done wore out her furniture on de movin' wagon. But looka here, Zora, whut you want wid a two-headed doctor? Is somebody done throwed a old shoe at *you?*"

"Not exactly neither one, Mrs. Viney. Just want to learn how to do things myself."

"Oh, honey, Ah wouldn't mess with it if Ah wuz you. Dat's a thing dat's got to be handled just so, do it'll kill you. Me and Rachel both knows somebody that could teach you if they will. Dis woman ain't lak some of these hoodoo doctors. She don't do nothin' but good. You couldn't pay her to be rottin' people's teeths out, and fillin' folks wid snakes and lizards and spiders and things like dat."

So I went to study with Eulalia, who specialized in Man-and-woman cases. Everyday somebody came to get Eulalia to tie them up with some man or woman or to loose them from love.

Eulalia was average sized with very dark skin and bushy eyebrows. Her house was squatting among the palmettoes and

---

[2]A root, extensively used in conjure.

the mossy scrub oaks. Nothing pretty in the house nor outside. No paint and no flowers. So one day a woman came to get tied to a man.

"Who is dis man?" Eulalia wanted to know.

"Jerry Moore," the woman told her. "He want me and Ah know it, but dat 'oman he got she got roots buried and he can't git shet of her—do we would of done been married."

Eulalia sat still and thought awhile. Then she said: "Course Ah'm uh Christian woman and don't believe in partin' no husband and wife but since she done worked roots on him, to hold him where he don't want to be, it tain't no sin for me to loose him. Where they live at?"

"Down Young's Quarters. De third house from dis end."

"Do she ever go off from home and stays a good while durin' de time he ain't there neither?"

"Yas Ma'am! She all de time way from dat house—off fanfootin' whilst he workin' lak a dog! It's a shame!"

"Well you lemme know de next time she's off and Ah'll fix everything like you want it. Put that money back in yo' purse, Ah don't want a thing till de work is done."

Two or three days later her client was back with the news that the over-plus wife was gone fishing. Eulalia sent her away and put on her shoes.

"Git dat salt-bowl and a lemon," she said to me. "Now write Jerry's name and his wife's nine times on a piece of paper and cut a little hole in the stem end of that lemon and pour some of that gun-powder in de hole and roll that paper tight and shove it inside the lemon. Wrap de lemon and de bowl of salt up and less go."

In Jerry Moore's yard, Eulalia looked all around and looked up at the sun a great deal, then pointed out a spot.

"Dig a little hole right here and bury dat lemon. It's got to be buried with the bloom-end down and it's got to be where de settin' sun will shine on it."

So I buried the lemon and Eulalia walked around to the kitchen door. By the time I had the lemon buried the door was open and we went inside. She looked all about and found some red pepper.

"Lift dat stove-lid for me," she ordered, and I did. She threw some of the pepper into the stove and we went on into the other room which was the bedroom and living-room all in one. Then Eulalia took the bowl and went from corner to corner "salting" the room. She'd toss a sprinkling into a corner and say, "Just fuss and fuss till you part and go away." Under the bed was sprinkled also. It was all over in a minute or two. Then we went out and shut the kitchen door and hurried away. And Saturday night Eulalia got her pay and the next day she set the ceremony to bring about the marriage.

TWO

Now I was in New Orleans and I asked. They told me Algiers, the part of New Orleans that is across the river to the west. I went there and lived for four months and asked. I found women reading cards and doing mail order business in names and insinuations of well known factors in conjure. Nothing worth putting on paper. But they all claimed some knowledge and link with Marie Leveau. From so much of hearing the name I asked everywhere for this Leveau and everybody told me differently. But from what they said I was eager to know to the end of the talk. It carried me back across the river into the Vieux Carré. All agreed that she had lived and died in the French quarter of New Orleans. So I went there to ask.

I found an oil painting of the queen of conjure on the walls of the Cabildo, and mention of her in the guide books of New Orleans, but I did a lot of stumbling and asking before I heard of Luke Turner, himself a hoodoo doctor, who says that he is her nephew.

When I found out about Turner, I had already studied under five two-headed doctors and had gone thru an initiation ceremony with each. So I asked Turner to take me as a pupil. He was very cold. In fact he showed no eagerness even to talk with me. He feels sure of his powers and seeks no one. He refused to take me as a pupil and in addition to his habitual indifference I could see he had no faith in my sincerity. I could see him searching my face for whatever was behind what I said. The City of New Orleans has a law against fortune tellers, hoodoo doctors and the like, and Turner did not know me. He asked me to excuse him as he was waiting upon someone in the inner room. I let him go but I sat right there and waited. When he returned, he tried to shoo me away by being rude. I stayed on. Finally he named an impossible price for tuition. I stayed and dickered. He all but threw me out, but I stayed and urged him.

I made three more trips before he would talk to me in any way that I could feel encouraged. He talked about Marie Leveau because I asked. I wanted to know if she was really as great as they told me. So he enlightened my ignorance and taught me. We sat before the soft coal fire in his grate.

"Time went around pointing out what God had already made. Moses had seen the Burning Bush. Solomon by magic knowed all wisdom. And Marie Leveau was a woman in New Orleans.

"She was born February 2, 1827. Anybody don't believe I tell the truth can go look at the book in St. Louis Cathedral. Her mama and her papa, they wasn't married and his name was Christophe Glapion.

"She was very pretty, one of the Creole Quadroons and many people said she would never be a hoodoo doctor like her mama and her grandma before her. She liked to go to the balls very much where all the young men fell in love with her. But Alexander, the great two-headed doctor felt the power in her and so he tell her she must come to study with him. Marie, she rather dance and make love, but one day a rattlesnake come to her in her bedroom and spoke to her. So she went to Alexander and studied. But soon she could teach her teacher and the snake stayed with her always.

"She has her house on St. Anne Street and people come from the ends of America to get help from her. Even Queen

Victoria ask her help and send her a cashmere shawl with money also.

"Now, some white people say she hold hoodoo dance on Congo Square every week. But Marie Leveau never hold no hoodoo dance. That was a pleasure dance. They beat the drum with the shin bone of a donkey and everybody dance like they do in Hayti. Hoodoo is private. She give the dance the first Friday night in each month and they have crab gumbo and rice to eat and the people dance. The white people come look on, and think they see all, when they only see a dance.

"The police hear so much about Marie Leveau that they come to her house in St. Anne Street to put her in jail. First one come, she stretch out her left hand and he turn round and round and never stop until some one come lead him away. Then two come together—she put them to running and barking like dogs. Four come and she put them to beating each other with night sticks. The whole station force come. They knock at her door. She know who they are before she ever look. She did work at her altar and they all went to sleep on her steps.

"Out on Lake Pontchartrain at Bayou St. John she hold a great feast every year on the Eve of St. John's, June 24th. It is Midsummer Eve, and the Sun give special benefits then and need great honor. The special drum be played then. It is a cowhide stretched over a half-barrel. Beat with a jaw-bone. Some say a man but I think they do not know. I think the jawbone of an ass or a cow. She hold the feast of St. John's partly because she is a Catholic and partly because of hoodoo.

"The ones around her altar fix everything for the feast. Nobody see Marie Leveau for nine days before the feast. But when the great crowd of people at the feast call upon her, she would rise out of the waters of the lake with a great communion candle burning upon her head and another in each one of her hands. She walked upon the waters to the shore. As a little boy I saw her myself. When the feast was over, she went back into the lake, and nobody saw her for nine days again.

"On the feast that I saw her open the waters, she looked

193

hard at me and nodded her head so that her tignon shook. Then I knew I was called to take up her work. She was very old and I was a lad of seventeen. Soon I went to wait upon her Altar, both on St. Anne Street and her house on Bayou St. John's.

"The rattlesnake that had come to her a little one when she was also young was very huge. He piled great upon his altar and took nothing from the food set before him. One night he sang and Marie Leveau called me from my sleep to look at him and see. 'Look well, Turner,' she told me. 'No one shall hear and see such as this for many centuries.'

"She went to her Great Altar and made great ceremony. The snake finished his song and seemed to sleep. She drove me back to my bed and went again to her Altar.

"The next morning, the great snake was not at his altar. His hide was before the Great Altar stuffed with spices and things of power. Never did I know what become of his flesh. It is said that the snake went off to the woods alone after the death of Marie Leveau, but they don't know. This is his skin that I wear about my shoulders whenever I reach for power.

"Three days Marie, she set at the Altar with the great sun candle burning and shining in her face. She set the water upon the Altar and turned to the window, and looked upon the lake. The sky grew dark. The lightning raced to the seventeen quarters of the heavens and the lake heaved like a mighty herd of cattle rolling in a pasture. The house shook with the earth.

"She told me, 'You are afraid. That is right, you should fear. Go to your own house and build an altar. Power will come.' So I hurried to my mother's house and told them.

"Some who loved her hurried out to Bayou St. John and tried to enter the house but she try hard to send them off. They beat upon the door, but she will not open. The terrible strong wind at last tore the house away and set it in the lake. The thunder and lightning grow greater. Then the loving ones find a boat and went out to where her house floats on one side and break a window to bring her out, but she begs, 'NO! Please, no,' she tell them. 'I want to die here in the lake,' but they would not permit her. She did not wish their destruction, so she let herself be drawn away from her altar in the lake. And the wind, the thunder and lightning, and the water all ceased the moment she set foot on dry land.

"That night she also sing a song and is dead, yes. So I have the snake skin and do works with the power she leave me."

"How did Marie Leveau do her work?" I asked feeling that I had gotten a little closer to him.

"She go to her great Altar and seek until she become the same as the spirit, then she come out into the room where she listens to them that come to ask. When they finish she answer them as a god. If a lady have a bad enemy and come to her she go into her altar room and when she come out and take her seat, the lady will say to her:

" 'Oh, Good Mother. I come to you with my heart bowed down and my shoulders drooping, and my spirits broken; for an enemy has sorely tried me; has caused my loved ones to leave me; has taken from me my worldly goods and my gold; has spoken meanly of me and caused my friends to lose faith in me. On my knees I pray to you, Good Mother, that you will cause confusion to reign in the house of my enemy and that you will take their power from them and cause them to be unsuccessful.'

"Marie Leveau is not a woman when she answer the one who ask. No. She is a god, yes. Whatever she say, it will come so. She say:

" 'Oh, my daughter, I have heard your woes and your pains and tribulations, and in the depth of the wisdom of the gods I will help you find peace and happiness.

" 'It is written that you will take of the Vinagredes Four Volle[1] for him, and you will dip into it a sheet of pure parchment paper, and on this sheet you will write the names of your enemies and send it to the house of your enemies, tightly sealed with the wax of the porcupine plant.

" 'Then when the sun shall have risen and gone down three

[1] Four Thieves Vinegar. For paraphernalia of conjure, see appendix.

195

times, you will take of the water of Mars, called War Water, and in front of the house of your enemy you will sprinkle it. This you will do as you pass by. If it be a woman, you will take the egg of a guinea fowl, and put it into the powder of the fruit of cayenne and the dust of Goofer,[2] and you will set it on the fire in your own house and in clear water from the skies you will boil it until it shall be hard. This you will do so that there shall be no fruit from her womb.

" 'And you shall take of the Damnation Powders, two drachmas, and of the water powders, two drachmas and make a package of it and send it to the home of the one who has spoken badly of you and has treated you mean, so that damnation and trouble shall be on the head of your enemy and not on you.

" 'You will do this so that you will undo your enemies and you will take the power to harm you away from your enemies.

" 'Oh daughter, go you in peace and do the works required of you, so that you will have rest and comfort from your enemies and that they will have not the power to harm you and lower you in the sight of your people and belittle you in the sight of your friends. So be it.' "

By the time that Turner had finished his recitation he wasn't too conscious of me. In fact he gave me the feeling that he was just speaking, but not for my benefit. He was away off somewhere. He made a final dramatic gesture with open hands and hushed for a minute. Then he sank deeper into himself and went on:

"But when she put the last curse on a person, it would be better if that man was dead, yes."

With an impatient gesture he signalled me not to interrupt him.

"She set the altar for the curse with black candles that have been dressed in vinegar. She would write the name of the person to be cursed on the candle with a needle. Then she place fifteen cents in the lap of Death upon the altar to pay the

[2]Dirt taken out of a grave.

spirit to obey her orders. Then she place her hands flat upon the table and say the curse-prayer.

" 'To The Man God: O great One, I have been sorely tried by my enemies and have been blasphemed and lied against. My good thoughts and my honest actions have been turned to bad actions and dishonest ideas. My home has been disrespected, my children have been cursed and ill-treated. My dear ones have been backbitten and their virtue questioned. O Man God, I beg that this that I ask for my enemies shall come to pass:

" 'That the South wind shall scorch their bodies and make them wither and shall not be tempered to them. That the North wind shall freeze their blood and numb their muscles and that it shall not be tempered to them. That the West wind shall blow away their life's breath and will not leave their hair grow, and that their finger nails shall fall off and their bones shall crumble. That the East wind shall make their minds grow dark, their sight shall fail and their seed dry up so that they shall not multiply.

" 'I ask that their fathers and mothers from their furtherest generation will not intercede for them before the great throne, and the wombs of their women shall not bear fruit except for strangers, and that they shall become extinct. I pray that the children who may come shall be weak of mind and paralyzed of limb and that they themselves shall curse them in their turn for ever turning the breath of life into their bodies. I pray that disease and death shall be forever with them and that their worldly goods shall not prosper, and that their crops shall not multiply and that their cows, their sheep, and their hogs and all their living beasts shall die of starvation and thirst. I pray that their house shall be unroofed and that the rain, the thunder and lightning shall find the innermost recesses of their home and that the foundation shall crumble and the floods tear it asunder. I pray that the sun shall not shed its rays on them in benevolence, but instead it shall beat down on them and burn them and destroy them. I pray that the moon shall not give them peace, but instead shall deride them and decry them and cause their minds to shrivel. I pray that their friends shall betray them and cause them loss of power, of gold and of silver, and that their enemies shall smite them until they beg for mercy which shall not be given them. I pray that their tongues shall forget how to speak in sweet words, and that it shall be paralyzed and that all about them will be desolation, pestilence and death. O Man God, I ask you for all these things because they have dragged me in the dust and destroyed my good name; broken my heart and caused me to curse the day that I was born. So be it.' "

Turner again made that gesture with his hands that meant the end. Then he sat in a dazed silence. My own spirits had been falling all during the terrible curse and he did not have to tell me to be quiet this time. After a long period of waiting I rose to go. "The Spirit say you come back tomorrow," he breathed as I passed his knees. I nodded that I had heard and went out. The next day he began to prepare me for my initiation ceremony, for rest assured that no one may approach the Altar without the crown, and none may wear the crown of power without preparation. *It must be earned.*

And what is this crown of power? Nothing definite in material. Turner crowned me with a consecrated snake skin. I have been crowned in other places with flowers, with ornamental paper, with cloth, with sycamore bark, with egg-shells. It is the meaning, not the material that counts. The crown without the preparation means no more than a college diploma without the four years' work.

This preparation period is akin to that of all mystics. Clean living, even to clean thoughts. A sort of going to the wilderness in the spirit. The details do not matter. My nine days being up, and possessed of the three snake skins and the new underwear required, I entered Turner's house as an inmate to finish the last three days of my novitiate. Turner had become so sure of my fitness as a hoodoo doctor that he would accept no money from me except what was necessary to defray the actual cost of the ceremony.

So I ate my final meal before six o'clock of the evening

before and went to bed for the last time with my right stocking on and my left leg bare.

I entered the old pink stucco house in the Vieux Carré at nine o'clock in the morning with the parcel of needed things. Turner placed the new underwear on the big Altar; prepared the couch with the snake-skin cover upon which I was to lie for three days. With the help of other members of the college of hoodoo doctors called together to initiate me, the snake skins I had brought were made into garments for me to wear. One was coiled into a high headpiece—the crown. One had loops attached to slip on my arms so that it could be worn as a shawl, and the other was made into a girdle for my loins. All places have significance. These garments were placed on the small altar in the corner. The throne of the snake. The Great One[3] was called upon to enter the garments and dwell there.

I was made ready and at three o'clock in the afternoon, naked as I came into the world, I was stretched, face downwards, my navel to the snake skin cover, and began my three day search for the spirit that he might accept me or reject me according to his will. Three days my body must lie silent and fasting while my spirit went wherever spirits must go that seek answers never given to men as men.

I could have no food, but a pitcher of water was placed on a small table at the head of the couch, that my spirit might not waste time in search of water which should be spent in search of the Power-Giver. The spirit must have water, and if none had been provided it would wander in search of it. And evil spirits might attack it as it wandered about dangerous places. If it should be seriously injured, it might never return to me.

For sixty-nine hours I lay there. I had five psychic experiences and awoke at last with no feeling of hunger, only one of exaltation.

I opened my eyes because Turner called me. He stood before the Great Altar dressed ceremoniously. Five others were with him.

[3]The Spirit.

199

"Seeker, come," Turner called.

I made to rise and go to him. Another laid his hand upon me lightly, restraining me from rising.

"How must I come?" he asked in my behalf.

"You must come to the spirit across running water," Turner answered in a sort of chant.

So a tub was placed beside the bed. I was assisted to my feet and led to the tub. Two men poured water into the tub while I stepped into it and out again on the other side.

"She has crossed the dangerous stream in search of the spirit," the one who spoke for me chanted.

"The spirit does not know her name. What is she called?"

"She has no name but what the spirit gives."

"I see her conquering and accomplishing with the lightning and making her road with thunder. She shall be called the Rain-Bringer."

I was stretched again upon the couch. Turner approached me with two brothers, one on either side of him. One held a small paint brush dipped in yellow, the other bore one dipped in red. With ceremony Turner painted the lightning symbol down my back from my right shoulder to my left hip. This was to be my sign forever. The Great One was to speak to me in storms.

I was now dressed in the new underwear and a white veil was placed over my head, covering my face, and I was seated in a chair.

After I was dressed, a pair of eyes was painted on my cheeks as a sign that I could see in more ways than one. The sun was painted on my forehead. Many came into the room and performed ceremonial acts, but none spoke to me. Nor could I speak to them while the veil covered my face. Turner cut the little finger of my right hand and caught the gushing blood in a wine cup. He added wine and mixed it with the blood. Then he and all the other five leaders let blood from themselves also and mixed it with wine in another glass. I was led to drink from the cup containing their mingled bloods, and each of them in turn beginning with Turner drank mine. At high noon

I was seated at the splendid altar. It was dressed in the center with a huge communion candle with my name upon it set in sand, five large iced cakes in different colors, a plate of honeyed St. Joseph's bread, a plate of serpent-shaped breads, spinach and egg cakes fried in olive oil, breaded Chinese okra fried in olive oil, roast veal and wine, two huge yellow bouquets, two red bouquets and two white bouquets and thirty-six yellow tapers and a bottle of holy water.

Turner seated me and stood behind me with his ceremonial hat upon his head, and the crown of power in his hand. "Spirit! I ask you to take her. Do you hear me, Spirit? Will you take her? Spirit, I want you to take her, she is worthy!" He held the crown poised above my head for a full minute. A profound silence held the room. Then he lifted the veil from my face and let it fall behind my head and crowned me with power. He lit my candle for me. But from then on I might be a candle-lighter myself. All the candles were reverently lit. We all sat down and ate the feast. First a glass of blessed oil was handed me by Turner. "Drink this without tasting it." I gulped it down and he took the glass from my hand, took a sip of the little that remained. Then he handed it to the brother at his right who did the same, until it went around the table.

"Eat first the spinach cakes," Turner exhorted, and we did. Then the meal began. It was full of joy and laughter, even though we knew that the final ceremony waited only for the good hour of twelve midnight.

About ten o'clock we all piled into an old Studebaker sedan—all but Turner who led us on a truck. Out Road No. 61 we rattled until a certain spot was reached. The truck was unloaded beside the road and sent back to town. It was a little after eleven. The swamp was dismal and damp, but after some stumbly walking we came to a little glade deep in the wood, near the lake. A candle was burning at each of the four corners of the clearing, representing the four corners of the world and the four winds. I could hear the occasional slap-slap of the water. With a whispered chant some twigs were gathered and tied into a broom. Some pine straw was collected. The sheets of typing paper I had been urged to bring were brought out and nine sheets were blessed and my petition written nine times on each sheet by the light from a shaded lantern. The crate containing the black sheep was opened and the sheep led forward into the center of the circle. He stood there dazedly while the chant of strange syllables rose. I asked Turner the words, but he replied that in good time I would know what to say. It was not to be taught. If nothing came, to be silent. The head and withers of the sheep were stroked as the chanting went on. Turner became more and more voluble. At last he seized the straw and stuffed some into the sheep's nostrils. The animal struggled. A knife flashed and the sheep dropped to its knees, then fell prone with its mouth open in a weak cry. My petition was thrust into its throat that he might cry it to the Great One. The broom was seized and dipped in the blood from the slit throat and the ground swept vigorously—back and forth, back and forth—the length of the dying sheep. It was swept from the four winds toward the center. The sweeping went on as long as the blood gushed. Earth, the mother of the Great One and us all, has been appeased. With a sharp stick Turner traced the outline of the sheep and the digging commenced. The sheep was never touched. The ground was dug from under him so that his body dropped down into the hole. He was covered with nine sheets of paper bearing the petition and the earth heaped upon him. A white candle was set upon the grave and we straggled back to the road and the Studebaker.

I studied under Turner five months and learned all of the Leveau routines; but in this book all of the works of any doctor cannot be given. However, we performed several of Turner's own routines.

Once a woman, an excited, angry woman wanted something done to keep her husband true. So she came and paid Turner gladly for his services.

Turner took a piece of string that had been "treated" at the altar and gave it to the woman.

"Measure the man where I tell you. But he must never know. Measure him in his sleep then fetch back the string to me."

The next day the woman came at ten o'clock instead of nine as Turner had told her, so he made her wait until twelve o'clock, that being a good hour. Twelve is one of the benign hours of the day while ten is a malignant hour. Then Turner took the string and tied nine knots in it and tied it to a larger piece of string which he tied about her waist. She was completely undressed for the ceremony and Turner cut some hair from under her left armpit and some from the right side of the groin and put it together. Then he cut some from the right arm-pit and a tuft from the left groin and it was all placed on the altar, and burned in a votive light with the wish for her husband to love her and forget all others. She went away quite happy. She was so satisfied with the work that she returned with a friend a few days later.

Turner, with his toothless mouth, his Berber-looking face, said to the new caller:

"I can see you got trouble." He shivered. "It is all in the room. I feel the pain of it; Anger, Malice. Tell me who is this man you so fight with?"

"My husband's brother. He hate me and make all the trouble he can," the woman said in a tone so even and dull that it was hard to believe she meant what she said. "He must leave this town or die. Yes, it is much better if he is dead." Then she burst out, "Yeah, he should be dead long time ago. Long before he spy upon me, before he tell lies, lies, lies. I should be very happy for his funeral."

"Oh I can feel the great hate around you," Turner said. "It follow you everywhere, but I kill nobody, I send him away if you want so he never come back. I put guards along the road in the spirit world, and these he cannot pass, no. When he go, never will he come back to New Orleans. You see him no more. He will be forgotten and all his works."

"Then I am satisfied, yes," the woman said. "When will you send him off?"

"I ask the spirit, you will know."

She paid him and he sent her off and Turner went to his snake altar and sat in silence for a long time. When he arose, he sent me out to buy nine black chickens, and some Four Thieves Vinegar.[4] He himself went out and got nine small sticks upon which he had me write the troublesome brother-in-law's name—one time on each stick. At ten that night we went out into the small interior court so prevalent in New Orleans and drove nine stakes into the ground. The left leg of a chicken was tied to each stake. Then a fire was built with the nine sticks on which the name had been written. The ground was sprinkled all over with the Four Thieves Vinegar and Turner began his dance. From the fire to the circle of fluttering chickens and back again to the fire. The feathers were picked from the heads of the chickens in the frenzy of the dance and scattered to the four winds. He called the victim's name each time as he whirled three times with the chicken's head-feathers in his hand, then he flung them far.

The terrified chickens flopped and fluttered frantically in the dim firelight. I had been told to keep up the chant of the victim's name in rhythm and to beat the ground with a stick. This I did with fervor and Turner danced on. One by one the chickens were seized and killed by having their heads pulled off. But Turner was in such a condition with his whirling and dancing that he seemed in a hypnotic state. When the last fowl was dead, Turner drank a great draught of wine and sank before the altar. When he arose, we gathered some ashes from the fire and sprinkled the bodies of the dead chickens and I was told to get out the car. We drove out one of the main highways for a mile and threw one of the chickens away. Then another mile and another chicken until the nine dead chickens had been disposed of. The spirits of the dead chickens had been instructed never to let the trouble-maker pass inward to New Orleans again after he had passed them going out.

[4]A conjure mixture. See Paraphernalia of Conjure.

*   *   *

One day Turner told me that he had taught me all that he could and he was quite satisfied with me. He wanted me to stay and work with him as a partner. He said that soon I would be in possession of the entire business, for the spirit had spoken to him and told him that I was the last doctor that he would make; that one year and seventy-nine days from then he would die. He wanted me to stay with him to the end. It has been a great sorrow to me that I could not say yes.

THREE

Anatol Pierre, of New Orleans, was a middle-aged octoroon. He is a Catholic and lays some feeble claim to kinship with Marie Leveau.

He had the most elaborate temple of any of the practitioners. His altar room was off by itself and absolutely sacrosanct.

He made little difficulty about taking me after I showed him that I had worked with others.

Pierre was very emotional and sometimes he would be sharp with his clients, indifferent as to whether they hired him or not. But he quickly adjusted himself to my being around him and at the end of the first week began to prepare me for the crown.

The ceremony was as follows:

On Saturday I was told to have the materials for my initiation bath ready for the following Tuesday at eleven o'clock. I must have a bottle of lavender toilet water, Jap honeysuckle perfume, and orange blossom water. I must get a full bunch of parsley and brew a pint of strong parsley water. I must have at hand sugar, salt and Vacher Balm. Two long pink candles must be provided, one to be burned at the initiation, one to be lit on the altar for me in Pierre's secret room.

He came to my house in Belville Court at a quarter to eleven to see if all was right. The tub was half-filled with warm water and Pierre put in all of the ingredients, along with a handful of salt and three tablespoons of sugar.

The candles had been dressed on Saturday and one was already burning on the secret altar for me. The other long pink candle was rolled around the tub three times, "In nomina patria, et filia, et spiritu sanctus, Amen." Then it was marked for a four day burning and lit. The spirit was called three times. "Kind spirit, whose name is Moccasin, answer me." This I was told to repeat three times, snapping my fingers.

Then I, already prepared, stepped into the tub and was bathed by the teacher. Particular attention was paid to my head and back and chest since there the "controls" lie. While in the tub, my left little finger was cut a little and his finger was cut and the blood bond made. "Now you are of my flesh and of the spirit, and neither one of us will ever deny you."

He dried me and I put on new underwear bought for the occasion and dressed with oil of geranium, and was told to stretch upon the couch and read the third chapter of Job night and morning for nine days. I was given a little Bible that had been "visited" by the spirit and told the names of the spirits to call for any kind of work I might want to perform. I am to call on Great Moccasin for all kinds of power and also to have him stir up the particular spirit I may need for a specific task. I must call on Kangaroo to stop worrying; call on Jenipee spirit for marriages; call on Death spirit for killing, and the seventeen "quarters"[1] of spirit to aid me if one spirit seems insufficient.

I was told to burn the marked candle every day for two hours—from eleven till one, in the northeast corner of the room. While it is burning I must go into the silence and talk to the spirit through the candle.

On the fifth day Pierre called again and I resumed my studies, but now as an advanced pupil. In the four months that followed these are some of the things I learned from him:

A man called Muttsy Ivins came running to Pierre soon after

[1]See appendix.

my initiation was over. Pierre looked him over with some instinctive antipathy. So he wouldn't help him out by asking questions. He just let Mr. Muttsy tell him the best way he could. So he began by saying, "A lot of hurting things have been done to me, Pierre, and now its done got to de place Ah'm skeered for mah life."

"That's a lie, yes," Pierre snapped.

"Naw it 'tain't!" Muttsy insisted. "Ah done found things 'round mah door step and in mah yard and Ah know who's doin' it too."

"Yes, you find things in your yard because you continue to sleep with the wife of another man and you are afraid because he has said that he will kill you if you don't leave her alone. You are crazy to think that you can lie to me. Tell me the truth and then tell me what you want me to do."

"Ah want him out de way—kilt, cause he swear he's gointer kill me. And since one of us got to die, Ah'd ruther it to be him than me."

"I knew you wanted a death the minute you got in here. I don't like to work for death."

"Please, Pierre, Ah'm skeered to walk de streets after dark, and me and de woman done gone too far to turn back. And he got de consumption nohow. But Ah don't wanter die before he do. Ah'm a well man."

"That's enough about that. How much money have you got?"

"Two hundred dollars."

"Two fifty is my terms, and I ain't a bit anxious for the job at that."

Pierre turned to me and began to give me a list of things to get for my own use and seemed to forget the man behind him.

"Maybe Ah kin git dat other fifty dollars and maybe not. These ain't no easy times. Money is tight."

"Well, goodbye, we're busy folks here. You don't have to do this thing anyway. You can leave town."

"And leave mah good trucking business? Dat'll never happen. Ah kin git yo' money. When yo' goin' ter do de work?''

"You pay the money and go home. It is not for you to know how and when the work is done. Go home with faith."

The next morning soon, Pierre sent me out to get a beef brain, a beef tongue, a beef heart and a live black chicken. When I returned he had prepared a jar of bad vinegar. He wrote Muttsy's enemy's name nine times on a slip of paper. He split open the heart, placed the paper in it, pinned up the opening with eighteen steel needles, and dropped it into the jar of vinegar, point downward.

The main altar was draped in black and the crudely carved figure of Death was placed upon it to shield us from the power of death.

Black candles were lit on the altar. A black crown was made and placed on the head of Death. The name of the man to die was written on paper nine times and placed on the altar one degree below Death, and the jar containing the heart was set on this paper. The candles burned for twelve hours.

Then Pierre made a coffin six inches long. I was sent out to buy a small doll. It was dressed in black to represent the man and placed in the coffin with his name under the doll. The coffin was left open upon the altar. Then we went far out to a lonely spot and dug a grave which was much longer and wider than the coffin. A black cat was placed in the grave and the whole covered with a cloth that we fastened down so that the cat could not get out. The black chicken was then taken from its confinement and fed a half glass of whiskey in which a paper had been soaked that bore the name of the man who was to die. The chicken was put in with the cat, and left there for a full month.

The night after the entombment of the cat and the chicken, we began to burn the black candles. Nine candles were set to burn in a barrel and every night at twelve o'clock we would go to the barrel and call upon the spirit of Death to follow the man. The candles were dressed by biting off the bottoms, as Pierre called for vengeance. Then the bottom was lighted instead of the top.

At the end of the month, the coffin containing the doll was carried out to the grave of the cat and chicken and buried upon their remains. A white bouquet was placed at the head and foot of the grave.

The beef brain was placed on a plate with nine hot peppers around it to cause insanity and brain hemorrhages, and placed on the altar. The tongue was slit, the name of the victim inserted, the slit was closed with a pack of pins and buried in the tomb.

"The black candles must burn for ninety days," Pierre told me. "He cannot live. No one can stand that."

Every night for ninety days Pierre slept in his holy place in a black draped coffin. And the man died.

Another conjure doctor solicited trade among Pierre's clients and his boasts of power, and his belittling comments of Pierre's power vexed him. So he said to me one day: "That fellow boasts too much, yes. Maybe if I send him a swelling he won't be out on the banquette bragging so much."

So Pierre took me with him to steal a new brick. We took the brick home and dressed nine black candles by writing the offensive doctor's name on each. His name was written nine times on a piece of paper and placed face down on the brick. It was tied there securely with twine. We put the black candles to burn, one each day for nine days, and then Pierre dug a well to the water table and slipped the brick slowly to the bottom. "Just like the brick soaks up the water, so that man will swell."

FOUR

I heard of Father Watson the "Frizzly Rooster" from afar, from people for whom he had "worked" and their friends, and from people who attended his meetings held twice a week in Myrtle Wreath Hall in New Orleans. His name is "Father" Watson, which in itself attests his Catholic leanings, though he is formally a Protestant.

On a given night I had a front seat in his hall. There were the usual camp-followers sitting upon the platform and bustling around performing chores. Two or three songs and a prayer were the preliminaries.

At last Father Watson appeared in a satin garment of royal purple, belted by a gold cord. He had the figure for wearing that sort of thing and he probably knew it. Between prayers and songs he talked, setting forth his powers. He could curse anybody he wished—and make the curse stick. He could remove curses, no matter who had laid them on whom. Hence his title The Frizzly Rooster. Many persons keep a frizzled chicken in the yard to locate and scratch up any hoodoo that may be buried for them. These chickens have, no doubt, earned this reputation by their ugly appearance—with all of their feathers set in backwards. He could "read" anybody at sight. He could "read" anyone who remained out of his sight if they but stuck two fingers inside the door. He could "read" anyone, no matter how far away, if he were given their height and color. He begged to be challenged.

He predicted the hour and the minute, nineteen years hence, when he should die—without even having been ill a moment in his whole life. God had told him.

He sold some small packets of love powders before whose powers all opposition must break down. He announced some new keys that were guaranteed to unlock every door and remove every obstacle in the way of success that the world knew. These keys had been sent to him by God through a small Jew boy. The old keys had been sent through a Jew man. They were powerful as long as they did not touch the floor—but if you ever dropped them, they lost their power. These new keys at five dollars each were not affected by being dropped, and were otherwise much more powerful.

I lingered after the meeting and made an appointment with him for the next day at his home.

Before my first interview with the Frizzly Rooster was fairly begun, I could understand his great following. He had the physique of Paul Robeson with the sex appeal and hypnotic what-ever-you-might-call-it of Rasputin. I could see that women would rise to flee from him but in mid-flight would whirl and end shivering at his feet. It was that way in fact.

His wife Mary knew how slight her hold was and continually planned to leave him.

"Only thing that's holding me here is this." She pointed to a large piece of brain-coral that was forever in a holy spot on the altar. "That's where his power is. If I could get me a piece, I could go start up a business all by myself. If I could only find a piece."

"It's very plentiful down in South Florida," I told her. "But if that piece is so precious, and you're his wife, I'd take it and let *him* get another piece."

"Oh my God! Naw! That would be my end. He's too powerful. I'm leaving him," she whispered this stealthily. "You get me a piece of that—you know."

The Frizzly Rooster entered and Mary was a different person at once. But every time that she was alone with me it was "That on the altar, you know. When you back in Florida, get me a piece. I'm leaving this man to his women." Then a quick hush and forced laughter at her husband's approach.

So I became the pupil of Reverend Father Joe Watson, "The Frizzly Rooster" and his wife, Mary, who assisted him in all things. She was "round the altar"; that is while he talked with the clients, and usually decided on whatever "work" was to be done, she "set" the things on the altar and in the jars. There was one jar in the kitchen filled with honey and sugar. All the "sweet" works were set in this jar. That is, the names and the thing desired were written on paper and thrust into this jar to stay. Already four or five hundred slips of paper had accumulated in the jar. There was another jar called the "break up" jar. It held vinegar with some unsweetened coffee added. Papers were left in this one also.

When finally it was agreed that I should come to study with them, I was put to running errands such as "dusting" houses, throwing pecans, rolling apples, as the case might be; but I was not told why the thing was being done. After two weeks of this I was taken off this phase and initiated. This was the first step towards the door of the mysteries.

My initiation consisted of the Pea Vine Candle Drill. I was told to remain five days without sexual intercourse. I must remain indoors all day the day before the initiation and fast. I might wet my throat when necessary, but I was not to swallow water.

When I arrived at the house the next morning a little before nine, as per instructions, six other persons were there,

so that there were nine of us—all in white except Father
Watson who was in his purple robe. There was no talking.
We went at once to the altar room. The altar was blazing.
There were three candles around the vessel of holy water,
three around the sacred sand pail, and one large cream candle burning in it. A picture of St. George and a large piece
of brain coral were in the center. Father Watson dressed
eight long blue candles and one black one, while the rest of
us sat in the chairs around the wall. Then he lit the eight
blue candles one by one from the altar and set them in the
pattern of a moving serpent. Then I was called to the altar
and both Father Watson and his wife laid hands on me. The
black candle was placed in my hand; I was told to light it
from all the other candles. I lit it at number one and pinched
out the flame, and re-lit it at number two and so on till it had
been lit by the eighth candle. Then I held the candle in my
left hand, and by my right was conducted back to the altar
by Father Watson. I was led through the maze of candles
beginning at number eight. We circled numbers seven, five
and three. When we reached the altar he lifted me upon the
step. As I stood there, he called aloud, "Spirit! She's standing here without no home and no friends. She wants you to
take her in." Then we began at number one and threaded
back to number eight, circling three, five and seven. Then
back to the altar again. Again he lifted me and placed me
upon the step of the altar. Again the spirit was addressed as
before. Then he lifted me down by placing his hands in my
arm-pits. This time I did not walk at all. I was carried
through the maze and I was to knock down each candle as I
passed it with my foot. If I missed one, I was not to try
again, but to knock it down on my way back to the altar.
Arrived there the third time, I was lifted up and told to
pinch out my black candle. "Now," Father told me, "you
are made Boss of Candles. You have the power to light candles and put out candles, and to work with the spirits anywhere on earth."

Then all of the candles on the floor were collected and one of them handed to each of the persons present. Father took the black candle himself and we formed a ring. Everybody was given two matches each. The candles were held in our left hands, matches in the right; at a signal everybody stooped at the same moment, the matches scratched in perfect time and our candles lighted in concert. Then Father Watson walked rhythmically around the person at his right. Exchanged candles with her and went back to his place. Then that person did the same to the next so that the black candle went all around the circle and back to Father. I was then seated on a stool before the altar, sprinkled lightly with holy sand and water and confirmed as a Boss of Candles.

Then conversation broke out. We went into the next room and had a breakfast that was mostly fruit and smothered chicken. Afterwards the nine candles used in the ceremony were wrapped up and given to me to keep. They were to be used for lighting other candles only, not to be just burned in the ordinary sense.

In a few days I was allowed to hold consultations on my own. I felt insecure and said so to Father Watson.

"Of course you do now," he answered me, "but you have to learn and grow. I'm right here behind you. Talk to your people first, then come see me."

Within the hour a woman came to me. A man had shot and seriously wounded her husband and was in jail.

"But, honey," she all but wept, "they say ain't a thing going to be done with him. They say he got good white folks back of him and he's going to be let loose soon as the case is tried. I want him punished. Picking a fuss with my husband just to get chance to shoot him. We needs help. Somebody that can hit a straight lick with a crooked stick."

So I went in to the Frizzly Rooster to find out what I must do and he told me, "That a low fence." He meant a difficulty that was easily overcome.

"Go back and get five dollars from her and tell her to go home and rest easy. That man will be punished. When we get through with him, white folks or no white folks, he'll find a tough jury sitting on his case." The woman paid me and left in perfect confidence of Father Watson.

So he and I went into the workroom.

"Now," he said, "when you want a person punished who is already indicted, write his name on a slip of paper and put it in a sugar bowl or some other deep something like that. Now get your paper and pencil and write the name; alright now, you got it in the bowl. Now put in some red pepper, some black pepper—don't be skeered to put it in, it needs a lot. Put in one eightpenny nail, fifteen cents worth of ammonia and two door keys. You drop one key down in the bowl and you leave the other one against the side of the bowl. Now you got your bowl set. Go to your bowl every day at twelve o'clock and turn the key that is standing against the side of the bowl. That is to keep the man locked in jail. And every time you turn the key, add a little vinegar. Now I know this will do the job. All it needs is for you to do it in faith. I'm trusting this job to you entirely. Less see what you going to do. That can wait another minute. Come sit with me in the outside room and hear this woman out here that's waiting."

So we went outside and found a weakish woman in her early thirties that looked like somebody had dropped a sack of something soft on a chair.

218

The Frizzly Rooster put on his manner, looking like a brown, purple and gold throne-angel in a house.

"Good morning, sister er, er———"

"Murchison," she helped out.

"Tell us how you want to be helped, Sister Murchison."

She looked at me as if I was in the way and he read her eyes.

"She's alright, dear one. She's one of us. I brought her in with me to assist and help."

I thought still I was in her way but she told her business just the same.

"Too many women in my house. My husband's mother is there and she hates me and always puttin' my husband up to fight me. Look like I can't get her out of my house no ways I try. So I done come to you."

"We can fix that up in no time, dear one. Now go take a flat onion. If it was a man, I'd say a sharp pointed onion. Core the onion out, and write her name five times on paper and stuff it into the hole in the onion and close it back with the cut-out piece of onion. Now you watch when she leaves the house and then you roll the onion behind her before anybody else crosses the door-sill. And you make a wish at the same time for her to leave your house. She won't be there two weeks more." The woman paid and left.

That night we held a ceremony in the altar room on the case. We took a red candle and burnt it just enough to consume the tip. Then it was cut into three parts and the short lengths of candle were put into a glass of holy water. Then we took the glass and went at midnight to the door of the woman's house and the Frizzly Rooster held the glass in his hands and said, "In the name of the Father, in the name of the Son, in the name of the Holy Ghost." He shook the glass three times violently up and down, and the last time he threw the glass to the ground and broke it, and said, "Dismiss this woman from this place." We scarcely paused as this was said and done and we kept going and went home by another way because that was part of the ceremony.

Somebody came against a very popular preacher. "He's

getting too rich and big. I want something done to keep him down. They tell me he's 'bout to get to be a bishop. I sho' would hate for that to happen. I got forty dollars in my pocket right now for the work.''

So that night the altar blazed with the blue light. We wrote the preacher's name on a slip of paper with black ink. We took a small doll and ripped open its back and put in the paper with the name along with some bitter aloes and cayenne pepper and sewed the rip up again with the black thread. The hands of the doll were tied behind it and a black veil tied over the face and knotted behind it so that the man it represented would be blind and always do the things to keep himself from progressing. The doll was then placed in a kneeling position in a dark corner where it would not be disturbed. He would be frustrated as long as the doll was not disturbed.

When several of my jobs had turned out satisfactorily to Father Watson, he said to me, ''You will do well, but you need the Black Cat Bone. Sometimes you have to be able to walk invisible. Some things must be done in deep secret, so you have to walk out of the sight of man.''

First I had to get ready even to try this most terrible of experiences—getting the Black Cat Bone.

First we had to wait on the weather. When a big rain started, a new receptacle was set out in the yard. It could not be put out until the rain actually started for fear the sun might shine in it. The water must be brought inside before the weather faired off for the same reason. If lightning shone on it, it was ruined.

We finally got the water for the bath and I had to fast and ''seek,'' shut in a room that had been purged by smoke. Twenty-four hours without food except a special wine that was fed to me every four hours. It did not make me drunk in the accepted sense of the word. I merely seemed to lose my body, my mind seemed very clear.

When dark came, we went out to catch a black cat. I must catch him with my own hands. Finding and catching black cats is hard work, unless one has been released for you to find.

Then we repaired to a prepared place in the woods and a circle drawn and "protected" with nine horseshoes. Then the fire and the pot were made ready. A roomy iron pot with a lid. When the water boiled I was to toss in the terrified, trembling cat.

When he screamed, I was told to curse him. He screamed three times, the last time weak and resigned. The lid was clamped down, the fire kept vigorously alive. At midnight the lid was lifted. Here was the moment! The bones of the cat must be passed through my mouth until one tasted bitter.

Suddenly, the Rooster and Mary rushed in close to the pot and he cried, "Look out! This is liable to kill you. Hold your nerve!" They both looked fearfully around the circle. They communicated some unearthly terror to me. Maybe I went off in a trance. Great beast-like creatures thundered up to the circle from all sides. Indescribable noises, sights, feelings. Death was at hand! Seemed unavoidable! I don't know. Many times I have thought and felt, but I always have to say the same thing. I don't know. I don't know.

Before day I was home, with a small white bone for me to carry.

FIVE

Dr. Duke is a member of a disappearing school of folk magic. He spends days and nights out in the woods and swamps and is therefore known as a "swamper." A swamper is a root-and-conjure doctor who goes to the swamps and gathers his or her own herbs and roots. Most of the doctors buy their materials from regular supply houses.

He took me to the woods with him many times in order that I might learn the herbs by sight and scent. Not only is it important to be able to identify the plant, but the swamper must know when and how to gather it. For instance, the most widely used root known as John de Conqueror must be gathered before September 21st. Wonder of the World Root must be spoken to with ceremony before it is disturbed, or forces will be released that will harm whoever handles it. Snakes guard other herbs and roots and must not be killed.

He is a man past fifty but very active. He believes his power is unlimited and that nothing can stand against his medicine.

His specialty is law cases. People come to him from a great distance, and I know that he received a fee of one hundred and eighty five dollars from James Beasley, who was in the Parish prison accused of assault with attempt to murder.

For that particular case we went first to the cemetery. With his right hand he took dirt from the graves of nine children.

I was not permitted to do any of this because I was only a beginner with him and had not the power to approach spirits directly. They might kill me for my audacity.

The dirt was put in a new white bowl and carried back to the altar room and placed among the burning candles, facing the east. Then I was sent for sugar and sulphur. Three teaspoons each of sugar and sulphur were added to the graveyard dirt. Then he prayed over it, while I knelt opposite him. The spirits were asked to come with power more than equal to a man. Afterwards, I was sent out to buy a cheap suit of men's underclothes. This we turned wrong side out and dressed with the prepared graveyard dust. I had been told to buy a new pair of tan socks also, and these were dressed in the same way.

As soon as Dr. Duke had been retained, I had been sent to the prison with a "dressed" Bible and Beasley was instructed to read the Thirty-fifth Psalm every day until his case should be called.

On the day he came up for trial, Dr. Duke took the new underclothes to the jail and put them on his client just before he started to march to the court room. The left sock was put on wrongside out.

Dr. Duke, like all of the conjure masters, has more than one way of doing every job. People are different and what will win with one person has no effect upon another. We had occasion to use all of the other ways of winning law suits in the course of practice.

In one hard case the prisoner had his shoes "dressed with the court." That was to keep the court under his control.

We wrote the judge's name three times, the prisoner's name three times, the district attorney's name three times, and folded the paper small, and the prisoner was told to wear it in his shoe.

Then we got some oil of rose geranium, lavender oil, verbena oil. Put three drops of oil of geranium in one-half ounce Jockey Club. Shook it and gave it to the client. He must use seven to nine drops on his person in court, but we had to dress his clothes, also. We went before court set to dress the court room and jury box and judge's stand, and have our client take perfume and rub it on his hand and rub from his face down his whole front.

To silence opposing witnesses, we took a beef tongue, nine pins, nine needles, and split the beef tongue. We wrote the names of those against our man and cut the names out and crossed them up in slit of tongue with red pepper and beef gall, and pinned the slit up with crossed needles and pins. We hung the tongue up in a chimney, tip up, and smoked the tongue for thirty-six hours. Then we took it down and put it in ice and lit on it from three to four black candles stuck in ice. Our client read the Twenty-second Psalm and Thirty-fifth also, because it was for murder. Then we asked the spirits for power more than equal to man.

So many people came to Dr. Duke to be uncrossed that he took great pains to teach me that routine. He never let me perform it, but allowed me to watch him do it many times.

Take seven lumps of incense. Take three matches to light the incense. Wave the incense before the candles on the altar. Make client bow over the incense three times. Then circle him with a glass of water three times, and repeat this three times. Fan him with the incense smoke three times—each time he bows his head. Then sprinkle him seven times with water, then lead him to and from the door and turn him around three times over incense that has been placed at the door. Then seat the client and sprinkle every corner of the room with water, three times, and also three times down the middle of the room, then go to another room and do the same. Smoke his underclothes and dress them. Don't turn the client's hand loose as he steps over the incense. Smoke him once at the door and three times at each corner. The room must be thoroughly smoked—even under the furniture—before the client leaves the room. After the evil has been driven out of him, it must also be driven from the room so it cannot return to him.

So much has been said and written about hoodoo doctors driving people away from a place that we cannot omit mentioning it. This was also one of Dr. Duke's specialties.

A woman was tired of a no-good husband; she told us about it.

"He won't work and make support for me, and he won't git on out the way and leave somebody else do it. He spend up all my money playing coon-can and kotch and then expect me to buy him a suit of clothes, and then he all the time fighting me about my wages."

"You sure you don't want him no more?" Dr. Duke asked her. "You know women get mad and say things they takes back over night."

"Lawd knows I means this. I don't want to meet him riding nor walking."

So. Dr. Duke told her what to do. She must take the right foot track of her hateful husband and parch it in an old tin frying pan. When she picks it up she must have a dark bottle with her to put the track in. Then she must get a dirt dauber nest, some cayenne pepper and parch that together and add it to the track. Put all of this into a dirty sock and tie it up. She must turn the bundle from her always as she ties it. She must carry it to the river at twelve noon. When she gets within forty feet of the river, she must run fast to the edge of the water, whirl suddenly and hurl the sock over her left shoulder into the water and never look back, and say, "Go, and go quick in the name of the Lord."

So she went off and I never saw her again.

Dr. Samuel Jenkins lives across the river in Marrero, Louisiana. He does some work, but his great specialty is reading the cards. I have seen him glance at people without being asked or without using his cards and making the most startling statements that all turned out to be true.

A young matron went out with me to Dr. Jenkins's one day just for the sake of the ride. He glanced at her and told her that she was deceiving her husband with a very worthless fellow. That she must stop at once or she would be found out. Her husband was most devoted, but once he mistrusted her he would accept no explanations. This was late in October, and her downfall came in December.

Dr. Charles S. Johnson, the well-known Negro sociologist, came to New Orleans on business while I was there and since I had to see Dr. Jenkins, he went with me. Without being asked, Dr. Jenkins told him that he would receive a sudden notice to go on a long trip. The next day, Dr. Johnson received a wire sending him to West Africa.

Once Dr. Jenkins put a light on a wish of mine that a certain influential white woman would help me, and assured me that she would never lose interest in me as long as she lived. The next morning at ten o'clock I received a wire from her stating that she would stand by me as long as she lived. He did this sort of thing day after day, and the faith in him is huge. Let me state here that most of his clients are white and upper-class people at that.

In appearance he is a handsome robust dark-skinned man around forty.

There are many superstitions concerning the dead.

All over the South and in the Bahamas the spirits of the dead have great power which is used chiefly to harm. It will be noted how frequently graveyard dust is required in the practice of hoodoo, goofer dust as it is often called.

It is to be noted that in nearly all of the killing ceremonies the cemetery is used.

The Ewe-speaking peoples[1] of the west coast of Africa all make offerings of food and drink—particularly libations of palm wine and banana beer upon the graves of the ancestor.

[1] A West African nation from which many slaves came to America.

It is to be noted in America that the spirit is always given a pint of good whiskey. He is frequently also paid for his labor in cash.

It is well known that church members are buried with their feet to the east so that they will arise on that last day facing the rising sun. Sinners are buried facing the opposite direction. The theory is that sunlight will do them harm rather than good, as they will no doubt wish to hide their faces from an angry God.

Ghosts cannot cross water—so that if a hoodoo doctor wishes to sic a dead spirit upon a man who lives across water, he must first hold the mirror ceremony to fetch the victim from across the water.

People who die from the sick bed may walk any night, but Friday night is the night of the people who died in the dark— who were executed. These people have never been in the light. They died with the black cap over the face. Thus, they are blind. On Friday nights they visit the folks who died from sick beds and they lead the blind ones wherever they wish to visit.

Ghosts feel hot and smell faintish. According to testimony all except those who died in the dark may visit their former homes every night at twelve o'clock. But they must be back in the cemetery at two o'clock sharp or they will be shut out by the watchman and must wander about for the rest of the night. That is why the living are frightened by seeing ghosts at times. Some spirit has lingered too long with the living person it still loves and has been shut out from home.

Pop Drummond of Fernandina, Fla., says they are not asleep at all. They "Sings and has church and has a happy time, but some are spiteful and show themselves to scare folks." Their voices are high and thin. Some ghosts grow very fat if they get plenty to eat. They are very fond of honey. Some who have been to the holy place wear seven-starred crowns and are very "suscautious" and sensible.

Dirt from sinners' graves is supposed to be very powerful, but some hoodoo doctors will use only that from the graves of infants. They say that the sinner's grave is powerful to kill, but his spirit is likely to get unruly and kill others for the pleasure of killing. It is too dangerous to commission.

The spirit newly released from the body is likely to be destructive. This is why a cloth is thrown over the face of a clock in the death chamber and the looking glass is covered over. The clock will never run again, nor will the mirror ever cast any more reflections if they are not covered so that the spirit cannot see them.

When it rains at a funeral it is said that God wishes to wash their tracks off the face of the earth, they were so displeasing to him.

If a murder victim is buried in a sitting position, the murderer will be speedily brought to justice. The victim sitting before the throne is able to demand that justice be done. If he is lying prone he cannot do this.

A fresh egg in the hand of a murder victim will prevent the murderer's going far from the scene. The egg represents life, and so the dead victim is holding the life of the murderer in his hand.

Sometimes the dead are offended by acts of the living and slap the face of the living. When this happens, the head is slapped one-sided and the victim can never straighten his neck. Speak gently to ghosts, and do not abuse the children of the dead.

It is not good to answer the first time that your name is called. It may be a spirit and if you answer it, you will die shortly. They never call more than once at a time, so by waiting you will miss probable death.[2]

[2]See Appendix for superstitions concerning sudden death.

SIX

❖

Before telling of my experiences with Kitty Brown I want to relate the following conjure stories which illustrate the attitude of Negroes of the Deep South toward this subject.

Old Lady Celestine went next door one day and asked her neighbor to lend her a quarter.

"I want it all in nickels, please, yes."

"Ah don't have five nickels, Tante Celestine, but Ah'll send a boy to get them for you," the obliging neighbor told her. So she did and Celestine took the money with a cold smile and went home.

Soon after another neighbor came in and the talk came around to Celestine.

"Celestine is not mad any more about the word we had last week. She was just in to pay me a visit."

"Humph!" snorted the neighbor, "maybe she come in to dust yo' door step. You shouldn't let people in that hate you. They come to do you harm."

"Oh no, she was very nice. She borrowed a quarter from me."

"Did she ask for small change?"

"Yes."

"Then she is still mad and means to harm you. They always

try to get small change from the ones they wish to harm. Celestine always trying to hurt somebody."

"You think so? You make me very skeered."

"Go send your son to see what she is doing. Ah'll bet she has a candle on yo' money now."

The boy was sent and came running back in terror. "Oh Mamma, come look at what Tante Celestine is doin'."

The two women crept to the crack in old Celestine's door. There in midsummer was the chimney ablaze with black candles. A cup in front of each candle, holding the money. The old woman was stretched out on her belly with her head in the fire-place twirling a huge sieve with a pair of shears stuck in the mesh, whirling and twirling the sieve and muttering the name of the woman who had loaned her the five nickels.

"She is cutting my heart with the shears!" the woman gasped; "the murderer should die." She burst into the house without ceremony and all the Treme[1] heard about the fight that followed.

Mrs. Grant lived down below Canal Street and was a faithful disciple of Dr. Strong, a popular hoodoo doctor who lived on Urquhart Street near St. Claude.

One hot summer night Mr. Grant couldn't sleep, so he sat on the upper balcony in his underwear chewing tobacco. Mrs. Grant was in bed.

A tall black woman lived two blocks down the street. She and Mrs. Grant had had some words a few days past and the black woman had been to a hoodoo doctor and bought a powder to throw at Mrs. Grant's door. She had waited till the hour of two in the morning to do it. Just as she was "dusting" the door, Mr. Grant on the balcony spit and some of the tobacco juice struck the woman.

She had no business at the Grant house at all, let alone at two o'clock in the morning throwing War Powder against the door. But even so, she stepped back and gave Mr. Grant a piece of her mind that was highly seasoned. It was a splendid

[1]The old French quarter of New Orleans.

232

bit of Creole invective art. He was very apologetic, but Mrs. Grant came to the door to see what was the trouble.

Her enemy had retreated, but as soon as she opened the door she saw the white powder against the door and on the steps. Moreover, there was an egg shell on each step.

Mrs. Grant shrieked in terror and slammed the door shut. She grabbed the chamber pot and ran out of the back door. Next door were three boys. She climbed into their back yard and woke up the family. She must have some urine from the boys. This she carried through the neighbor's front gate to her own door and dashed it over the door and steps. One of the boys was paid to take the egg shells away. She could not enter her front door until the conjure was removed. The neighborhood was aroused—she must have a can of lye. She must have some river water in which to dissolve the lye. All this was dashed against the door and steps.

Early next morning she was at the door of Dr. Strong. He congratulated her on the steps she had already taken, but told her that to be sure she had counteracted all the bad work, she must draw the enemy's "wine." That is, she must injure her enemy enough to draw blood.

So Mrs. Grant hurried home and half-filled three quart bottles with water. She put these in a basket, and the basket on her arm, and set out for the restaurant where the night-sprinkler-of-powders was a cook.

She asked to speak to her, and as soon as she appeared— bam! bam! bam! went the bottles over her head and the "wine" flowed. But she fought back and in the fracas she bit Mrs. Grant's thumb severely, drawing *her* "wine."

This complicated affairs again. Something must be done to neutralize this loss of blood. She hurried home and called one of the boys next door and said: "Son, here's five dollars. Go get me a black chicken—not a white feather on him—and keep the change for your trouble."

The chicken was brought. She seized her husband's razor and split the live bird down the breast and thrust her fist inside. As the hot blood and entrails enveloped her hand, she went into a sort of frenzy, shouting: "I got her, I got her, I got her now!"

A wealthy planter in Middle Georgia was very arrogant in his demeanor towards his Negro servants. He boasted of being "unreconstructed" and that he didn't allow no niggers to sass him.

A Negro family lived on his place and worked for him. The father, it seems, was the yard man, the mother, the cook. The boys worked in the field and a daughter worked in the house and waited on the table.

There was a huge rib-roast of beef one night for dinner. The white man spoke very sharply for some reason to the girl and she sassed right back. He jumped to his feet and seized the half-eaten roast by the naked ribs and struck her with the vertebrate end. The blow landed squarely on her temple and she dropped dead.

The cook was attracted to the dining-room door by the tumult. The white man resumed his seat and was replenishing his plate. He coolly told the mother of the dead girl to "Call Dave and you all take that sow up off the floor."

Dave came and the parents bore away the body of their daughter, the mother weeping.

Now Dave was known to dabble in hoodoo. The Negroes around both depended upon him and feared him.

He came back to clear away the blood of the murdered girl. He came with a pail and scrubbing brush. But first he sopped his handkerchief in the blood and put it into his pocket. Then he washed up the floor.

That night the Negro family moved away. They knew better than to expect any justice. They knew better than to make too much fuss about what had happened.

But less than two weeks later, the planter looked out of his window one night and thought he saw Dave running across the lawn away from the house. He put up the window and called to demand what he was doing on his place, but the figure disappeared in the trees. He shut the window and went to his wife's room to tell her about it and found her in laughing

234

hysteria. She laughed for three days despite all that the doctors did to quiet her. On the fourth day she became maniacal and attacked her husband. Shortly it was realized that she was hopelessly insane and she had to be put in an institution. She made no attempt to hurt anyone except her husband. She was gentleness itself with her two children.

The plantation became intolerable to the planter, so he decided to move to more cheerful surroundings with his children. He had some friends in South Carolina, so he withdrew his large account at the bank and transferred it to South Carolina and set up a good home with the help of a housekeeper.

Two years passed and he became more cheerful. Then one night he heard steps outside his window and looked out. He saw a man—a Negro. He was sure it was Old Dave. The man ran away as before. He called and ran from the house in pursuit. He was determined to kill him if he caught him, for he began to fear ambush from the family of the girl he had murdered. He ran back to get his son, his gun and the dogs to trail the Negro.

As he burst into the front door he was knocked down by a blow on the head, but was not unconscious. His twenty year old son was raving and screaming above him with a poker in his hand. He struck blow after blow, his father dodging and covering himself as best he could. The housekeeper rushed up and caught the poker from behind and saved the man on the floor. The boy was led away weeping by the woman, but renewed his attack upon his father later in the night. This kept up for more than a month before the devoted parent would consent to his confinement in an institution for the criminally insane.

This was a crushing blow to the proud and wealthy ex-planter. He once more gathered up his goods and moved away. But a year later the visitation returned. He saw Dave. He was sure of it. This time he locked himself in his room and asked the housekeeper through the door about his daughter. She reported the girl missing. He decided at once that his black enemies had carried off his daughter Abbie. He made ready to pursue. He unlocked his door and stepped into the hall to put on his overcoat. When he opened the closet his daughter pointed a gun in his face and pulled the trigger. The gun snapped. It happened to be unloaded. She had hidden in the closet to shoot him whenever he emerged from his room. Her disordered brain had overlooked the cartridges.

So he moved to Baltimore—out in a fashionable neighborhood. The nurse who came to look after his deranged daughter had become his mistress. He skulked about, fearful of every Negro man he saw. At no time must any Negro man come upon his premises. He kept guns loaded and handy, but hidden from his giggling, simpering daughter, Abbie, who now and then attacked him with her fists. His love for his children was tremendous. He even contrived to have his son released in his charge. But two weeks later, as he drove the family out, the young man sitting in the rear seat attacked him from behind and would have killed him but for the paramour and a traffic officer.

"When I was a boy[2] about ten years old there was a man named Levi Conway whom I knew well. He operated a ferry and had money and was highly respected by all. He was very careful about what he wore. He was tall and brown and wore a pompadour. He usually wore a broad-brimmed Stetson.

"He began to change. People thought he was going crazy. He owned lots of residential property but he quickly lost everything in some way that nobody seemed to understand. He grew careless in his dress and became positively untidy. He even got to the point where he'd buy ten cents worth of whiskey and drink it right out of the bottle.

"He began to pick up junk—old boilers, stones, wheels, pieces of harness, etc., and drag it around for miles every day. Then he'd bring it home and pile it in his backyard. This kept up for ten years or more.

"Finally he got sick in bed and couldn't get up.

[2]Told by Pierre Landeau of New Orleans.

236

"Tante Lida kept house for him. She was worried over his sickness, so she decided to get a woman from the Treme to find out what was wrong. The woman came. She was about fifty with a sore on her nose.

"She looked at Levi in the bed. Then she came out to Tante Lida. 'Sure, something has been done. I don't believe I can do anything to save him now, but I can tell you who did the work. You fix a place for me to stay here tonight and in the morning I will tell you.'

"Early next morning she sent for a heart of sheep or beef. She had them get her a package of needles and a new kettle. She lit a wood fire in the yard and filled the kettle one-third full of water and stood over the pot with the heart. She stuck the needles in one by one, muttering and murmuring as she stuck them in. When the water was boiling hard she dropped the heart in. It was about eleven o'clock in the morning.

" 'Now we shall know who has done this thing to Levi. In a few minutes the one who did it will come and ask for two things. Don't let him have either.'

"In a few minutes in came Pere Voltaire, a man whom all of us knew. He asked how Levi was. They told him pretty bad! He asked would they let him have two eggs and they said they had none. Then he asked would they lend him the wheelbarrow, and they said it wasn't there. The old woman winked and said, 'That is he.'

"He went on off. Then she told them to look into the pot, and they did. The heart was gone.

"A week later Levi died.

"This is the funny part. Some time after that my older brother, my cousin and I rowed over to the west bank of the river. Just knocking about as boys will, we found an old leaky boat turned upside down on the bank just out of reach of the water. I wondered who owned the piece of trash. My brother told me it belonged to Pere Voltaire. I said: 'Why doesn't he get a decent boat? This is too rotten to float.'

"I turned it over and found a great deal of junk under it—bundles tied up in rags, old bottles and cans and the like.

So I started to throwing the stuff into the water and my cousin helped me. We pushed the boat in, too. My brother tried to stop us.

"I forget now how it was that Pere Voltaire knew we did that. But two days later I began to shake as if I had an ague. Nothing the doctors could do stopped me. Two days later my cousin began to shake and two days after that my brother started to shake. It was three or four months before we could be stopped. But my brother stopped first. Then my cousin, then at last I stopped."

SEVEN

Kitty Brown is a well-known hoodoo doctor of New Orleans, and a Catholic. She liked to make marriages and put lovers together. She is squat, black and benign. Often when we had leisure, she told funny stories. Her herb garden was pretty full and we often supplied other doctors with plants. Very few raise things since the supply houses carry about everything that is needed. But sometimes a thing is wanted fresh from the ground. That's where Kitty's garden came in.

When the matter of my initiation came up she said, "In order for you to reach the spirit somebody has got to suffer. I'll suffer for you because I'm strong. It might be the death of you."

It was in October 1928, when I was a pupil of hers, that I shared in a hoodoo dance. This was not a pleasure dance, but ceremonial. In another generation African dances were held in Congo Square, now Beauregard Square. Those were held for social purposes and were of the same type as the fire dances and jumping dances of the present in the Bahamas. But the hoodoo dance is done for a specific purpose. It is always a case of death-to-the-enemy that calls forth a dance. They are very rare even in New Orleans now, even within the most inner circle, and no layman ever participates, nor has ever been allowed to witness such a ceremony.

This is how the dance came to be held. I sat with my teacher in her front room as the various cases were disposed of. It was my business to assist wherever possible, such as running errands for materials or verifying addresses, locating materials in the various drawers and cabinets, undressing and handling patients, writing out formulas as they were dictated, and finally making "hands."[1] At last, of course, I could do all of the work while she looked on and made corrections where necessary.

This particular day, a little before noon, came Rachael Roe. She was dry with anger, hate, outraged confidence and desire for revenge. John Doe had made violent love to her; had lain in her bed and bosom for the last three years; had received of Rachael everything material and emotional a woman can give. They had both worked and saved and had contributed to a joint savings account. Now, only the day before yesterday, he had married another. He had lured a young and pretty girl to his bed with Rachael's earnings; yes. Had set up housekeeping with Rachael's sweat and blood. She had gone to him and he had laughed at his former sweetheart, yes. The police could do nothing, no. The bank was sorry, but they could do nothing, no. So Rachael had come to Kitty.

Did she still love her John Doe? Perhaps; she didn't know. If he would return to her she should strive to forget, but she was certain he'd not return. How could he? But if he were dead she could smile again, yes—could go back to her work and save some more money, yes. Perhaps she might even meet a man who could restore her confidence in menfolk.

Kitty appraised her quickly. "A dance could be held for him that would carry him away right now, but they cost something."

"How much?"

"A whole lot. How much kin you bring me?"

"I got thirty-seven dollars."

"Dat ain't enough. Got to pay de dancers and set de table."

---

[1] Manufacturing certain luck charms.

240

One hundred dollars was agreed upon. It was paid by seven o'clock that same night. We were kept very busy, for the dance was set from ten to one the next day, those being bad hours. I ran to certain addresses to assemble a sort of college of bishops to be present and participate. The table was set with cake, wine, roast duck and barbecued goat.

By nine-thirty the next morning the other five participants were there and had dressed for the dance. A dispute arose about me. Some felt I had not gone far enough to dance. I could wait upon the altar, but not take the floor. Finally I was allowed to dance, as a delegate for my master who had a troublesome case of neuritis. The food was being finished off in the kitchen.

Promptly on the stroke of ten Death mounted his black draped throne and assumed his regal crown, Death being represented by a rudely carved wooden statue, bust length. A box was draped in black sateen and Kitty placed him upon it and set his red crown on. She hobbled back to her seat. I had the petition and the name of the man written on seven slips of paper—one for each participant. I was told to stick them in Death's grinning mouth. I did so, so that the end of each slip protruded. At the command I up-ended nine black tapers that had been dressed by a bath in whiskey and bad vinegar, and bit off the butt end to light, calling upon Death to take notice. As I had been instructed, I said: "Spirit of Death, take notice I am fixing your candles for you. I want you to hear me." I said this three times and the assembly gave three snaps with the thumb and middle finger.

The candles were set upside down and lighted on the altar, three to the left of Death, three to the right, and three before him.

I resumed my seat, and everyone was silent until Kitty was possessed. The exaltation caught like fire. Then B. arose drunkenly and danced a few steps. The clapping began lightly. He circled the room, then prostrated himself before the altar, and, getting to his hands and knees, with his teeth pulled one of the slips from the jaws of Death. He turned a violent somersault and began the dance, not intricate, but violent and muscle-twitching.

We were to dance three hours, and the time was divided equally, so that the more participants the less time each was called upon to dance. There were six of us, since Kitty could not actively participate, so that we each had forty minutes to dance. Plenty of liquor was provided so that when one appeared exhausted the bottle was pressed to his lips and he danced on. But the fury of the rhythm more than the stimulant kept the dancers going. The heel-patting was a perfect drum rhythm, and the hand clapping had various stimulating breaks. At any rate no one fell from exhaustion, though I know that even I, the youngest, could not have danced continuously on an ordinary dance floor unsupported by a partner for that length of time.

Nearly all ended on the moment in a twitchy collapse, and the next most inspired prostrated himself and began his dance with the characteristic somersault. Death was being continuously besought to follow the footsteps of John Doe. There was no regular formula. They all "talked to him" in their own way, the others calling out to the dancer to "talk to him." Some of the postures were obscene in the extreme. Some were grotesque, limping steps of old men and women. Some were mere agile leapings. But the faces! That is where the dedication lay.

When the fourth dancer had finished and lay upon the floor retching in every muscle, Kitty was taken. The call had come for her. I could not get upon the floor quickly enough for the others and was hurled before the altar. It got me there and I danced, I don't know how, but at any rate, when we sat about the table later, all agreed that Mother Kitty had done well to take me.

I have neglected to say that one or two of the dancers remained upon the floor "in the spirit" after their dance and had to be lifted up and revived at the end.

Death had some of all the food placed before him. An uncorked pint of good whiskey was right under his nose. He was paid fifteen cents and remained on his throne until one o'clock that night. Then all of the food before him was taken up with the tablecloth on which it rested and was thrown into the Mississippi River.

The person danced upon is not supposed to live more than nine days after the dance. I was very eager to see what would happen in this case. But five days after the dance John Doe deserted his bride for the comforting arms of Rachael and she hurried to Mother Kitty to have the spell removed. She said he complained of breast pains and she was fearfully afraid for him. So I was sent to get the beef heart out of the cemetery (which had been put there as of the routine), and John and Rachael made use of the new furniture bought for his bride. I think he feared that Rachael might have him fixed, so he probably fled to her as soon as the zest for a new wife had abated.

Kitty began by teaching me various ways of bringing back a man or woman who had left his or her mate. She had plenty to work on, too. In love cases the client is often told what to do at home. Minnie Foster was the best customer Kitty had. She wanted something for every little failing in her lover. Kitty said to her one day, "You must be skeered of yourself with that man of yours."

"No, Ma'am, I ain't. But I love him and I just want to make sure. Just you give me something to make his love more stronger."

"Alright, Minnie, I'll do it, but you ain't got no reason to be so unsettled with me behind you. Do like I say and you'll be alright.

"Use six red candles. Stick sixty pins in each candle—thirty on each side. Write the name of your sweetheart three times on a small square of paper and stick it underneath the candle. Burn one of these prepared candles each night for six nights. Make six slips of paper and write the name of the loved one once on each slip. Then put a pin in the paper on all four sides of the name. Each morning take up the sixty pins left from the burning of the candles, and save them. Then smoke the slip of paper with the four pins in it in incense smoke and bury it with the pins under your door step. The piece of paper with the name written on it three times, upon which each candle stands while burning, must be kept each day until the last candle is burned. Then bury it in the same hole with the rest. When you are sticking the pins in the candles, keep repeating: 'Tumba Walla, Bumba Walla, bring Gabe Staggers back to me.' "

Minnie paid her five dollars, thanked her loudly and hurried off to tighten the love-shackles on her Gabriel. But the following week she was back again.

"Ain't you got dat man to you wishes, yet, Minnie?" Kitty asked, half in fun and half in impatience.

"He love me, I b'lieve, but he gone off to Mobile with a construction gang and I got skeered he might not come back. Something might delay him on his trip."

"Oh, alright Minnie, go do like I say and he'll sure be back. Write the name of the absent party six times on paper. Put the paper in a water glass with two tablespoons full of quicksilver on it. Write his or her name three times each on six candles and burn one on a window sill in the daytime for six days."

Minnie paid and went home, but a week later she was back, washed down in tears. So Kitty gave her a stronger help.

"This is bound to bring him. Can't help it, Minnie. Now go home and stop fretting and do this:

"Write his name three times. Dig a hole in the ground. Get a left-foot soiled-sock from him secretly. His hatband may be used also. Put the paper with the name in the hole first. Then the sock or hatband. Then light a red candle on top of it all and burn it. Put a spray of Sweet Basil in a glass of water beside the candle. Light the candle at noon and burn until one. Light it again at six P.M. and burn till seven. (Always pinch out a candle—never blow it.) After the candle is lit, turn a barrel over the hole. When you get it in place, knock on it three times to call the spirit and say: 'Tumba Walla, Bumba Walla, bring Gabriel Staggers home to me.' "

We saw nothing of Minnie for six weeks, then she came in another storm of tears.

"Miss Kitty, Gabriel done got to de place I can't tell him his eye is black. What can I do to rule de man I love?"

"Do like I say, honey, and you can rule. Get his sock. Take one silver dime, some hair from his head or his hatband. Lay the sock out on a table, bottom up. Write his name three times and put it on the sock. Place the dime on the name and the hair or hatband on the dime. Put a piece of 'he' Lodestone[2] on top of the hair and sprinkle it with steel dust. As you do this, say, 'Feed the he, feed the she.' That is what you call feeding the Lodestone. Then fold the sock heel on the toe and roll it all up together, tight. Pin the bundle by crossing two needles. Then wet it with whiskey and set it up over a door. And don't 'low him to go off no more, do you going to lose all control.

"Now listen, honey, this is the way to change a man's mind about going away: Take the left shoe, set it up straight, then roll it one-half over first to the right, then to the left. Roll it to a coming-in door and point it straight in the door, and he can't leave. Hatband or sock can be made into a ball and rolled the same way: but it must be put under the sill or over the door."

Once Sis Cat got hongry and caught herself a rat and set herself down to eat 'im. Rat tried and tried to git loose but Sis Cat was too fast and strong. So jus' as de cat started to eat 'im he says, "Hol' on dere, Sis Cat! Ain't you got no manners atall? You going set up to de table and eat 'thout washing yo' face and hands?"

Sis Cat was mighty hongry but she hate for de rat to think she ain't got no manners, so she went to de water and washed her face and hands and when she got back de rat was gone.

So de cat caught herself a rat again and set down to eat. So de Rat said, "Where's yo' manners at, Sis Cat? You going to eat 'thout washing yo' face and hands?"

"Oh, Ah got plenty manners," de cat told 'im. "But Ah eats

---

[2]Magnetic iron ore.

mah dinner and washes mah face and uses mah manners afterwards.'' So she et right on 'im and washed her face and hands. And cat's been washin' after eatin' ever since.

I'm sitting here like Sis Cat, washing my face and usin' my manners.

GLOSSARY

Jack or John (not John Henry) is the great human culture hero in Negro folklore. He is like Daniel in Jewish folklore, the wish-fulfillment hero of the race. The one who, nevertheless, or in spite of laughter, usually defeats Ole Massa, God and the Devil. Even when Massa seems to have him in a hopeless dilemma he wins out by a trick. Brer Rabbit, Jack (or John) and the Devil are continuations of the same thing. p. 9

Woofing is a sort of aimless talking. A man half seriously flirts with a girl, half seriously threatens to fight or brags of his prowess in love, battle or in financial matters. The term comes from the purposeless barking of dogs at night. p. 13

Testimony. There is a meeting called a "love-feast" in the Methodist Church and an "experience meeting" with the Baptists. It is held once a month, either on a week-night or a Sunday morning preceding the Communion service. It is a Protestant confessional. No one is supposed to take communion unless he is on good terms with all of the other church members and is free from sin otherwise. The love-feast gives opportunity for public expression of good-will to the world. There are three set forms with variations. (1) The person who expects to testify raises a hymn. After a verse or two he or she speaks expressing (a) love for everybody, (b) joy at being present, (c) tells of the determination to stay in the field to the end. (2) Singing of a "hot" spiritual, giving the right hand of fellowship to the entire church, a shouting, tearful finish. (3) (a) Expresses joy at being present, (b) recites incident of conversion, telling in detail the visions seen and voices heard, (c) expresses determination to hold out to the end.   p. 20

It is singular that God never finds fault, never censures the Negro. He sees faults but expects nothing different. He is lacking in bitterness as is the Negro story-teller himself in circumstances that ordinarily would call for pity.   p. 29

The devil is not the terror that he is in European folk-lore. He is a powerful trickster who often competes successfully with God. There is a strong suspicion that the devil is an extension of the story-makers while God is the supposedly impregnable white masters, who are nevertheless defeated by the Negroes.   p. 48

John Henry. This is a song of the railroad camps and is suited to the spiking rhythm, though it is, like all the other work songs, sung in the jooks and other social places. It is not a very old song, being younger by far than Casey Jones and like that song being the celebration of an incidence of bravery. John Henry is not as widely distributed as "Mule on de Mount," "Uncle Bud" or several of the older songs, though it has a better air than most of the work songs. *John Henry has no place in Negro folk-lore except in this one circumstance.* The story told in the ballad is of John Henry, who is a great steel-driver, growing jealous when the company installs a steam drill. He boasts that he can beat the steam drill hammering home spikes, and asks his boss for a 9-pound hammer saying that if he has a good hammer he can beat the steam drill driving. The hammer is provided and he attempts to beat the drill. He does so for nearly an hour, then his heart fails him and he drops dead from exhaustion. It is told in direct dialogue for the greater part. The last three verses show internal evidence of being interpolated from English ballads. Judge the comparative newness of the song by the fact that he is competing with something as recent as a steam drill. For music for "John Henry" see Appendix.   p. 55

Long House. Another name for jook. Sometimes means a mere bawdy house. A long low building cut into rooms that all open on a common porch. A woman lives in each of the rooms.   p. 67

Blue Baby. Nicknames such as this one given from appearances or acts, i.e. "Blue Baby" was so black he looked blue. "Tush Hawg," a rough man; full of fight like a wild boar.   p. 68

One notes that among the animals the rabbit is the trickster hero. Lacking in size, strength and natural weapons such as teeth and claws, he continues to overcome by cunning. There are other minor characters that are heroic, but Brer Rabbit is first. In Florida, Brer Gopher, the dry-land tortoise, is also a hero and perhaps nearly equal to the rabbit.   p. 109

The colored preacher, in his cooler passages, strives for grammatical correctness, but goes natural when he warms up. The "hah" is a breathing device, done rhythmically to punctuate the lines. The congregation wants to hear the preacher breathing or "straining."
                                                        p. 139

Georgia Skin Game. Any number of "Pikers" can play at a time, but there are two "principals" who do the dealing. Both of them are not dealing at the same time, however. But when the first one who deals "falls" the other principal takes the deal. If he in turn falls it goes back to the first dealer. The principals draw the first two cards. The pikers draw from the third card on. Unless a player or players want to "scoop one in the rough," he can choose his own card which can be any card in the deck except the card on top of the deck and that one goes to the dealer. The dealer charges anything he pleases for the privilege of "scooping," the money being put in sight. It is the player's bet. After the ones who wish to have scooped, then the dealer begins to "turn" the cards. That is, flipping them off the deck face upwards and the pikers choose a card each from among those turned off to bet on. Sometimes several pikers are on the same card. When all have selected their cards and have their bets down, they begin to chant "Turn 'em" to the dealer. He turns them until a player falls. That is, a card like the one he is holding falls. For instance one holds the 10 of hearts. When another 10 falls he loses. Then the players cry "hold 'em" until the player selects another clean card, one that has not fallen. The fresh side bets are down and the chant "turn 'em" and the singing "Let de deal go Down" until the deck is run out.   p. 143

APPENDIX

I

NEGRO SONGS WITH MUSIC

JOHN HENRY

1   John Henry driving on the right hand side,
Steam drill driving on the left,
Says, 'fore I'll let your steam drill beat me down
I'll hammer my fool self to death,
Hammer my fool self to death.

2   John Henry told his Captain,
When you go to town
Please bring me back a nine pound hammer
And I'll drive your steel on down.
And I'll drive your steel on down.

3   John Henry told his Captain,
Man ain't nothing but a man,
And 'fore I'll let that steam drill beat me down
I'll die with this hammer in my hand,
Die with this hammer in my hand.

4   Captain ast John Henry,
What is that storm I hear?
He says Cap'n that ain't no storm,
'Tain't nothing but my hammer in the air,
Nothing but my hammer in the air.

5 John Henry told his Captain,
   Bury me under the sills of the floor,
   So when they get to playing good old Georgy skin,
   Bet 'em fifty to a dollar more,
   Fifty to a dollar more.

6 John Henry had a little woman,
   The dress she wore was red,
   Says I'm going down the track,
   And she never looked back.
   I'm going where John Henry fell dead,
   Going where John Henry fell dead.

7 Who's going to shoe your pretty li'l' feet?
   And who's going to glove your hand?
   Who's going to kiss your dimpled cheek?
   And who's going to be your man?
   Who's going to be your man?

8 My father's going to shoe my pretty li'l' feet;
   My brother's going to glove my hand;
   My sister's going to kiss my dimpled cheek;
   John Henry's going to be my man,
   John Henry's going to be my man.

9 Where did you get your pretty li'l' dress?
   The shoes you wear so fine?
   I got my shoes from a railroad man,
   My dress from a man in the mine,
   My dress from a man in the mine.

JOHN HENRY

(Work Song Series)

From the Zora Neale Hurston   *Arranged by C. Spencer Tocus*
Collection of Negro Folklore

1. John Hen-ry driv-ing on the right hand side,

Steam drill driv-ing 'on the left, Says, 'fore I'll let your steam drill

beat me down I'll ham-mer my fool self to

death, Ham-mer my fool self to death.

REFRAIN (spoken)

Hm .... Hm .... hah!

Hm........................ Hm.. 2. John Hm.... Hah
3. The
4. John

D.S. Last time (spoken)

D.S.

EAST COAST BLUES

1 Don't you hear that East Coast when she blows,
Oh, don't you hear that East Coast when she blows,
Ah, don't you hear that East Coast when she blows.

2 I'm going down that long lonesome road,
Oh, I'm going down that long lonesome road,
Ah, I'm going down that long lonesome road.

3 I'm going where the chilly winds don't blow,
Oh, I'm going where the chilly winds don't blow,
Ah, I'm going where the chilly winds don't blow.

4 You treat me mean you sho going see it again,
Oh, you treat me mean you sho going see it again,
Ah, you treat me mean you sho going see it again.

5 I love you honey but your woman got me barred,
Oh, I love you honey but your woman got me barred,
Ah, I love you honey but your woman got me barred.

6 Love ain't nothing but the easy going heart disease,
Oh, love ain't nothing but the easy going heart disease,
Ah, love ain't nothing but the easy going heart disease.

EAST COAST BLUES

(Social Song Series)

From the Zora Neale Hurston Collection of Negro Folklore

Po' gal long ways from home............

Po' gal long ways from home.......... oh ....

I'm po' gal a long ways from home ....

PLEASE DON'T DRIVE ME

(Convict Song)

*From the Zora Neale Hurston
Collection of Negro Folklore*

Arranged by Porter Grainger

Please don't drive me be-cause I'm blind.

B'lieve I can make it if I take my time.

1 Please don't drive me because I'm blind,
   B'lieve I kin make it if I take my time.

2 Lift up de hammer and let it fall down,
   It's a hard rocky bottom and it must be found.

3 De cap'n say hurry, de boss say run,
   I got a damn good notion not to do nary one.

COLD RAINY DAY

Cold rain-y day. Some old cold rain-y day I'll be back some old cold rain-y day. Old Smok-ey Joe Lawd, he died on the road Say-ing I'll be back some day.

Cold rain-y day. Some old cold rain-y day I'll be back some old cold

rain-y day. All I want is my rail - road fare, Take me back

where I was born. Oh, the rocks may be my pil-low, Lawd, the sand may

be my bed. I'll be back some old cold rain-y day. Cold rain-y day,

Some old cold rain-y day, I'll be back some old cold rain-y day.

1 Cold rainy day, some old cold, rainy day,
   I'll be back some old cold, rainy day.

2 All I want is my railroad fare,
   Take me back where I was born.

3 Ole Smoky Joe, Lawd, he died on the road
   Saying I'll be back some day.

4 Oh, the rocks may be my pillow
   Lawd, the sand may be my bed,
   I'll be back some old cold, rainy day.

GOING TO SEE MY LONG-HAIRED BABE

SOLOIST:

Oh Lulu! Oh Gal!
Want to see you, so bad.

CHORUS:

Going to see my long-haired babe;
Going to see my long-haired babe,
Oh Lawd I'm going 'cross the water
See my long-haired babe.

SOLOIST:

What you reckon Mr. Treadwell
Said to Mr. Goff,
Lawd I b'lieve I'll go South,
Pay them poor boys off.

CHORUS:

SOLOIST:

Lawd I ast that woman
Lemme be her kid,
And she looked at me
And began to smile.

CHORUS:

SOLOIST:

Oh Lulu! Oh Gal!

ALL:

Want to see you, so bad.

GOING TO SEE MY LONG-HAIRED BABE

(Spiking Rhythm)

Oh, Lu-lu, Oh gal, want to see you, so bad. Going to see my long-haired babe, Going to see my long-haired babe. Oh Lawd, I'm going 'cross the

wa-ter see my long-haired babe. Lawd, I ast dat wom-an

lem-me be— her kid And she looked at me—and be-gan to smile.

After last verse

Oh, Lu-lu, Oh gal, Want to see you so bad.

8va. *8va.*

CAN'T YOU LINE IT?

NOTE: This song is common to the railroad camps. It is suited to the "lining" rhythm. That is, it fits the straining of the men at the lining bars as the rail is placed in position to be spiked down.

1 When I get in Illinois
I'm going to spread the news about the Florida boys.
Chorus: (All men straining at rail in concert.)
Shove it over! Hey, hey, can't you line it?
(Shaking rail.) Ah, shack-a-lack-a-lack-a-lack-a-lack-a-lack-a-lack.

(Grunt as they move rail.) Can't you move it? Hey, hey, can't you try.

2 Tell what the hobo told the bum,
If you get any corn-bread save me some.
CHORUS:

3 A nickle's worth of bacon, and a dime's worth of lard,
I would buy more but the time's too hard.
CHORUS:

4 Wonder what's the matter with the walking boss,
It's done five-thirty and he won't knock off.
CHORUS:

5 I ast my Cap'n what's the time of day,
He got mad and throwed his watch away.
CHORUS:

6 Cap'n got a pistol and he try to play bad,
But I'm going to take it if he make me mad.
CHORUS:

7 Cap'n got a burner* I'd like to have,
A 32:20 with a shiny barrel.
CHORUS:

8 De Cap'n can't read, de Cap'n can't write,
How do he know that the time is right?
CHORUS:

*Gun.

9 Me and my buddy and two three more,
  Going to ramshack Georgy everywhere we go.
CHORUS:

10 Here come a woman walking 'cross the field,
   Her mouth exhausting like an automobile.

CAN'T YOU LINE IT?

(Work Song Series)

From the Zora Neale Hurston   *Arranged by Portia D. Duhart*
Collection of Negro Folklore

THERE STANDS A BLUE BIRD (CHILDREN)

Another version: Going around de mountain, two by two (actions suit words).

1   There stands a blue-bird, tra, la, la, la.
    There stands a blue-bird tra, la, la, la.
    Gimme sugar, coffee and tea.

2   Now trip around the ocean, tra, la, la, la.
    Now trip around the ocean, tra, la, la, la.
    Gimme sugar, coffee and tea (one in ring dances around ring).

3   Show me your motion, tra, la, la, la (does solo dance).
    Show me your motion, tra, la, la, la.
    Gimme sugar, coffee and tea.

4   Show me a better one, tra, la, la, la (second solo step).
    Show me a better one, tra, la, la, la.

5   Choose your partner, tra, la, la, la.
    Choose your partner, tra, la, la, la.
    Gimme sugar, coffee and tea.

(One in ring chooses partner and the new chosen partner takes his place in the ring and the other comes out.)

THERE STANDS A BLUE BIRD

(Children's Game)

*From the Zora Neale Hurston
Collection of Negro Folklore*   *Arranged by C. Spencer Tocus*

267

tra la la la, Gim - me su - gar cof - fee and tea. Now

skip a-round the o - cean, tra la la la —, Skip a-round the o - cean.

tra la la la —, Gim - me su - gar, cof - fee and tea.

MULE ON DE MOUNT

NOTE: The most widely distributed and best known of all Negro work songs. Since folk songs grow by incremental repetition the diversified subject matter that it accumulates as it ages is one of the evidences of its distribution and usage. This has everything in folk life in it. Several stories to say nothing of just lyric matter. It is something like the Odyssey, or the Iliad.

1   Cap'n got a mule, mule on the Mount called Jerry
    Cap'n got a mule, mule on the Mount called Jerry
    I can ride, Lawd, Lawd, I can ride.
    (He won't come down, Lawd; Lawd, he won't come down, in
        another version.)

2   I don't want no cold corn bread and molasses,
    I don't want no cold corn bread and molasses,
    Gimme beans, Lawd, Lawd, gimme beans.

3   I don't want no coal-black woman for my regular,
    I don't want no coal-black woman for my regular,
    She's too low-down, Lawd, Lawd, she's too low-down.

4   I got a woman, she's got money 'cumulated,
    I got a woman, she's got money 'cumulated,
    In de bank, Lawd, Lawd, in de bank.

5   I got a woman she's pretty but she's too bulldozing,
    I got a woman she's pretty but she's too bulldozing,
    She won't live long, Lawd, Lawd, she won't live long.

6   Every pay day, pay day I gits a letter,
    Every pay day, pay day I gits a letter,
    Son come home, Lawd, Lawd, son come home.

7   If I can just make June, July and August,
    If I can just make June, July and August,
    I'm going home, Lawd, Lawd, I'm going home.

8   Don't you hear them, coo-coo birds keep a'hollering,
    Don't you hear them, coo-coo birds keep a'hollering,
    It's sign of rain, Lawd, Lawd, it's sign of rain.

9   I got a rain-bow wrapped and tied around my shoulder,
    I got a rain-bow wrapped and tied around my shoulder,
    It ain't goin' rain, Lawd, Lawd, it ain't goin' rain.

MULE ON DE MOUNT

(Work Song Series)

From the Zora Neale Hurston   *Arranged by C. Spencer Tocus*
Collection of Negro Folklore

LET THE DEAL GO DOWN

(Gaming song suited to the action of Georgia Skin Game.)

SOLOIST:

1 When your card gits lucky, oh partner,
You ought to be in a rolling game.

CHORUS:

Let the deal go down, boys,
Let the deal go down.

SOLOIST:

2 I ain't had no money, Lawd, partner,
I ain't had no change.

CHORUS:

SOLOIST:

3 I ain't had no trouble, Lawd, partner,
Till I stop by here.

CHORUS:

SOLOIST:

4 I'm going back to de 'Bama, Lawd, partner,
Won't be worried with you.

LET THE DEAL GO DOWN

You ought to be in a roll-ing game.

CHORUS

Let the deal go down, boys, Let the deal go down.

II

FORMULAE OF HOODOO DOCTORS [1]

CONCERNING SUDDEN DEATH

1. Put an egg in a murdered man's hand and the murderer can't get away. He will wander right around the scene.
2. If a murder victim falls on his face, the murderer can't escape punishment. He will usually be executed.
3. If the blood of the victim is put in a jug and buried at the north corner of his house, the murderer will be caught and convicted.
4. Bury the victim with his hat on and the murderer will never get away.
5. If you kill and step backwards over the body, they will never catch you.
6. If you are murdered or commit suicide, you are dead before your times comes. God is not ready for you, and so your soul must prowl about until your time comes.
7. If you suspect that a person has been killed by hoodoo, put a cassava stick in the hand and he will punish the murderer. If he is killed by violence, put the stick in one hand and a knife and fork in the other. The spirit of the murdered one will first drive the slayer insane, and then kill him with great violence.
8. If people die wishing to see someone, they will stay limp and warm for days. They are waiting.
9. If a person dies who has not had his fling in this world, he will turn on his face in the grave.
10. If a person dies without speaking his mind about matters, he will purge (foam at the mouth after death). Hence the expression: "I ain't goin' to purge when I die (I shall speak my mind)."

[1]The formulae, paraphernalia and prescriptions of conjure are reprinted through the courtesy of the *Journal of American Folklore*.

TO RENT A HOUSE

Tie up some rice and sycamore bark in a small piece of goods. Tie six fig leaves and a piece of John de Conquer root in another piece. Cheesecloth is good. Boil both bundles in a quart of water at the same time. Strain it out. Now sprinkle the rice and sycamore bark mixed together in front of the house. Put the fig leaves and John de Conquer root in a corner of the house and scrub the house with the water they were boiled in. Mix it with a pail of scrub water.

FOR BAD WORK—(DEATH)

Take a coconut that has three eyes. Take the name of the person you want to get rid of and write it on the paper like a coffin. (Put the name all over the coffin.) Put this down in the nut. (Pour out water.) Put beef gall and vinegar in the nut and the person's name all around the coconut. Stand nut up in sand and set one black candle on top of it. Number the days from one to fifteen days. Every day mark that coconut at twelve o'clock A.M. or P.M., and by the fifteenth day they will be gone. Never let the candle go out. You must light the new candle and set it on top of the old stub which has burnt down to a wafer.

COURT SCRAPES

a. Take the names of all the *good* witnesses (for your client), the judge and your client's lawyer. Put the names in a dish and pour sweet oil on them and burn a white candle each morning beside it for one hour, from nine to ten. The day of the trial when you put it upon the altar, don't take it down until the trial is over.

b. Take the names of the opponent of your client, his witnesses and his lawyer. Take all of their names on one piece of paper. Put it between two whole bricks. Put the top brick crossways. On the day of the trial set a bucket or dishpan on top of the bricks with ice in it. That's to freeze them out so they can't talk.

c. Take the names of your client's lawyer, witnesses and lawyer on paper. Buy a beef tongue and split it from the base towards the tip, thus separating top from bottom. Put the paper with names in the split tongue along with eighteen pods of hot pepper and pin it through and through with pins and needles. Put it in a tin pail with plenty of vinegar and keep it on ice until the day of court. That day, pour kerosene in the bucket and burn it, and they will destroy themselves in court.

d. Put the names of the judge and all those *for* your client on paper. Take the names of the twelve apostles after Judas hung himself and write each apostle's name on a sage leaf. Take six candles and burn them standing in holy water. Have your client wear six of the sage leaves in each shoe and the jury will be made for him.

e. Write all the enemies' names on paper. Put them in a can. Then take soot and ashes from the chimney of your client and mix it with salt. Stick pins crosswise in the candles and burn them at a good hour. Put some ice in a bucket and set the can in it. Let your client recite the One Hundred Twentieth Psalm before Court and in Court.

f. To let John the conqueror win your case; take one-half pint whiskey, nine pieces of John the Conqueror Root one inch long. Let it soak thirty-eight hours till all the strength is out. (Gather all roots before September 21.) Shake up good and drain off roots in another bottle. Get one ounce of white rose or Jockey Club perfume and pour into the mixture. Dress your client with this before going to Court.

TO KILL AND HARM

Get bad vinegar, beef gall, filet gumbo with red pepper, and put names written across each other in bottles. Shake the bottle for nine mornings and talk and tell it what you want it to do. To kill the victim, turn it upside down and bury it breast deep, and he will die.

RUNNING FEET

To give anyone the running feet: Take sand out of one of his tracks and mix the sand with red pepper; throw some into a running stream of water and this will cause the person to run from place to place, until finally he runs himself to death.

TO MAKE A MAN COME HOME

Take nine deep red or pink candles. Write his name three times on each candle. Wash the candles with Van-Van. Put the name three times on paper and place under the candles, and call the name of the party three times as the candle is placed at the hours of seven, nine or eleven.

TO MAKE PEOPLE LOVE YOU

Take nine lumps of starch, nine of sugar, nine teaspoons of steel dust. Wet it all with Jockey Club cologne. Take nine pieces of ribbon, blue, red or yellow. Take a dessertspoonful and put it on a piece of ribbon and tie it in a bag. As each fold is gathered together call his name. As you wrap it with yellow thread call his name till you finish. Make nine bags and place them under a rug, behind an armoire, under a step or over a door. They will love you and give you everything they can get. Distance makes no difference. Your mind is talking to his mind and nothing beats that.

TO BREAK UP A LOVE AFFAIR

Take nine needles, break each needle in three pieces. Write each person's name three times on paper. Write one name backwards and one forwards and lay the broken needles on the paper. Take five black candles, four red and three green.

Tie a string across the door from it, suspend a large candle upside down. It will hang low on the door; burn one each day for one hour. If you burn your first in the daytime, keep on in the day; if at night, continue at night. A tin plate with paper and needles in it must be placed to catch wax in.

When the ninth day is finished, go out into the street and get some white or black dog dung. A dog only drops his dung in the street when he is running and barking, and whoever you curse will run and bark likewise. Put it in a bag with the paper and carry it to running water, and one of the parties will leave town.

III

PARAPHERNALIA OF CONJURE

It would be impossible for anyone to find out all the things that are being used in conjure in America. Anything may be conjure and nothing may be conjure, according to the doctor, the time and the use of the article.

What is set down here are the things most commonly used.

1. Fast Luck: Aqueous solution of oil of Citronella. It is put in scrub water to scrub the house. It brings luck in business by pulling customers into a store.

2. Red Fast Luck: Oil of Cinnamon and Oil of Vanilla, with wintergreen. Used as above to bring luck.

3. Essence of Van Van: Ten percent. Oil of Lemon Grass in alcohol. (Different doctors specify either grain, mentholated, or wood alcohol), used for luck and power of all kinds. It is the most popular conjure drug in Louisiana.

4. Fast Scrubbing Essence: A mixture of thirteen oils. It is burned with incense for fish-fry luck, i.e., business success. It includes:
   Essence Cinnamon
   Essence Wintergreen
   Essence Geranium
   Essence Bergamot
   Essence Orange Flowers, used also in initiation baths
   Essence Lavender, used also in initiation baths
   Essence Anice
   Essence St. Michael
   Essence Rosemary.

5. Water Notre Dame: Oil of White Rose and water. Sprinkle it about the home to make peace.

6. War Water: Oil of Tar in water (filtered). Break a glass of it on the steps wherever you wish to create strife. (It is sometimes made of creolin in water.)

7. Four Thieves Vinegar. It is used for breaking up homes,

for making a person run crazy, for driving off. It is sometimes put with a name in a bottle and the bottle thrown into moving water. It is used also to "dress" cocoanuts to kill and drive crazy.

8. Egyptian Paradise Seed (Amonium Melegreta). This is used in seeking success. Take a picture of St. Peter and put it at the front door and a picture of St. Michael at the back door. Put the Paradise seeds in little bags and put one behind each saint. It is known as "feeding the saint."

9. Guinea Paradise seed. Use as above.

10. Guinea pepper. This may also be used for feeding saints; also for breaking up homes or protecting one from conjure.

11. White Mustard seed. For protection against harm.

12. Black Mustard seed. For causing disturbance and strife.

13. Has-no-harra: Jasmine lotion. Brings luck to gamblers.

14. Carnation, a perfume. As above.

15. Three Jacks and a King. A perfume. As above.

16. Narcisse. As above but mild.

17. Nutmegs, bored and stuffed with quicksilver and sealed with wax, and rolled in Argentorium are very lucky for gamblers.

18. Lucky Dog is best of all for gamblers' use.

19. Essence of Bend-over. Used to rule and have your way.

20. Cleo-May, a perfume. To compel men to love you.

21. Jockey Club, a perfume. To make love and get work.

22. Jasmine Perfume. For luck in general.

23. White Rose. To make peace.

24. French Lilac. Best for vampires.

25. Taper Oil: perfumed olive oil. To burn candles in.

26. St. Joseph's Mixture:
    Buds from the Garden of Gilead
    Berries of the Fish
    Wishing Beans
    Juniper Berries
    Japanese scented Lucky Beans
    Large Star Anice

27. Steel dust is sprinkled over black load stone in certain

ceremonies. It is called "feeding the he, feeding the she."

28. Steel dust is attracted by a horse-shoe magnet to draw people to you. Used to get love, trade, etc.

29. Gold and silver magnetic sand. Powdered silver gilt used with a magnet to draw people to you.

30. *Saltpetre* is dissolved in water and sprinkled about to ward off conjure.

31. Scrub waters other than the Fast Lucks (see above, 1 and 2) are colored and perfumed and used as follows: red, for luck and protection; yellow, for money; blue (always colored with copperas), for protection and friends.

32. Roots and Herbs are used freely under widespread names:

> Big John the Conqueror.
> Little John the Conqueror. It is also put in Notre Dame Water or Waterloo in order to win.
> World-wonder Root. It is used in treasure-hunts. Bury a piece in the four corners of the field; also hide it in the four corners of your house to keep things in your favor.
> Ruler's Root. Used as above.
> Rattlesnake Root.
> Dragon's Blood (red root fibres). Crushed. Used for many purposes.
> Valerian Root. Put a piece in your pillow to quiet nerves.
> Adam and Eve Roots (paid). Sew together in bag and carry on person for protection.
> Five-fingered grass. Used to uncross. Make tea, strain it and bathe in it nine times.
> Waste Away Tea. Same as above.

33. Pictures of Saints, etc., are used also.

> St. Michael, the Archangel. To Conquer.
> St. Expedite. For quick work.
> St. Mary. For cure in sickness.
> St. Joseph with infant Jesus. To get job.
> St. Peter without the key. For success.
> St. Peter with the key. For great and speedy success.

St. Anthony de Padua. For luck.

St. Mary Magdalene. For luck in love (for women).

Sacred Heart of Jesus. For organic diseases.

34. Crosses. For luck.

35. Scapular. For protection.

36. Medals. For success.

37. Candles are used with set meanings for the different colors. They are often very large, one candle costing as much as six dollars.

White. For peace and to uncross and for weddings.

Red. For victory.

Pink. For love (some say for drawing success).

Green. To drive off (some say for success).

Blue. For success and protection (for causing death also).

Yellow. For money.

Brown. For drawing money and people.

Lavender. To cause harm (to induce triumph also).

Black. Always for evil or death.

Valive candles. For making Novenas.

38. The Bible. All hold that the Bible is the great conjure book in the world. Moses is honored as the greatest conjurer. "The names he knowed to call God by was what give him the power to conquer Pharaoh and divide the Red Sea."

IV

PRESCRIPTIONS OF ROOT DOCTORS

Folk medicine is practiced by a great number of persons. On the "jobs," that is, in the sawmill camps, the turpentine stills, mining camps and among the lowly generally, doctors are not generally called to prescribe for illnesses, certainly, nor for the social diseases. Nearly all of the conjure doctors practice "roots," but some of the root doctors are not hoodoo doctors. One of these latter at Bogaloosa, Louisiana, and one at Bartow, Florida, enjoy a huge patronage. They make medicine only, and white and colored swarm about them claiming cures.

The following are some prescriptions gathered here and there in Florida, Alabama and Louisiana:

GONORRHEA

a.   Fifty cents of iodide potash in two quarts of water. Boil down to one quart. Add two teaspoons of Epsom salts. Take a big swallow three times a day.

b.   Fifty cents iodide potash to one quart sarsaparilla. Take three teaspoons three times a day in water.

c.   A good handful of May pop roots; one pint ribbon cane syrup; one-half plug of Brown's Mule tobacco cut up. Add fifty cents iodide potash. Take this three times a day as a tonic.

d.   Parch egg shells and drink the tea.

e.   For Running Range (Claps): Take blackberry root, sheep weed, boil together. Put a little blueing in (a pinch) and a pinch of laundry soap. Put all this in a quart of water. Take one-half glass three times a day and drink one-half glass of water behind it.

f.   One quart water, one handful of blackberry root, one pinch of alum, one pinch of yellow soap. Boil together. Put in last nine drops of turpentine. Drink it for water until it goes through the bladder.

281

SYPHILIS

a. Ashes of one good cigar, fifteen cents worth of blue ointment. Mix and put on the sores.

b. Get the heart of a rotten log and powder it fine. Tie it up in a muslin cloth. Wash the sores with good castile soap and powder them with the wood dust.

c. When there are blue-balls (buboes), smear the swellings with mashed up granddaddies (daddy-long-legs) and it will bring them to a head.

d. Take a gum ball, cigar, soda and rice. Burn the gum ball and cigar and parch the rice. Powder it and sift and mix with vaseline. It is ready for use.

e. Boil red oak bark, palmetto root, fig root, two pinches of alum, nine drops of turpentine, two quarts of water together to one quart. Take one-half cup at a time. (Use no other water.)

FOR BLADDER TROUBLE

One pint of boiling water, two tablespoons of flaxseed, two tablespoons of cream of tartar. Drink one-half glass in the morning and one-half at night.

FISTULA

Sweet gum bark and mullen cooked down with lard. Make a salve.

RHEUMATISM

Take mullen leaves (five or six) and steep in one quart of water. Drink three to four wine glasses a day.

SWELLING

Oil of white rose (fifteen cents), oil of lavender (fifteen cents), Jockey Club (fifteen cents), Japanese honeysuckle (fifteen cents). Rub.

FOR BLINDNESS

a. Slate dust and pulverized sugar. Blow it in the eyes. (It must be finely pulverized to remove film.)

b. Get somebody to catch a catfish. Get the gall and put it in a bottle. Drop one drop in each eye. Cut the skin off. It gives the sight a free look.

LOCK-JAW

a. Draw out the nail. Beat the wound and squeeze out all the blood possible. Then take a piece of fat bacon, some tobacco and a penny and tie it on the wound.

b. Draw out the nail and drive it in a green tree on the sunrise side, and the place will heal.

FLOODING[1]

One grated nutmeg, pinch of alum in a quart of water (cooked). Take one-half glass three times daily.

SICK AT STOMACH

Make a tea of parched rice and bay leaves (six). Give a cup at a time. Drink no other water.

LIVE THINGS IN STOMACH (FITS)

Take a silver quarter with a woman's head on it. Stand her on her head and file it in one-half cup of sweet milk. Add nine parts of garlic. Boil and give to drink after straining.

MEDICINE TO PURGE

Jack of War tea, one tablespoon to a cup of water with a pinch of soda after it is ready to drink.

---

[1]Menstruation.

LOSS OF MIND

Sheep weed leaves, bay leaf, sarsaparilla root. Take the bark and cut it all up fine. Make a tea. Take one tablespoon and put in two cups of water and strain and sweeten. You drink some and give some to patient.

Put a fig leaf and poison oak in shoe. (Get fig leaves off a tree that hasn't borne fruit. Stem them so that nobody will know.)

TO MAKE A TONIC

One quart of wine, three pinches of raw rice, three dusts of cinnamon (about one heaping teaspoon), five small pieces of the hull of pomegranate about the size of a fingernail, five tablespoons of sugar. Let it come to a boil, set one-half hour and strain. Dose: one tablespoon.

(When the pomegranate is in season, gather all the hulls you can for use at other times in the year.)

POISONS

There are few instances of actual poisoning. When a conjure doctor tells one of his patients, "Youse poisoned nearly to death," he does not necessarily mean that poison has been swallowed. He might mean that, but the instances are rare. He names that something has been put down for the patient. He may be: (1) "buried in the graveyard"; (2) "throwed in de river"; (3) "nailed up in a tree"; (4) put into a snake, rabbit, frog or chicken; (5) just buried in his own yard; (6) or hung up and punished. Juice of the nightshade, extract of polk root, and juice of the milkweed have been used as vegetable poisons, and poisonous spiders and powdered worms and insects are used as animal poisons. I have heard of one case of the poison sac of the rattlesnake being placed in the water pail of an enemy. But this sort of poisoning is rare.

It is firmly held in such cases that doctor's medicine can do the patient no good. What he needs is a "two-headed" doctor, that is, the conjure man. In some cases the hoodoo man does effect a cure where the physician fails because he has faith working with him. Often the patient is organically sound. He is afraid that he has been "fixed," and there is nothing that a medical doctor can do to remove that fear. Besides, some poisons of a low order, like decomposed reptiles and the like, are not listed in the American pharmacopoeia. The doctor would never suspect their presence and would not be prepared to treat the patient if he did.

AFTERWORD

ZORA NEALE HURSTON: "A NEGRO WAY OF SAYING"

I.

The Reverend Harry Middleton Hyatt, an Episcopal priest whose five-volume classic collection, *Hoodoo, Conjuration, Witchcraft, and Rootwork,* more than amply returned an investment of forty years' research, once asked me during an interview in 1977 what had become of another eccentric collector whom he admired. "I met her in the field in the thirties, I think," he reflected for a few seconds, "that her first name was Zora." It was an innocent question, made reasonable by the body of confused and often contradictory rumors that make Zora Neale Hurston's own legend as richly curious and as dense as are the black myths she did so much to preserve in her classic anthropological works, *Mules and Men* and *Tell My Horse,* and in her fiction.

A graduate of Barnard, where she studied under Franz Boas, Zora Neale Hurston published seven books—four novels, two books of folklore, and an autobiography—and more than fifty shorter works between the middle of the Harlem Renaissance and the end of the Korean War, when she was the dominant black woman writer in the United States. The dark obscurity into which her career then lapsed reflects her staunchly independent political stances rather than any deficiency of craft or vision. Virtually ignored after the early fifties, even by the Black Arts movement in the sixties, an otherwise noisy and intense spell of black image- and myth-making that rescued so many black writers from remaindered oblivion, Hurston embodied a more or less harmonious but nevertheless problematic unity of opposites. It is this complexity that refuses to lend itself to the glib categories of "radical" or "conservative," "black" or "Negro," "revolutionary" or "Uncle Tom"—categories of little use in literary criticism. It is this same complexity, embodied in her fiction, that, until Alice Walker published her important essay ("In Search of Zora Neale Hurston") in *Ms.* magazine in 1975, had made Hurston's place in black literary history an ambiguous one at best.

The rediscovery of Afro-American writers has usually turned on larger political criteria, of which the writer's work is supposedly a mere reflection. The deeply satisfying aspect of the rediscovery of Zora Neale Hurston is that black women generated it primarily to establish a maternal literary ancestry. Alice Walker's moving essay recounts her attempts to find Hurston's unmarked grave in the Garden of the Heavenly Rest, a segregated cemetery in Fort Pierce, Florida. Hurston became a metaphor for the black woman writer's search for tradition. The craft of Alice Walker, Gayl Jones, Gloria Naylor, and Toni Cade Bambara bears, in markedly different ways, strong affinities with Hurston's. Their attention to Hurston signifies a novel sophistication in black literature: they read Hurston not only for the spiritual kinship inherent in such relations but because she used black vernacular speech and rituals, in ways subtle and various, to chart the coming to consciousness of black women, so glaringly absent in other black fiction. This use of the vernacular became the fundamental framework for all but one of her novels and is particularly effective in her classic work *Their Eyes Were Watching God,* published in 1937, which is more closely related to Henry James's *The Portrait of a Lady* and Jean Toomer's *Cane* than to Langston Hughes's and Richard Wright's proletarian literature, so popular in the Depression.

The charting of Janie Crawford's fulfillment as an autonomous imagination, *Their Eyes* is a lyrical novel that correlates the need of her first two husbands for ownership of progressively larger physical space (and the gaudy accoutrements of upward mobility) with the suppression of self-awareness in their wife. Only with her third and last lover, a roustabout called Tea Cake whose unstructured frolics center around and about the Florida swamps, does Janie at last bloom, as does the large pear tree that stands beside her grandmother's tiny log cabin.

> She saw a dust bearing bee sink into the sanctum of a bloom; the thousand sister calyxes arch to meet the love embrace and the ecstatic shiver of the tree from root to tiniest branch creaming in every blossom and frothing with delight. So this was a marriage!

To plot Janie's journey from object to subject, the narrative of the novel shifts from third to a blend of first and third person (known as "free indirect discourse"), signifying this awareness of self in Janie. *Their Eyes* is a bold feminist novel, the first to be explicitly so in the Afro-American tradition. Yet in its concern with the project of finding a voice, with language as an instrument of injury and salvation, of selfhood and empowerment, it suggests many of the themes that inspirit Hurston's oeuvre as a whole.

II.

One of the most moving passages in American literature is Zora Neale Hurston's account of her last encounter with her dying mother, found in a chapter entitled "Wandering" in her autobiography, *Dust Tracks on a Road* (1942):

> As I crowded in, they lifted up the bed and turned it around so that Mama's eyes would face east. I thought that she looked to me as the head of the bed reversed. Her mouth was slightly open, but her breathing took up so much of her strength that she could not talk. But she looked at me, or so I felt, to speak for her. She depended on me for a voice.

We can begin to understand the rhetorical distance that separated Hurston from her contemporaries if we compare this passage with a similar scene published just three years later in *Black Boy* by Richard Wright. Hurston's dominant black male contemporary and rival: "Once, in the night, my mother called me to her bed and told me that she could not endure the pain, and she wanted to die. I held her hand and begged her to be quiet. That night I ceased to react to my mother; my feelings were frozen." If Hurston represents her final moments with her mother in terms of the search for voice, then Wright attributes to a similar experience a certain "somberness of spirit that I was never to lose," which "grew into a symbol in my mind, gathering to itself . . . the poverty, the ignorance, the helplessness. . . ." Few authors in the black tradition have less in common than Zora Neale Hurston and Richard Wright. And whereas Wright would reign through the forties as our predominant author, Hurston's fame reached its zenith in 1943 with a *Saturday Review* cover story honoring the success of *Dust Tracks.* Seven years later, she would be serving as a maid in Rivo Alto, Florida; ten years after that she would die in the County Welfare Home in Fort Pierce, Florida.

How could the recipient of two Guggenheims and the author of four novels, a dozen short stories, two musicals, two books on black mythology, dozens of essays, and a prizewinning autobiography virtually "disappear" from her readership for three full decades? There are no easy answers to this quandary, despite the concerted attempts of scholars to resolve it. It is clear, however, that the loving, diverse, and enthusiastic responses that Hurston's work engenders today were not shared by several of her influential black male contemporaries. The reasons for this are complex and stem largely from what we might think of as their "racial ideologies."

Part of Hurston's received heritage—and perhaps the paramount received notion that links the novel of manners in the Harlem Renaissance, the social realism of the thirties, and the cultural nationalism of the Black Arts movement—was the idea that racism had reduced black people to mere ciphers, to beings who only react to an omnipresent racial oppression, whose culture is "deprived" where different, and whose psyches are in the main "pathological." Albert Murray, the writer and social critic, calls this "the Social Science Fiction Monster." Socialists, separatists, and civil rights advocates alike have been devoured by this beast.

Hurston thought this idea degrading, its propagation a trap, and railed against it. It was, she said, upheld by "the sobbing school of Negrohood who hold that nature somehow has given them a dirty deal." Unlike Hughes and Wright, Hurston chose deliberately to ignore this "false picture that distorted. . . ." Freedom, she wrote in *Moses, Man of the Mountain,* "was something internal. . . . The man himself must make his own emancipation." And she declared her first novel a manifesto against the "arrogance" of whites assuming that "black lives are only defensive reactions to white actions." Her strategy was not calculated to please.

What we might think of as Hurston's mythic realism, lush and dense within a lyrical black idiom, seemed politically retrograde to the proponents of a social or critical realism. If Wright, Ellison, Brown, and Hurston were engaged in a battle over ideal fictional modes with which to represent the Negro, clearly Hurston lost the battle.

But not the war.

After Hurston and her choice of style for the black novel

291

were silenced for nearly three decades, what we have witnessed since is clearly a marvelous instance of the return of the repressed. For Zora Neale Hurston has been "rediscovered" in a manner unprecedented in the black tradition: several black women writers, among whom are some of the most accomplished writers in America today, have openly turned to her works as sources of narrative strategies, to be repeated, imitated, and revised, in acts of textual bonding. Responding to Wright's critique, Hurston claimed that she had wanted at long last to write a black novel, and "not a treatise on sociology." It is this urge that resonates in Toni Morrison's *Song of Solomon* and *Beloved,* and in Walker's depiction of Hurston as our prime symbol of "racial health—a sense of black people as complete, complex, *undiminished* human beings, a sense that is lacking in so much black writing and literature." In a tradition in which male authors have ardently denied black literary paternity, this is a major development, one that heralds the refinement of our notion of tradition: Zora and her daughters are a tradition-within-the-tradition, a black woman's voice.

The resurgence of popular and academic readerships of Hurston's works signifies her multiple canonization in the black, the American, and the feminist traditions. Within the critical establishment, scholars of every stripe have found in Hurston texts for all seasons. More people have read Hurston's works since 1975 than did between that date and the publication of her first novel, in 1934.

III.

Rereading Hurston, I am always struck by the density of intimate experiences she cloaked in richly elaborated imagery. It is this concern for the figurative capacity of black language, for what a character in *Mules and Men* calls "a hidden meaning, jus' like de Bible . . . de inside meanin' of words," that unites Hurston's anthropological studies with her fiction. For the folklore Hurston collected so meticulously as Franz Boas's student at Barnard became metaphors, allegories, and performances in her novels, the traditional recurring canonical metaphors of black culture. Always more of a novelist than a social scientist, even Hurston's academic collections center on the quality of imagination that makes these lives whole and splendid. But it is in the novel that Hurston's use of the black idiom realizes its fullest effect. In *Jonah's Gourd Vine,* her first novel, for instance, the errant preacher, John, as described by Robert Hemenwoh "is a poet who graces his world with language but cannot find the words to secure his own personal grace." This concern for language and for the "natural" poets who "bring barbaric splendor of word and song into the very camp of the mockers" not only connects her two disciplines but also makes of "the suspended linguistic moment" a thing to behold indeed. Invariably, Hurston's writing depends for its strength on the text, not the context, as does John's climactic sermon, a *tour de force* of black image and metaphor. Image and metaphor define John's world; his failure to interpret himself leads finally to his self-destruction. As Robert Hemenway, Hurston's biographer, concludes, "Such passages eventually add up to a theory of language and behavior."

Using "the spy-glass of Anthropology," her work celebrates rather than moralizes; it shows rather than tells, such that "both behavior and art become self-evident as the tale texts and hoodoo rituals accrete during the reading." As author, she functions as "a midwife participating in the birth of a body of folklore, . . . the first wondering contacts with natural law." The myths she describes so accurately are in fact "alternative modes for perceiving reality," and never just condescending depictions of the quaint. Hurston sees "the Dozens," for example, that age-old black ritual of graceful insult, as, among other things, a verbal defense of the sanctity of the family, conjured through ingenious plays on words. Though attacked by Wright and virtually ignored by his literary heirs, Hurston's ideas about language and craft undergird many of the most successful contributions to Afro-American literature that followed.

IV.

We can understand Hurston's complex and contradictory legacy more fully if we examine *Dust Tracks on a Road,* her own controversial account of her life. Hurston did make significant parts of herself up, like a masquerader putting on a disguise for the ball, like a character in her fictions. In this way, Hurston *wrote* herself, and sought in her works to rewrite the "self" of "the race," in its several private and public guises, largely for ideological reasons. That which she chooses to reveal is the life of her imagination, as it sought to mold and interpret her environment. That which she silences or deletes, similarly, is all that her readership would draw upon to delimit or pigeonhole her life as a synecdoche of "the race problem," an exceptional part standing for the debased whole.

Hurston's achievement in *Dust Tracks* is twofold. First, she gives us a *writer's* life, rather than an account, as she says, of "the Negro problem." So many events in this text are figured in terms of Hurston's growing awareness and mastery of books and language, language and linguistic rituals as spoken and written both by masters of the Western tradition and by ordinary members of the black community. These two "speech communities," as it were, are Hurston's great sources of inspiration not only in her novels but also in her autobiography.

The representation of her sources of language seems to be her principal concern, as she constantly shifts back and forth between her "literate" narrator's voice and a highly idiomatic black voice found in wonderful passages of free indirect discourse. Hurston moves in and out of these distinct voices effortlessly, seamlessly, just as she does in *Their Eyes* to chart Janie's coming to consciousness. It is this usage of a *divided* voice, a double voice unreconciled, that strikes me as her great achievement, a verbal analogue of her double experiences as a woman in a male-dominated world and as a black person in a nonblack world, a woman writer's revision of W. E. B. Du

Bois's metaphor of "double consciousness" for the hyphenated African-American.

Her language, variegated by the twin voices that intertwine throughout the text, retains the power to unsettle:

There is something about poverty that smells like death.
Dead dreams dropping off the heart like leaves in a dry
season and rotting around the feet; impulses smothered too
long in the fetid air of underground caves. The soul lives
in a sickly air. People can be slave-ships in shoes.

Elsewhere she analyzes black "idioms" used by a culture "raised on simile and invective. They know how to call names," she concludes, then lists some, such as 'gator-mouthed, box-ankled, puzzle-gutted, shovel-footed: "Eyes looking like skint-ginny nuts, and mouth looking like a dish-pan full of broke-up crockery!"

Immediately following the passage about her mother's death, she writes:

The Master-Maker in His making had made Old Death.
Made him with big, soft feet and square toes. Made him
with a face that reflects the face of all things, but neither
changes itself, nor is mirrored anywhere. Made the body of
death out of infinite hunger. Made a weapon of his hand to
satisfy his needs. This was the morning of the day of the
beginning of things.

Language, in these passages, is not merely "adornment," as Hurston described a key black linguistic practice; rather, manner and meaning are perfectly in tune: she says the thing in the most meaningful manner. Nor is she being "cute," or pandering to a condescending white readership. She is "naming" emotions, as she says, in a language both deeply personal and culturally specific.

The second reason that *Dust Tracks* succeeds as literature arises from the first: Hurston's unresolved tension between her double voices signifies her full understanding of modernism. Hurston uses the two voices in her text to celebrate the psychological fragmentation both of modernity and of the black American. As Barbara Johnson has written, hers is a rhetoric of division, rather than a fiction of psychological or cultural unity. Zora Neale Hurston, the "real" Zora Neale Hurston that we long to locate in this text, dwells in the silence that separates these two voices: she is both, and neither; bilingual, and mute. This strategy helps to explain her attraction to so many contemporary critics and writers, who can turn to her works again and again only to be startled at her remarkable artistry.

But the life that Hurston could write was not the life she could live. In fact, Hurston's life, so much more readily than does the standard sociological rendering, reveals how economic limits determine our choices even more than does violence or love. Put simply, Hurston wrote well when she was comfortable, wrote poorly when she was not. Financial problems—book sales, grants and fellowships too few and too paltry, ignorant editors and a smothering patron—produced the sort of dependence that affects, if not determines, her style, a relation she explored somewhat ironically in "What White Publishers Won't Print." We cannot oversimplify the relation between Hurston's art and her life; nor can we reduce the complexity of her postwar politics, which, rooted in her distaste for the pathological image of blacks, were markedly conservative and Republican.

Nor can we sentimentalize her disastrous final decade, when she found herself working as a maid on the very day the *Saturday Evening Post* published her short story "Conscience of the Court" and often found herself without money, surviving after 1957 on unemployment benefits, substitute teaching, and welfare checks. "In her last days," Hemenway concludes dispassionately, "Zora lived a difficult life—alone, proud, ill, obsessed with a book she could not finish."

The excavation of her buried life helped a new generation read Hurston again. But ultimately we must find Hurston's legacy in her art, where she "ploughed up some literacy and laid by some alphabets." Her importance rests with the legacy of fiction and lore she constructed so cannily. As Hurston herself noted, "Roll your eyes in ecstasy and ape his every move, but until we have placed something upon his street corner that is our own, we are right back where we were when they filed our iron collar off." If, as a friend eulogized, "She didn't come to you empty," then she does not leave black literature empty. If her earlier obscurity and neglect today seem inconceivable, perhaps now, as she wrote of Moses, she has "crossed over."

HENRY LOUIS GATES, JR.

SELECTED BIBLIOGRAPHY

WORKS BY ZORA NEALE HURSTON

Jonah's Gourd Vine. Philadelphia: J. B. Lippincott, 1934.

Mules and Men. Philadelphia: J. B. Lippincott, 1935.

Their Eyes Were Watching God. Philadelphia: J. B. Lippincott, 1937.

Tell My Horse. Philadelphia: J. B. Lippincott, 1938.

Moses, Man of the Mountain. Philadelphia: J. B. Lippincott, 1939.

Dust Tracks on a Road. Philadelphia: J. B. Lippincott, 1942.

Seraph on the Suwanee. New York: Charles Scribner's Sons, 1948.

I Love Myself When I Am Laughing . . . & Then Again When I Am Looking Mean and Impressive: A Zora Neale Hurston Reader. Edited by Alice Walker. Old Westbury, N.Y.: The Feminist Press, 1979.

The Sanctified Church. Edited by Toni Cade Bambara. Berkeley: Turtle Island, 1981.

Spunk: The Selected Short Stories of Zora Neale Hurston. Berkeley: Turtle Island, 1985.

WORKS ABOUT ZORA NEALE HURSTON

Baker, Houston A., Jr. *Blues, Ideology, and Afro-American Literature: A Vernacular Theory,* pp. 15–63. Chicago: University of Chicago Press, 1984.

Bloom, Harold, ed. *Zora Neale Hurston.* New York: Chelsea House, 1986.

————, ed. *Zora Neale Hurston's "Their Eyes Were Watching God."* New York: Chelsea House, 1987.

Byrd, James W. "Zora Neale Hurston: A Novel Folklorist." *Tennessee Folklore Society Bulletin* 21 (1955): 37–41.

Cooke, Michael G. "Solitude: The Beginnings of Self-Realization in Zora Neale Hurston, Richard Wright, and Ralph Ellison." In Michael G. Cooke, *Afro-American Literature in the Twentieth Century,* pp. 71–110. New Haven: Yale University Press, 1984.

Dance, Daryl C. "Zora Neale Hurston." In *American Women Writers: Bibliographical Essays,* edited by Maurice Duke, et al. Westport, Conn.: Greenwood Press, 1983.

Gates, Henry Louis, Jr. "The Speakerly Text." In Henry Louis Gates, Jr., *The Signifying Monkey,* pp. 170–217. New York: Oxford University Press, 1988.

Giles, James R. "The Significance of Time in Zora Neale Hurston's *Their Eyes Were Watching God." Negro American Literature Forum* 6 (Summer 1972): 52–53, 60.

Hemenway, Robert E. *Zora Neale Hurston: A Literary Biography.* Chicago: University of Illinois Press, 1977.

Holloway, Karla. *The Character of the Word: The Texts of Zora Neale Hurston.* Westport, Conn.: Greenwood Press, 1987.

Holt, Elvin. "Zora Neale Hurston." In *Fifty Southern Writers After 1900,* edited by Joseph M. Flura and Robert Bain, pp. 259–69. Westport, Conn.: Greenwood Press, 1987.

Howard, Lillie Pearl. *Zora Neale Hurston.* Boston: Twayne, 1980.

————. "Zora Neale Hurston." In *Dictionary of Literary Biography,* vol. 51, edited by Trudier Harris, pp. 133–45. Detroit: Gale, 1987.

Jackson, Blyden. "Some Negroes in the Land of Goshen." *Tennessee Folklore Society Bulletin* 19 (4) (December 1953): 103–7.

Johnson, Barbara. "Metaphor, Metonymy, and Voice in *Their Eyes.*" In *Black Literature and Literary Theory,* edited by Henry Louis Gates, Jr., pp. 205–21. New York: Methuen, 1984.

————. "Thresholds of Difference: Structures of Address in Zora Neale Hurston." In *"Race," Writing and Difference,* edited by Henry Lewis Gates, Jr. Chicago: University of Chicago Press, 1986.

Jordan, June. "On Richard Wright and Zora Neale Hurston." *Black World* 23 (10) (August 1974): 4–8.

Kubitschek, Missy Dehn. " 'Tuh de Horizon and Back': The Female Quest in *Their Eyes.*" *Black American Literature Forum* 17 (3) (Fall 1983): 109–15.

Lionnet, Françoise. "Autoethnography: The Anarchic Style of *Dust Tracks on a Road.*" In Françoise Lionnet, *Autobiographical Voices: Race, Gender, Self-Portraiture,* pp. 97–130. Ithaca: Cornell University Press, 1989.

Lupton, Mary Jane. "Zora Neale Hurston and the Survival of the Female." *Southern Literary Journal* 15 (Fall 1982): 45–54.

Meese, Elizabeth. "Orality and Textuality in Zora Neale Hurston's *Their Eyes.*" In Elizabeth Meese, *Crossing the Double Cross: The Practice of Feminist Criticism,* pp. 39–55. Chapel Hill: University of North Carolina Press, 1986.

Newson, Adele S. *Zora Neale Hurston: A Reference Guide.* Boston: G. K. Hall, 1987.

Rayson, Ann. *"Dust Tracks on a Road:* Zora Neale Hurston and the Form of Black Autobiography." *Negro American Literature Forum* 7 (Summer 1973): 42–44.

Sheffey, Ruthe T., ed. *A Rainbow Round Her Shoulder: The Zora Neale Hurston Symposium Papers.* Baltimore: Morgan State University Press, 1982.

Smith, Barbara. "Sexual Politics and the Fiction of Zora Neale Hurston." *Radical Teacher* 8 (May 1978): 26–30.

Stepto, Robert B. *From Behind the Veil.* Urbana: University of Illinois Press, 1979.

Walker, Alice. "In Search of Zora Neale Hurston." *Ms.,* March 1975, pp. 74–79, 85–89.

Wall, Cheryl A. "Zora Neale Hurston: Changing Her Own Words." In *American Novelists Revisited: Essays in Feminist Criticism,* edited by Fritz Fleischmann, pp. 370–93. Boston: G. K. Hall, 1982.

Washington, Mary Helen. "Zora Neale Hurston: A Woman Half in Shadow." Introduction to *I Love Myself When I Am Laughing,* edited by Alice Walker. Old Westbury, N.Y.: Feminist Press, 1979.

————. " 'I Love the Way Janie Crawford Left Her Husbands': Zora Neale Hurston's Emergent Female Hero." In Mary Helen Washington, *Invented Lives: Narratives of Black Women, 1860–1960.* New York: Anchor Press, 1987.

Willis, Miriam. "Folklore and the Creative Artist: Lydia Cabrera and Zora Neale Hurston." *CLA Journal* 27 (September 1983): 81–90.

Wolff, Maria Tai. "Listening and Living: Reading and Experience in *Their Eyes.*" *BALF* 16 (1) (Spring 1982): 29–33.

CHRONOLOGY

January 7, 1891	Born in Eatonville, Florida, the fifth of eight children, to John Hurston, a carpenter and Baptist preacher, and Lucy Potts Hurston, a former schoolteacher.
September 1917– June 1918	Attends Morgan Academy in Baltimore, completing the high school requirements.
Summer 1918	Works as a waitress in a nightclub and a manicurist in a black-owned barbershop that serves only whites.
1918–19	Attends Howard Prep School, Washington, D.C.
1919–24	Attends Howard University; receives an associate degree in 1920.
1921	Publishes her first story, "John Redding Goes to Sea," in the *Stylus,* the campus literary society's magazine.
December 1924	Publishes "Drenched in Light," a short story, in *Opportunity.*
1925	Submits a story, "Spunk," and a play, *Color Struck,* to *Opportunity*'s literary contest. Both

	win second-place awards; publishes "Spunk" in the June number.
1925–27	Attends Barnard College, studying anthropology with Franz Boas.
1926	Begins field work for Boas in Harlem.
January 1926	Publishes "John Redding Goes to Sea" in *Opportunity*.
Summer 1926	Organizes *Fire!* with Langston Hughes and Wallace Thurman; they publish only one issue, in November 1926. The issue includes Hurston's "Sweat."
August 1926	Publishes "Muttsy" in *Opportunity*.
September 1926	Publishes "Possum or Pig" in the *Forum*.
September–November 1926	Publishes "The Eatonville Anthology" in the *Messenger*.
1927	Publishes *The First One,* a play, in Charles S. Johnson's *Ebony and Topaz*.
February 1927	Goes to Florida to collect folklore.
May 19, 1927	Marries Herbert Sheen.
September 1927	First visits Mrs. Rufus Osgood Mason, seeking patronage.
October 1927	Publishes an account of the black settlement at St. Augustine, Florida, in the *Journal of Negro History;* also in this issue: "Cudjo's Own Story of the Last African Slaver."
December 1927	Signs a contract with Mason, enabling her to return to the South to collect folklore.
1928	Satirized as "Sweetie Mae Carr" in Wallace Thurman's novel about the Harlem Renaissance *Infants of the Spring;* receives a bachelor of arts degree from Barnard.
January 1928	Relations with Sheen break off.

May 1928	Publishes "How It Feels to Be Colored Me" in the *World Tomorrow*.
1930–32	Organizes the field notes that become *Mules and Men*.
May–June 1930	Works on the play *Mule Bone* with Langston Hughes.
1931	Publishes "Hoodoo in America" in the *Journal of American Folklore*.
February 1931	Breaks with Langston Hughes over the authorship of *Mule Bone*.
July 7, 1931	Divorces Sheen.
September 1931	Writes for a theatrical revue called *Fast and Furious*.
January 1932	Writes and stages a theatrical revue called *The Great Day*, first performed on January 10 on Broadway at the John Golden Theatre; works with the creative literature department of Rollins College, Winter Park, Florida, to produce a concert program of Negro music.
1933	Writes "The Fiery Chariot."
January 1933	Stages *From Sun to Sun* (a version of *Great Day*) at Rollins College.
August 1933	Publishes "The Gilded Six-Bits" in *Story*.
1934	Publishes six essays in Nancy Cunard's anthology, *Negro*.
January 1934	Goes to Bethune-Cookman College to establish a school of dramatic arts "based on pure Negro expression."
May 1934	Publishes *Jonah's Gourd Vine*, originally titled *Big Nigger;* it is a Book-of-the-Month Club selection.

305

September 1934	Publishes "The Fire and the Cloud" in the *Challenge.*
November 1934	*Singing Steel* (a version of *Great Day*) performed in Chicago.
January 1935	Makes an abortive attempt to study for a Ph.D in anthropology at Columbia University on a fellowship from the Rosenwald Foundation. In fact, she seldom attends classes.
August 1935	Joins the WPA Federal Theatre Project as a "dramatic coach."
October 1935	*Mules and Men* published.
March 1936	Awarded a Guggenheim Fellowship to study West Indian Obeah practices.
April–September 1936	In Jamaica.
September–March 1937	In Haiti; writes *Their Eyes Were Watching God* in seven weeks.
May 1937	Returns to Haiti on a renewed Guggenheim.
September 1937	Returns to the United States; *Their Eyes Were Watching God* published, September 18.
February–March 1938	Writes *Tell My Horse;* it is published the same year.
April 1938	Joins the Federal Writers Project in Florida to work on *The Florida Negro.*
1939	Publishes "Now Take Noses" in *Cordially Yours.*
June 1939	Receives an honorary Doctor of Letters degree from Morgan State College.
June 27, 1939	Marries Albert Price III in Florida.

Summer 1939	Hired as a drama instructor by North Carolina College for Negroes at Durham; meets Paul Green, professor of drama, at the University of North Carolina.
November 1939	*Moses, Man of the Mountain* published.
February 1940	Files for divorce from Price, though the two are reconciled briefly.
Summer 1940	Makes a folklore-collecting trip to South Carolina.
Spring–July 1941	Writes *Dust Tracks on a Road.*
July 1941	Publishes "Cock Robin, Beale Street" in the *Southern Literary Messenger.*
October 1941–January 1942	Works as a story consultant at Paramount Pictures.
July 1942	Publishes "Story in Harlem Slang" in the *American Mercury.*
September 5, 1942	Publishes a profile of Lawrence Silas in the *Saturday Evening Post.*
November 1942	*Dust Tracks on a Road* published.
February 1943	Awarded the Anisfield-Wolf Book Award in Race Relations for *Dust Tracks;* on the cover of the *Saturday Review.*
March 1943	Receives Howard University's Distinguished Alumni Award.
May 1943	Publishes "The 'Pet Negro' Syndrome" in the *American Mercury.*
November 1943	Divorce from Price granted.
June 1944	Publishes "My Most Humiliating Jim Crow Experience" in the *Negro Digest.*
1945	Writes *Mrs. Doctor;* it is rejected by Lippincott.

March 1945	Publishes "The Rise of the Begging Joints" in the *American Mercury.*
December 1945	Publishes "Crazy for This Democracy" in the *Negro Digest.*
1947	Publishes a review of Robert Tallant's *Voodoo in New Orleans* in the *Journal of American Folklore.*
May 1947	Goes to British Honduras to research black communities in Central America; writes *Seraph on the Suwanee;* stays in Honduras until March 1948.
September 1948	Falsely accused of molesting a ten-year-old boy and arrested; case finally dismissed in March 1949.
October 1948	*Seraph on the Suwanee* published.
March 1950	Publishes "Conscience of the Court" in the *Saturday Evening Post,* while working as a maid in Rivo Island, Florida.
April 1950	Publishes "What White Publishers Won't Print" in the *Saturday Evening Post.*
November 1950	Publishes "I Saw Negro Votes Peddled" in the *American Legion* magazine.
Winter 1950–51	Moves to Belle Glade, Florida.
June 1951	Publishes "Why the Negro Won't Buy Communism" in the *American Legion* magazine.
December 8, 1951	Publishes "A Negro Voter Sizes Up Taft" in the *Saturday Evening Post.*
1952	Hired by the *Pittsburgh Courier* to cover the Ruby McCollum case.
May 1956	Receives an award for "education and human relations" at Bethune-Cookman College.

June 1956	Works as a librarian at Patrick Air Force Base in Florida; fired in 1957.
1957–59	Writes a column on "Hoodoo and Black Magic" for the *Fort Pierce Chronicle.*
1958	Works as a substitute teacher at Lincoln Park Academy, Fort Pierce.
Early 1959	Suffers a stroke.
October 1959	Forced to enter the St. Lucie County Welfare Home.
January 28, 1960	Dies in the St. Lucie County Welfare Home of "hypertensive heart disease"; buried in an unmarked grave in the Garden of Heavenly Rest, Fort Pierce.
August 1973	Alice Walker discovers and marks Hurston's grave.
March 1975	Walker publishes "In Search of Zora Neale Hurston," in *Ms.,* launching a Hurston revival.